JOE ROOT

BRINGING HOME THE ASHES

JOE ROOT

BRINGING HOME THE ASHES
WINNING WITH ENGLAND

WITH RICHARD GIBSON

HODDER

First published in Great Britain in 2015 by Hodder & Stoughton
An Hachette UK company

First published in paperback in 2016

1

A CIP catalogue record for this title is available from the British Library

Paperback ISBN: 978 1 473 63335 3
Ebook ISBN: 978 1 473 63334 6

Typeset in Minion Pro by Palimpsest Book Production Limited,
Falkirk, Stirlingshire

Printed and bound by Clays Ltd, St Ives plc

Hodder & Stoughton policy is to use papers that are natural, renewable and
recyclable products and made from wood grown in sustainable forests.
The logging and manufacturing processes are expected to conform to the
environmental regulations of the country of origin.

Hodder & Stoughton Ltd
Carmelite House
50 Victoria Embankment
London EC4Y 0DZ

www.hodder.co.uk

To my grandpa Don, for all the time you have given, and miles you have driven, to get me where I am.

CONTENTS

1 MADE IN YORKSHIRE

THROUGHOUT the wonderful summer of 2015, a peppered old thigh pad with the sweat marks of battle telling their own tales travelled everywhere with me. Only it is not any old thigh pad. To me, it is a cherished piece of Ashes memorabilia: the one worn by Michael Vaughan in 2005, when he became the first England captain to get his hands on the famous urn for eighteen years. It remained in my kitbag as we trekked from venue to venue, serving as a reminder of my predecessors in cricket's most thrilling narrative, and also of where I have come from.

I was a teenage hopeful without a first-team appearance to my name for Yorkshire when Michael announced his retirement from all cricket in late June 2009. It was then that he started thinking about what he was going to do with certain things from his kit, having remembered that Geoffrey Boycott passed down a chest guard to him when he was a young player at Headingley. In modern-day cricket, that particular piece of protective padding would serve no purpose, given the advances in the manufacturing of such items over the decades, so instead he passed on the thigh pad he had worn his entire career.

It was actually presented to me not by Michael but by Craig White, at the end of a second-team practice session a few days later. He was fully padded up when he called a team huddle and, in a rather surreal moment, dropped his trousers.

'I've got a little presentation to make,' he announced. 'As you all know, Michael has decided to retire from cricket and he just wanted to pass a little gift on to another Sheffield lad.'

He proceeded to take the thigh pad off and hand it to me. To have two of my heroes involved in the transaction was really special. Michael sent me a text later that day that read, 'All the best with your career. Really excited to see how it all goes.'

After all he'd achieved in the game, it was a very nice touch to recognise someone who had not done anything at all. He'd decided to honour me partly through what he had heard via word of mouth, and partly because he'd liked what he'd seen after catching me bat here and there on my way up through the age groups and academy at Yorkshire. For him to take an interest in my career was really exciting.

Because, like me, Michael had started with Sheffield Collegiate, it was easy for me to relate to him, and through that connection I saw that all my goals were achievable. The dream was always to follow him across every brick of a career path that had begun at Abbeydale Park and reached a podium at The Oval at its zenith. The thigh pad served to inspire.

For years I kept it in my locker at Headingley, but once I began playing regularly for England I was forced to clear everything out: the changing rooms being the size they are, someone else needed my storage space, so the thigh pad found a new home in the kitbag I lug around in the boot of the car. It's always near me and will remain so until I finish playing. Whether I keep it then, pass it on to another young Yorkshire player or give them something else of mine, I do not yet know, but it is a legacy I want to maintain. I know the feeling it gave me – the drive and determination to succeed – and would like another player to experience that in the future.

I have a confession to make here. When it comes to cricket, I am a proper geek – or, in dressing-room speak, a 'badger'. I have always loved collecting all the equipment, the feel of a new bat in the hand; being handed new kit turns me into a kid at Christmas.

These days that kit has three lions emblazoned on it and, no matter how many international caps I go on to win, I do not think the buzz and sense of pride I feel when pulling on that England shirt will ever diminish for me. Ever since being a young boy watching my predecessors on the TV, or pretending to be them in the back garden, to do so has been a massive dream of mine. I have always been so proud of representing my country and never more so than the summer of 2015 in winning back the Ashes.

Family and close friends would tell you my devotion to the badge is deep-rooted. As an 11-year-old I wore my Yorkshire schoolboy cap everywhere I went. It was my first season representing the county and I was so pleased about doing so that I rarely took it off. If I went to watch my dad Matthew play league cricket for Sheffield Collegiate on a Saturday afternoon, there I would be, advertising the fact I was a junior county cricketer, peak pulled down slightly, with the white rose displayed above my eyeline. I sometimes even wore it if I was with my mum Helen popping to the shops. I would wear it when travelling to my junior matches, not only when the game was under way, and even on the occasions when we travelled to see the England team play.

If I went to watch a Test match, there it was perched on top of my head, as it was in August 2002 when our family went to the match between England and India at Trent Bridge. After the game I badgered Mum to hang around.

'We've got to get the autographs of all the players,' I insisted, so desperate was I to meet them all. We did just that and it provided a moment I will always cherish, as Craig White spoke to us in the car park afterwards.

'Is that a Yorkshire cap?' he asked me.

'Yes, it is,' I said, beaming.

'That's brilliant,' he said. 'Maybe one day you will get to play with me.'

I can still hear Craig's words in my head. I can see him mouthing them to me as clear as day. I even plucked up the courage to repeat them to him when they became a reality on my Yorkshire second-team debut as a 16-year-old. There I was, a schoolboy having just sat my GCSEs, in the same changing room as one of the guys I had looked up to for years. Very nervous I might have been, but I plucked up the courage to tell him the story of how we had met previously. He obviously didn't remember it, but it was a special moment for me; another significant rung on my ascent, if you like.

He gave me a pair of his batting gloves during that match against Derbyshire and for the rest of the season I didn't wear another pair. They were already old and had holes in them, but I wore them until the leather palms were crisp, as if they had been left in the oven, so hardened were they with sweat. I may have been playing second XI cricket by this point, but Craig White held legendary status as far as I was concerned; someone I had tremendous respect for; someone whose journey to the top of cricket I wanted to emulate.

Never losing that special feeling I had when we talked in the Trent Bridge car park has been important to me. It was an integral step on the path of my cricket career and that is why I try to retain a connection with the next generation of the game when youngsters turn up to see England play. Getting to put the Three Lions on is such a privilege, one hundreds and thousands dream of but only a select few get the chance to experience. Interaction with the players of thirteen years ago certainly inspired me to be one of those select few, and my own memories are why I have always tried to give back to the fans who wait around after matches, by signing autographs, chatting or posing for photos. On the day we secured the Ashes, at Trent Bridge on 8 August 2015, I must have been close to the world record for selfies taken in a twenty-four-hour period. It was wonderful that so many people stuck around to be part of the celebrations.

While Michael and Craig provided links to my intended destination, getting there, I have to confess, has required a great deal of good fortune. You see, people have always invested their faith in me, and for that I will always be grateful. I have been very lucky when it has come to being thrown into teams. If ever there was a 50–50 call to be made, those with the power to decide seemed to opt to give me the chance to prove myself.

For example, when I was 12 the junior coaches at Yorkshire recommended me for one of the club's scholarships. Effectively, that was recognition of good performances against your peers and provided an incentive to push on for higher honours. I got invited to Headingley, where I was presented with some kit and the chance to do some work with Kevin Sharp, Yorkshire's batting coach at that time.

My dad and I arrived early at the indoor cricket centre

on St Michael's Lane, Headingley, and watched Kevin from behind the net as he did some short-pitched bowling work against the new ball with Anthony McGrath. I was due to meet up with him after the session had finished.

Kevin congratulated me on my award and asked me what I would like to do in the nets. Cheekily, I asked to replicate the same routine McGrath had just been through.

'I can't do that. I'll hurt you,' he said.

'I'll be all right,' I insisted.

I toddled off to get my pads and helmet and when I returned to the net, Kevin warned me, 'You've asked for this, Joe. Just to let you know, I am not going to be your friend for the next quarter of an hour.'

'That's good,' I said.

One delivery rose up and struck me on the grille of the helmet.

'That were a good delivery,' I acknowledged.

According to Kevin, after I got what I had asked for – a peppering in my first session – he popped up to the first floor, where Ian Dews, the director of the Yorkshire Academy, had his office, and told him that he had just been working with a young lad he believed would open the batting for Yorkshire in the future.

'Wow. That's a big call,' Ian replied.

That the big call came true owed a lot to Kevin's influence. He clearly liked the look of me the first time he saw me bat, and because of my scholarship with Yorkshire I had the opportunity to do further one-on-ones with him and also to train not only with my peer group but with the academy. Obviously, I was a lot younger than the other players, but being around that academy set-up, seeing what they did and talking to them, was great. For a young kid, mixing with the lads that were pushing to get in the first team and would play the odd game on television provided me with a real incentive to try to kick on.

The fact that Kevin Sharp rated me as a batter was essential in my development, and the work I did with him was the most pivotal, I believe, in my career to date.

All the way through Yorkshire's age-group sides I was one of the smaller kids – usually the smallest, in fact. It was that way from my first year, at 11 years old, all the way up until I was 17 or 18, and my stature naturally contributed to the way I played. Lacking the physical prowess of my rivals, I could never really get the ball off the square and so I had to find a way of batting longer periods of time – it was the only way I would ever make significant scores. If I wanted to put runs on the board, I had to stick around in the middle longer than others.

So I worked extremely hard, trying to ingrain a really solid technique into my batting and a proper old-school Yorkshire-style defence. That meant that whenever I went to practise, it was always about trying to be as technically correct as possible. I even made a point of trying to copy all the most technically correct batsmen in the world at that time.

The most obvious, given my club links with him, was Michael Vaughan. Towards the end of his career, his technique was slightly flawed but when he was world number one Michael was a massive inspiration to me. For a large period of my junior cricket he was England captain and one of England's best players too. He was always someone I looked to copy because I enjoyed the way he played. He had an amazing cover drive and pulled anything that was just slightly short over midwicket and square leg. As a kid, being so small, I tended to play off the back foot and so those were the shots I tried to copy off him. I would be developing the pull and cut as I walked around the house shadow-batting, stopping deliberately to practise them in front of the mirror. Every kid wants to copy their heroes and play like they do, and I was no different.

My younger brother Bill and I actually came through the Michael Vaughan Cricket Academy that was held on a Friday night at Abbeydale Park. We would be down there for Collegiate's junior club nets on a Tuesday and then look forward to the Friday academy sessions. Every now and again, Michael would pop down, and I never missed that opportunity to get an autograph on the back of my bat.

In between these sessions, I would be working hard with my dad or Bill, whoever would throw balls at me, in the nets at the club or in the back garden, grooving a basic technique. The core shots of the game didn't need to change, they would happen naturally, it was just things like my footwork, my stance and my backlift that I tinkered with.

Then, I would try to copy some shots from other favourite players. One month I would copy Mark Butcher, the next Michael Atherton or Graham Thorpe. It's natural to emulate the stars you watch on the telly, and in hindsight that adaptability, that mimicking of their strokes, has been very helpful in my game. Twenty20 came in around that time – when I was 12 – and with limited-overs cricket moving forward the way it has, you have to be quite changeable with regard to certain aspects of your batting. As long as you have those core basics to your game, you can become more flamboyant or add more strokes to make an easy transition between all three formats. But from a personal point of view, the basics, the nuts and bolts, have been key.

Your technique is not something you stumble across by accident; it needs work over time, but the basics should stay the same. Later, during my professional career, when I have been forced to make changes, they have been to the little things, not the core. In fact, even though we don't like change as human beings, the game is evolving so quickly – just look back two years at one-day cricket and compare it to how it is now, look at Twenty20, or even Test cricket, with teams scoring at four an over on a regular basis – that you simply have to embrace it. If you want to stay in that environment, and be successful, you have to keep up with developments and even be ahead of them. That means you require a strong base to work from, so you can add other parts as you see fit.

Kids starting to play cricket these days are naturally

incorporating everything into their game, because they're seeing scoops and flicks – all these shots on the TV, people aiming to score at 360 degrees – as commonplace. They might not have the most solid defence but they have all these shots in their locker. That's a great way to be. Because if you have all the shots and the skills to deliver them, it is about being controlled enough to condense things if you need to and then expand your repertoire when the time is right. It's slightly different to how I did things a decade ago, but that in itself shows you just how fast the game is evolving.

I was still a young-looking 16 when Kevin Sharp thrust me into my second-team debut against Derbyshire at Abbeydale Park in 2007. There was little time for nerves as we batted first against a visiting attack that included some first-team pedigree in Ian Hunter, Wayne White and Jon Clare and some decent pace to go with it. A consequence of my physique was that they bowled short at me. However, another consequence of my physique was that the cut and pull had become my premier shots. I made 57, which even included a six, with all but a handful of runs coming from cross-batted strokes behind square on either side of the wicket. Unable to generate my own, I simply used the power put on the ball by the bowlers to score my runs.

It was not to be long before my accumulation of regular scores for the Yorkshire academy team brought England

Under-19 recognition, and it was a winter away as an Under-19 tourist that coincided with the biggest challenge of my cricket life.

All the way up to my 18th birthday I was considered a short-arse, but things were soon to change and a massive growth spurt threw my batting completely out of kilter. Over that one winter period of 2009–10, split between a pre-Christmas tour of Bangladesh and the Under-19 World Cup in New Zealand in the new year, I shot up something like four inches in height and came back quite literally a different player. Not that I realised it at first, as before my first season on the playing staff at Headingley I had a month off between returning from international duty and pre-season training, the first break I had from cricket for two or three years.

As it was my first season as a senior player, after signing a three-year contract, I wanted to make a solid start. My thoughts were to be in the reckoning for the first team, and first impressions, I believed, would be crucial. Unfortunately, I made the wrong kind of first impression after pulling on the pads and wandering into the net to face the array of first-team bowlers. As I stood there in my normal stance, my bat no longer touched the floor. What was going on? I had always stood with my bat like that. Suddenly, it just wasn't happening.

'This is weird,' I thought.

My legs were now longer and made me look extremely short in the body. My balance was indifferent at best and all over the place at times, and it wasn't long before Kevin Sharp dubbed me 'Bambi' in one of his jovial moments. But there was a serious side to all this, and serious work to do because of my change in stature. Things had to be adjusted in both my stance and my pre-delivery movements now that I stood six feet tall. As a kid coming through, I had always felt in control of what I was doing, but here was a tough period to work through. Unfortunately, there was no quick fix to be found and for the first couple of months of the season there was no sign that I was making any progress whatsoever as I became a leg-before victim waiting to happen.

Three times within one week in mid-April, in one-day practice matches for the second XI, against Durham twice and Lancashire, I perished cheaply in that manner as my poise at the crease deserted me. Feeling trapped in an alien body, I kept falling over in my strokes. During that period, if I wasn't being struck on the pads, I was missing the ball altogether and getting bowled, or clipping the ball in the air into the leg-side.

After getting out lbw in a Second XI Trophy match, a one-wicket win against Notts on 27 April 2010, I sat in the dressing room with my pads on, looking at the floor, almost in disbelief. I must have sat there for about three-quarters of an hour and Kevin kept popping in and out before I finally broke the silence: 'When I was batting, I could feel myself growing.'

I didn't know quite what else to say, or how else to convey

what was happening. I just felt so different to the normal me, and as odd as it might have sounded it was the only way I could sum up my true feelings.

There was no hiding this technical vulnerability, and although there was nothing malicious to their reactions, the other lads would be trying not to giggle through this spate of LBs. There must have been a point when they sat on the boundary putting odds up on how long it would take me to get out in that manner.

That is where Kevin Sharp was really good with me. I had never experienced such a jolt before as a player. I had never gone through anything like an extended bad patch of form in my schoolboy days, and he was unbelievably supportive. I would get very upset, really annoyed at what was happening, and he would just laugh it off with reassurances that it would be a fleeting slump.

'Don't worry, it'll be fine,' he would tell me. We did endless work together to fix it. We had to change my entire stance. For a while I tried to place my bat in between my legs rather than behind my back foot. Next we worked to get me used to standing up a lot taller. There were so many little things we had to tinker with to get things right. Then one day everything clicked.

The turning point came against Warwickshire on 29 June at Clifton Park, York, after I nicked one to first slip, where Dougie Brown, who was their second XI player-coach, dropped an absolute sitter. I was only in the teens at the time and went on to make 169. As I walked off, the smile on Kev's face said, 'I told you so.' He never stopped telling me I would be fine, and throughout the whole process he seemed to believe in me so much more than I believed in myself.

It was one of those moments you can fall back on in testing times. Whenever I go through any sort of bad patch now I remind myself that part of the game of cricket is God testing you. That's what Kevin always used to tell me. He's not a massively religious man but the saying sums up your struggles perfectly. Regardless of whatever you do in life, there will be certain things that test you and, in the greater scheme of things, cricket – albeit a massive part of me and who I am – is just a game. And games are to be enjoyed. To make the odd mistake in life is to be human, he used to say. It's important not to over-analyse; keep neutral and eventually you will be fine. Those were the principles Kevin tried to instil in me and I have incorporated them into my attitude throughout my career. Maintaining that not only helps me personally but hopefully also rubs off on the rest of the team. For example, if you play in a side that loses a couple of games, negativity can creep in. Any sort of attitude can be infectious and be carried into someone else's game, and if you can stay positive, it is a far better influence on the rest of the environment and on the team.

Kevin moved on from Yorkshire during the overhaul of the club's coaching system in November 2011, but I have not forgotten how he helped me achieve my ambitions.

Back in those county second XI days, he used to say to me, 'When you're playing in a Lord's Test, remember to leave me a couple of tickets on the gate, won't you?' So in 2013, ahead of the match against New Zealand, I sent him a text to remind him that if he wanted them, they would be there. At the time of writing, he has turned me down twice, but there'll always be two waiting for him if he wants them. A thank you for flattening the bumps in the road.

From the time I began playing competitive cricket, I had quietly achieved at regional and school levels. This was recognised when, at the end of my first year of secondary education at King Ecgbert's in Dore, the Sheffield suburb where I grew up, I was nominated for the school's Sports Personality Award. It was an event at the back end of summer to celebrate the individual achievements of pupils in the annual sporting calendar.

There were four nominees for this award, for the individual who had contributed most to the school on the sports field, and I was absolutely gutted when I lost out to a girl in the sixth form who did athletics.

'This is rubbish. How can they possibly give it to someone who does running and jumping? There is no skill involved in that at all,' I thought.

To be fair, a collection of Olympic, Commonwealth and World Championship gold medals in heptathlon suggest Jessica Ennis-Hill was a worthy recipient!

By the time I broke into the second team at Yorkshire,

I was in my last days as a fifth-former at Worksop College, to which I had transferred on a scholarship at the age of 15, after scoring a half-century against them for King Ecgbert's. As a fanatical hitter of a cricket ball, switching schools suited me down to the ground, as at Worksop I was able to get regular practice in once lessons were done. I simply couldn't bat enough.

Not that everyone was complimentary about my ability, mind. Paying a visit to promote school tours of Barbados, Sir Garfield Sobers watched me practising one day and offered me some words of advice after strolling down the net to greet me. 'You'll not play first-class cricket with a back-foot game like that,' he warned. Given that I've always been a predominantly back-foot player, it was hardly the kind of thing I wanted to hear.

Mum and Dad were incredibly supportive, as was my grandpa Don, taking me to training and matches here, there and everywhere. But if it was through their devotion to sport that I was able to develop my own love of the game, and their willingness to indulge my passion that created the opportunities, it was another family member, my brother Bill, nineteen months my junior, who helped develop another essential ingredient for reaching the top level: a competitive edge.

Wherever Dad went with the Sheffield Collegiate first team, the pair of us went too, playing changing-room cricket with all the other characters and generally getting in the way – we must have been so annoying. We would get told off for hitting balls on the field, or making a certain area really muddy at an away ground because we had played in the same spot for hours on end.

Having Bill around helped more than anything because I cannot remember a time when I didn't want to beat him at whatever we turned our hands to, and vice versa. One of the reasons I always wanted to get better at sport was that I never wanted to lose to my brother. He appeared to have been born with a real desire to show me up and I was equally desperate to eradicate any chance of this ever happening, whether it be in the back garden, in the nets at Abbeydale or in a knockabout on another Yorkshire League ground.

On one occasion when I was nine and Bill was seven, we travelled to Scarborough for our usual Saturday-afternoon excursion with Dad. There were nets over in the corner and that was the area of the ground the kids would migrate to whenever a match started. As older brother, I normally made sure I batted first, bullying him into bowling, but this time he dug his heels in and insisted he would be batting.

Second ball, I cleaned him up and he just completely lost it, his mood only worsened by my chirping away to wind him up. Within seconds it escalated into him chasing me around the boundary with his bat, the pair of us causing enough commotion for the game to be stopped by the umpires and Dad to leave his position at fine leg to sprint 120 yards to break us up. Bill's punishment for trying to decapitate me with a wooden blade was a paternally imposed one-match ban.

We both played for Rotherham's Under-11 team at the time, because Collegiate didn't have a team for our age group, so Bill was forced to sit out our next fixture, his misery compounded by the fact that I was allowed to play and he was forced to come and watch. Safe to say, he never took a bat to me again.

That was the sort of rivalry we had as kids. We love each other, we were always best mates and remain so now, but those were the antics we got up to. We were just so keen to come out on top, to prove we could do something better than the other. Another time at Scarborough we were larking around in the nets and Bill was trying to keep wicket, stood up to the stumps, when one of the other young Collegiate boys bowled a beamer. I missed it and Bill copped it as it struck him straight in the forehead. He was rushed to hospital and we didn't leave the east coast that night until about 11 o'clock. I don't know what it is about my brother and that ground, but I look forward to him playing a first-class game there one day and having a better time of things.

It was during this period that I got my first taste of Lord's, although I certainly didn't fully appreciate its grandeur as Sheffield Collegiate prepared for the 2000 National Club Knockout final. Collegiate went on to be crowned Yorkshire League champions that summer and Eastbourne stood in the way of a famous double. For us Roots, it was like a mini-holiday. All the families travelled down to London on the team bus, and the day before the match, the team went down to the ground for a warm-up and a training session on the Nursery Ground nets.

We acted exactly as we would for any other game and found some vacant turf, strolling under the spaceship-style Media Centre and onto the outfield at Lord's to knock the stumps into our chosen patch. Within seconds a steward ran over and gave us a right telling-off, ripped all three stumps out of the ground and marched us into the corner of one of the stands. Of course, being young boys we had no idea what we'd done wrong. We were just miffed that we had been prevented from having a knockabout, and had to settle for some throw-downs in the nets on the Nursery Ground when the team had finished practising.

In the end, Collegiate did not get to experience the turf for themselves because the match was washed out – the replay at Southgate took place on 19 September, within twenty-four hours of the league title being secured – but Bill and I were reunited on it when he acted as twelfth man for England in 2013 against the New Zealanders. Even then, when running drinks, he was telling me what to do. And later that summer he was back on twelfths at Lord's, causing me grief in my first Ashes series. I was at the crease when, upon the fall of a wicket, Bill ran out with a drink.

'It must feel like Christmas dinner out here for you,' chirped Brad Haddin, Australia's wicketkeeper.

'You don't even know what a proper Christmas dinner is,' Bill hit back.

'E'scuse me?'

'You heard,' Bill said.

'Shut the hell up, Bill,' I whispered, desperately trying to avoid an escalation into a full-on sledging match.

So I let Haddin have the final word: 'Don't make this any harder for your brother than it's already going to be.'

Bill has always been a fierce competitor and he often texts to tell me how many runs he has scored himself, warning that I'd better get some for England if I want to match him. That was nigh-on impossible during 2015, a prolific season in which he passed 2,500 runs in all competitions for Nottinghamshire's second XI and for Collegiate at weekends. But he keeps me on my toes.

2 GROWING UP

THE dressing room at Headingley possesses a reputation as a savage place the meek should not enter. It has been home to some of the biggest characters to have graced English cricket and some of the most outspoken voices. On face value, it would be exactly the kind of environment that would be guaranteed to strike fear into a Sheffield lad with inherent shyness. But to be honest, its modern version was the making of me.

Spending time within those four walls certainly helped bring me out of myself, once I had been given experience of senior cricket in its second-team equivalent. That second XI was one sprinkled with a lot of senior guys who had been in and out of the first-class scene. I was able to learn a lot from them through chatting about the game or watching how they went about things. As a young player, it was invaluable to be around the likes of Simon Guy, Joe Sayers, Craig White and Steven Patterson, cricketers who knew the county circuit and the challenges it threw up. Getting to see how they played the game and how they prepared might have seemed fairly simple stuff, but it was crucial for someone straight out of secondary school who had not played a great deal of three-day cricket before. It was especially good when it came to things like how to build an innings. Constructing one requires the right patience, attitude and application, and up until that point I had played two or three games maximum a year for the academy, so getting accustomed to playing for longer periods was important.

Other members of the second XI were a season or two further ahead of me in terms of their development. Alongside me were Jonny Bairstow, Gary Ballance and Adam Lyth – with whom I shared an opening stand of 133 in scoring that debut half-century against Derbyshire's second team. He went on to hit an unbeaten 115. Even then, he used to thrash the ball to all parts while retaining a distinctive poise about his batting.

In fact, it has been amazing to play in a winning England team this past year with so many of the guys I came through the ranks with at Yorkshire. During those early days as a second XI cricketer traipsing around little-known outgrounds, there were nearly always three of us in a team together. These days we rock up at Cardiff, Lord's or Trent Bridge and do the same for an Ashes Test match and it feels surreal.

We have all come through a club traditionally viewed by outsiders as one riven with in-fighting and full of players looking after number one. I can only speak from my own experience, but if it was like that in decades gone by, it has obviously changed a lot. Yes, there are times over any season when things get tense and not everyone remains pals, but show me a club that doesn't have the odd difference of opinion. In professional sport there are inevitably some harsh lessons along the way.

Honesty prevails within the Yorkshire set-up. Sometimes you need a kick up the backside, and the majority of the time if something needs saying it will be said. As a Yorkshireman that's what you are used to anyway. I have been on the end of some brutal honesty from the coaches at Headingley and feel a better player for it. One thing the environment I was brought up in taught you was not to make excuses. If you tried, you were made to look silly. For example, a batsman couldn't get away with walking off every week saying 'I got a good ball' when they were dismissed. You would have ten other blokes telling you, 'No you didn't. You played a rubbish shot.' (Though don't for one minute think I was the perfect lad, exempt from such behaviour. We all go through those spells of claiming only magic balls get us out when it has actually been a terrible shot.)

One of the reasons we have been so successful at Yorkshire over recent years is that we have retained honesty in our evaluations of both our own games and our team performances. You only had to watch the Sky Sports documentary *Cricketing Yorkshire* to get an insight into what is said in post-match debriefs. At times there is no hiding place, even for the younger members of the side.

By the time I was one of those young guys coming into

the first team I was extremely harsh on myself, and some-times too harsh, but being over the top probably hasn't done me any harm in the long run. Sometimes I would be looking for a reason why I got out and there wouldn't really be one. It might genuinely have been a good delivery or a bad decision, and there wouldn't have been a lot wrong from my end of things. Now I am in a place where I can accept a bad shot and not think too harshly of it, just make sure I don't do it again. The way to deal with it is to work on it, and rid it from my game.

During my first days in a senior Yorkshire dressing room I would sit and listen, and not do much more. I was the youngest one in there, surrounded by lads who had played a lot of first-class cricket, so I didn't have the confidence to speak up in that environment. I observed and learned. As a cricketer with aspirations, you can figure out so many things yourself if you are prepared to watch other people go about their business, talk to your team-mates and listen to what the coaches say.

I would listen as intently to arguments as team discus-sions, in the belief that player disagreements can be healthy. Confrontation can be the best thing for everyone – the alternative is to sit there, not necessarily believe what someone else is saying and bite your lip, causing issues to fester and bad feelings to develop within the team. If you feel strongly about something tactically, you are much better off actually saying it.

It meant that even though I was quite young and only

had one full season behind me, I had the confidence to start speaking out at the start of the 2012 summer. I wanted us to do better as a side, and I was confident enough to tell others what I thought. My theory was that if I said something, even if no one else agreed with it, at least I would have got it off my chest. I had seen all that kind of thing in the second team and considered what the lads had done there to be healthy, so I saw no reason why it couldn't be incorporated into my way of thinking too. I have maintained the same outlook ever since moving into the England fold.

It was almost as if I had ten big brothers during my first few matches for Yorkshire seconds: whenever the lads went out for dinner, they took me along and looked after me. I was lucky to have blokes like Simon Guy, Craig White and Steve Patterson around. When it came to playing for the academy, in addition to friends like Gary and Jonny, I got close to people like James Lee, who was a really talented cricketer who never went on to show how good he was, and Ben Sanderson. We're all very good mates now but at the time I was extremely shy and there was a little bit of an age gap. So when I was 16 and they were 18, they would head off for a few beers and I wouldn't be able to. It wasn't even worth borrowing ID, as no one would have bought it. I looked about 12.

As for my batting, that was also a bit different to the other lads, as I still lacked power. However, I worked on turning a perceived weakness into a strength by becoming more adaptable and finding other ways to score. Against spin, for example, I had to learn how to manipulate the ball because I couldn't muscle it for four or hit it over the top. As I didn't possess as many boundary options as my peers, it meant knocking the ball into the gaps and rotating the strike more frequently than others. As a result, when I did eventually get stronger I was able to score quicker.

A massive reason I began opening the batting was that I couldn't realistically bat anywhere else. Quite simply, I batted too slowly to go in later in the order. Yorkshire obviously felt I could play, but I only had one gear and that was something to work on. It was why I focused on practising the shots that used the pace put on the ball by the bowlers, such as the hook and pull. Kevin Sharp would always be on hand to help me in this regard, willing to participate in endless throw-downs. I would practise whenever and wherever I could, and not necessarily in traditional facilities. On one occasion, on the 2009 pre-season tour of Barbados, I was not involved in a match at the 3Ws Oval and wanted to make use of my time rather than just sit about. I found an old shed on the site, which was not much more than 22 yards in length, and asked Kevin to pound bouncers at me off the concrete surface.

Despite this ingenuity, others still showed some frustration when it came to my lack of muscle. After we returned from the Under-19 World Cup in New Zealand in late January 2010, I sat down with Mark Robinson, the coach, for my post-tournament appraisal.

'I think you're a great player,' he told me. 'If you were playing at Sussex you would eventually get into our four-day side, but I could never see you playing in our one-day team because you are only able to score at a certain rate. The only way that you would change that would be if you were to go away and work on it.'

Listening to his assessment made me furious – I guess no one enjoys being told they are not up to standard – but putting aside my feelings at the time, and with the benefit of hindsight, he was absolutely spot on. It was a harsh reality that I needed to learn, and although it might not have been what I wanted to hear, taking it on board in the long run helped my development. Deep down I knew it to be true, but acknowledging it in self-assessment and being told by a third party are quite different things.

Evidence that Robinson's words rang true had already been provided at the end of the 2009 domestic season. I was handed my Yorkshire debut in a List A match, the final fixture of the NatWest Pro40 League, against Essex at Headingley on 27 September. Statistically, my maiden innings should have been a source of satisfaction, but I was pretty despondent after that game because I got 63 off 95 balls opening the batting, and they knocked off our total of 187 with 6.3 overs unused. In contrast to my performance, their opening batsman Mark Pettini scored an unbeaten hundred. Alastair Cook was playing in that game and I treasured the fact that I caught him – an England international batsman – at mid-off off the bowling of James

Lee. That was an amazing feeling, being the little cricket badger that I am. Those scrapbook moments have always meant a hell of a lot to me. Of course, that comes up in conversation every now and again these days, but Cook tends to counter with a similar analysis of the game to mine: 'Didn't you lose your side the game that day?'

It was not until the 2012 season that I began to make significant strides with regards to this side of my cricket. The previous year I had been in and out of Yorkshire's one-day and Twenty20 sides and this was something I felt I needed to address. Any young cricketer wants to play all formats, so the challenge for me was to find a niche in white-ball cricket.

That pre-season we returned to Barbados. The plan drawn up by Jason Gillespie, our new coach, and Martyn Moxon, the club's director of cricket, was that I was going to bat at number six throughout that year. However, that was not how things panned out.

Things went OK in our games over in the Caribbean. I contributed a few cameos, scoring at better than a run a ball quite comfortably in some, and I went into the home season in the belief that I had secured my batting spot in white-ball cricket for the year. But in our first Twenty20 match of the season, at home to Durham, we lost some early wickets and I was promoted up to five with the advice of Paul Farbrace, whose role as second-team coach with Yorkshire also incorporated helping with our 20-over stuff, ringing in my ears.

'Just go for it,' he said.

He had not been with us for long but Farby had already gained a reputation as a coach with the ability to make players feel ten-feet tall when they crossed the white line, and he was always sending us out with the message to take the opposition on. His attitude was not to worry about being bowled out for 120, but to try to get 180, and I accepted that was the attitude I needed to adopt whatever the situation in Twenty20.

I only got 14 in that first innings but I hit three early fours, and perhaps it was my willingness to be adventurous that got me promoted up the order to number three for our third game of the group stage at Derby. In the fourth, the away fixture against Durham, I got 41, hitting another trio of boundaries in my first over at the crease, and finished up scoring at comfortably better than a run a ball. In my head, this certainly shifted things a little bit for me. I told myself that was the way I had to keep playing if I was going to have the success I craved. In Twenty20 cricket, you can get on a bit of a roll and this was the case for me as I contributed some good scores, culminating in an innings of 65 off 40 in the quarter-final win over Worcestershire that sent Yorkshire to Twenty20 Finals Day for the first time.

Farbrace gave me confidence from the start, but having an experienced guy like Anthony McGrath, who was in his final season as a player that year, to work with was also really beneficial. I always think that players work best on their games alongside other players. They are the guys that you go out there in the middle with, guys that have experienced the same challenges as you. They know what it's like to be competing in that environment.

As a coach, you are there observing, but when you are out on the field certain things go on that can be explained more easily to someone who's been taking part in the contest himself. That provides you with the knowledge to help develop each other's games, and it is important to have those conversations with your team-mates. Mags was the perfect example of someone who did that. Not only was he a great person to look up to because of all his statistical achievements as a player with Yorkshire, making him an excellent role model; he was also a great player in terms of analysis.

Other sides to his character made him a popular team-mate. As well as being a great cricket man in terms of his knowledge, he was absolutely hilarious in the dressing room with his quick-witted nature, and everyone at Yorkshire absolutely loved him for it. During his playing days, a phantom sock-snipper did the rounds and so it raised a few eyebrows that the snipping recommenced not long after he rejoined the club as part of the coaching staff in 2015. I am pretty confident it is not him but other than that I could not possibly comment.

Sock-snipping appears to have undergone something of a rebirth this year actually, as there was even a snipper, or perhaps multiple snippers, on the loose in the England dressing room during the Ashes. In fact, the epidemic was so bad by the time we got to The Oval for the fifth Test that I broke an old Yorkshire pledge and put my hand in my pocket, forking out for a present for the rest of the lads – I popped into Top Man and bought twenty pairs of socks and stockpiled them in the middle of the dressing room.

Anyone pointing the finger at me can be assured that not only did I have my socks snipped after the fourth Test at Trent Bridge, but someone took the scissors to my boxer shorts as well. That, as I understand it, was in retaliation for somebody else getting done the week before. It became something of a free-for-all throughout the summer, with everybody getting hacked on a weekly basis. There are a number of prime suspects, but like any fair judicial system we have worked on the basis that everyone is innocent until they are found guilty. Not that I would know, but apparently the secret of a good sock-snipper is not to do it indiscriminately, but to pick one or two targets a match.

It wasn't all fun at Yorkshire during my first couple of seasons, though, as the club were relegated to Division Two of the County Championship in 2011, my breakthrough campaign, the consequences of which were a complete overhaul of the club's coaching structure. Thankfully, when Kevin Sharp left, whenever I had a problem with my batting, Mags was the first person I turned to. He had got to know my game as well as anyone, mainly because he was as great a watcher as a player. Nor was I the only one to benefit from this. He was very good at helping the young lads coming into the side develop and get better, and so it was therefore no surprise when the club welcomed him back in an official capacity. As a player, he'd worked with me, Gary Ballance, Adam Lyth and Jonny Bairstow, talking through each of our games and aiding our development.

Good fortune played another welcome hand for me during that summer of 2011, as the theme of people taking a punt on me continued. If I owed my club progress partially to the whim of Kevin, I had to credit Graham Thorpe for giving me an international chance. Previously, he had been a coach at Surrey and had therefore seen me play in second-team cricket. At this point, he was involved with England Lions and was instrumental, as I understand, in promoting me for the squad to face Sri Lanka A in first-class and one-day matches that August. There were lots of guys ahead of me results-wise and stats-wise, and given that I did not even have a first-class hundred to my name, I probably should not have been picked. But he chucked me in at the deep end, to see if I would sink or swim. I managed to get 66 in the second innings of a drawn match at Scarborough and then hit another fifty at New Road, Worcester, in the first match of three 50-over encounters between the two sides.

With confidence soaring after that experience with the

Lions, that maiden first-class hundred was under my belt before the month was out – 160 for Yorkshire in another drawn encounter at North Marine Road, this time with Sussex as the opposition. That hundred, I believe, is what got me onto the England Lions tour that winter. I was able to back up the good fortune of being picked with a significant score at exactly the right time. I always think that to get anywhere in the game, you have to have a certain amount of talent but you also have to have a little bit of luck with people giving you opportunities and pushing you. Without those opportunities, you cannot necessarily show everyone what you can do and put the performances in. So I will always be thankful for that.

Throughout playing for England Lions I was aware of talk of me being a future England player, and I guess that is only natural for anyone that makes the step up from county cricket to international A team level. But I wasn't naive enough to think that a call was going to be coming any time soon, because I simply didn't have the weight of first-class hundreds behind me. To be given a chance in the Test arena, you need a few of those.

And if I required any indication of the step up in class between the Lions and the Test team it was given during the winter of 2011–12. I went away on tours of Bangladesh and Sri Lanka and got a couple of decent one-day scores, including a maiden List A hundred of 110 not out in a big Lions win over Sri Lanka A at the Premadasa Stadium in

Colombo. Four days later, on 10 February, we faced the full England side in Abu Dhabi as an additional practice fixture for them ahead of their one-day series against Pakistan.

A couple of years earlier, they had played some practice matches like that ahead of the World Twenty20 and Michael Lumb ended up getting picked for the full side on the back of them. By taking his chance, he had gone from a fringe player to a World Cup winner. Naturally, it meant members of our Lions party were thinking 'what if' ahead of this one-off meeting on the way home. Scoring a few runs or taking some wickets against the full side can do wonders for someone's career.

But if we headed into the match with thoughts of pushing for selection, those thoughts did not linger as, after James Taylor won the toss at the Sheikh Zayed Stadium, we were dismissed for just 96 in 28.3 overs. They bowled us out in no time and then, with the sun coming out, eased past our total. We were beaten so comprehensively, in fact, that between innings the List A nature of the contest was relinquished and the management set up a fake chase of 230, just so the batsmen could get enough practice during the time that had been scheduled.

Watching those batsmen – Kevin Pietersen, Jonathan Trott and Ravi Bopara – go about their business showed me that while it might not have been men against boys, there was definitely a noticeable gap between the full side and those of us in reserve.

That was a massive eye-opener, as far as I was concerned. Yes, I had done really well to get some runs for the Lions, and it made me feel that I must be close to international selection, but that week told me I was still nowhere near playing. Not only were we beaten, we were absolutely battered in that game.

It meant that I returned to play county cricket in 2012 in the knowledge that if I was to retain aspirations of playing for England, I was going to have to step up a level and be that much better than everyone else in direct competition with me. I had to get to the same level as the players I had seen during that Abu Dhabi nightmare. Up until that point, my progress through the levels had been fairly smooth and I always seemed to do quite well every time I was moved up. Granted, I never particularly stood out, but each time I was exposed against higher company I had answered with runs.

During that debut season of 2011, I averaged 36 in first-class action, which represented a solid county season – playing every game, I just crept over the sought-after 1,000-run mark. But my post-season assessment was that the challenge for the following season of 2012 was not to try to get another year in the Yorkshire first team but to aim higher, to push on and be better than that. And if things didn't quite materialise, I would at least know that I was still improving rather than standing still.

In that winter in between I learned to play in Asian conditions, and spent time with new colleagues. Initially

I was so quiet in the England Lions dressing room that during the trips to Bangladesh and Sri Lanka I earned the nickname 'Casper'. Alex Hales, someone I get on with extremely well, came up with it because he reckoned it was as though I wasn't there at times – as in Casper the Friendly Ghost.

I was content enough, though, both from a cricket perspective and away from the ground. There wasn't a huge amount to do in Bangladesh and while others hung out together playing computer games, not being a *FIFA* addict, I spent a lot of time chilling in my room watching DVDs. That meant I spent a lot of time chilling in my room.

Twelve months later it was a similar story after I was picked for the 2012–13 Test tour of India on the back of another solid season, in which the weather made batting more challenging. On that trip, I had familiar faces for company, in the shape of Jonny Bairstow and Tim Bresnan, who I literally stalked for the first three weeks. If Bres had bothered looking he would have found me in his back pocket as I set about integrating into the full England team. It wasn't long before I was at ease in the company of the whole tour party and within no time I felt as much a part of it as anyone else. I didn't necessarily expect it to be like that at all, mainly because it was a little intimidating mingling with Alastair Cook, Graeme Swann, James Anderson and Kevin Pietersen, all guys I had watched and admired playing on television for years. But there was no suggestion that I wasn't an equal member of the dressing room. They just made me feel like one of the lads.

By the end of the tour, I was a Test cricketer myself. Two days before the final match of the series at Nagpur, Alastair Cook wandered up to me with some welcome news: 'Unless Monty Panesar goes down ill or picks up an injury, you are going to come into the team in place of Samit Patel.' For the next two days I man-marked Monty, making sure he walked down the stairs properly and was eating the right things for lunch. I ensured he wasn't over-training in practice, was running upright and was able to report for duty fully fit.

Practice makes perfect, they say, and, following a winter away the previous year working with Graham Thorpe on playing spin, I spent hour after hour working with the likes of Mushtaq Ahmed, Graham Gooch and Richard Halsall, both on the pre-tour camp in the United Arab Emirates and the tour of India itself. I had hit literally thousands of balls by the time of that fourth Test in Nagpur, working on all different aspects of my game to combat it. So I wasn't really concerned that India were going to be playing four spinners, in Pragyan Ojha, Ravichandran Ashwin, Piyush Chawla and Ravindra Jadeja.

There was no question that I was prepared for what lay ahead, so I decided from the moment Cooky told me I was playing that I was going to enjoy Test cricket whether my career was to span one match or 100. I'd dreamed of playing it since I was a very small boy and I wasn't going to let anything get in the way of me having a good time. That is the mentality I have tried to maintain ever since.

I can hardly express how much fun it was playing against India in their conditions, having to combat something so foreign to what I had been brought up on in a leafy suburb of Sheffield, and batting initially at the other end to Kevin Pietersen. Here was a guy I had watched winning the Ashes and making astonishing contributions to English cricket for a number of years, and now I had the chance to play alongside him. To me that was absolutely amazing. Of course I was nervous, but I considered that natural because everyone gets nervous. I certainly wasn't going to allow those nerves to impede me. They weren't going to be allowed to prevent me from doing well.

I reminded myself to play the situation in front of me and in the scheme of things, with us needing just a draw to win the series, that meant grinding out an innings. Here I was playing against Sachin Tendulkar, who had made his Test debut for India a year before I was born. It was just so exciting to be involved in direct competition with players of that stature. As a young boy I had been in awe of how guys like Tendulkar and Virender Sehwag played the game: some of the shots they would play, the massive scores they would make and how they succeeded under pressure. Now, here I was playing in the same game as them.

The fact that I started with a fifty in my first innings certainly helped confirm that the attitude I'd adopted of enjoying myself was the right one for me. Equally, I was soon to learn that after this start, both from a personal and team perspective, things would not always be so easy. After Christmas, my second appearance in Test cricket, away in New Zealand in March 2013, was not a pleasant one. I had done really well in the one-day series that preceded that first Test in Dunedin, but I played an horrendous shot in the first innings and then got run out in the second. Before I knew it, I had only one decent score to my name, while my most significant contribution in the series was arguably the hour and three-quarters I spent at the crease in Auckland on the final morning as we secured a draw in the third Test – chiefly due to the efforts of Bell, Matt Prior and Stuart Broad – to keep the series deadlocked. Despite being four wickets down overnight, we scraped over the line with just one wicket intact and Prior unbeaten on 110, made in four and a half hours.

On reflection, I had not done well on that trip. In fact, I returned home thinking that I would have to play really well to get back into the team when the home series against New Zealand came around just two months later. Thankfully, the selectors stuck with me and things really took off at the start of that summer thanks to more than 100 runs in the opening victory at Lord's and a special, maiden Test hundred on my home ground of Headingley. That was a period that highlighted the beauty of Test cricket for me.

Quite simply, you have to work tirelessly to succeed but are never going to conquer it. Test matches will always unearth ways to find you out, throw different challenges at you and stop you achieving absolutely everything that you want to, and let's face it, that's why we all play the game – the challenge. It is not easy; things don't come to you on a plate. You have to work hard and go through some hard times in order to make those really special times stand out. I had done that in New Zealand and then enjoyed success against them at home. You always have to remember that Test cricket can take you to the heights of Ashes wins and dip you to the lows of 5–0 whitewashes.

3 WINTER OF DISCONTENT

OR Alastair Cook, the year of 2014 must have been
horrific, bookended as it was by an Ashes whitewash
and his removal as England one-day captain. Yet to his
immense credit, throughout all his tribulations he never
once allowed his personal situation to have a negative effect
on the dressing room.

When it comes down to it, international players are picked
on performance, and by the time we departed for our final
assignment of 2014 in late November – the seven-match
series in Sri Lanka that represented a chance for fine-tuning
before the 2015 World Cup – Alastair was struggling for
form, having experienced a summer in which questions
were constantly being asked about his game and his
captaincy. Unless you have been put in that situation, you
can't really expect to understand what it was like for him
and what was going on in his head. All I can say is that
from the players' perspective he did not change one bit,
remaining his level-headed self, determined to play on in
a bid to improve, in spite of all the external pressure.

For any player, going through a run of games where you

do not make scores can be stressful, but the timing of Alastair's run could not have been any worse. Even though the home Test series against India had finished with us winning comfortably, television commentators, Shane Warne in particular, were constantly deconstructing his captaincy and his batting, asking questions like 'Is Cook the man to take England to a World Cup?' Incessant chat like that not only plays on the mind of a player; I am sure it must also play on the minds of selectors and management.

None of us sitting alongside him were questioning whether he was the right man, as far as I am aware, and I know I speak for a good number of other guys when I say he had our full support. The captain is the one you look up to and the one you have the most respect for in the group, so from a team-mate's point of view the criticism was not nice to witness. But the dignity with which Alastair handled it all, and the way he acted off the field, made a big impression on me. To remain that composed even though it wasn't necessarily the way he felt inside was something I'm sure I can learn from. He dealt with everything like a true captain: a proper leader. He did not want to let his personal struggles affect anybody else's preparation or performance, didn't take frustrations out on others and never once offered excuses. He was always very honest about the fact he was striving for form and it was certainly a good example to set for the rest of us.

It was just a shame he could not get the scores together to take us to the World Cup. But ultimately he paid the price for a failure to make significant contributions at the top of the order – not scoring a half-century in either the 3–1 one-day series defeat to India at the end of the 2014 summer or the 5–2 loss to the Sri Lankans – and a slump in results.

After a fifth loss in six 50-over series, I returned home to Sheffield aware of the speculation about his future. But when you are not part of the team management – either captain or vice-captain – you do not really have a clue about what's going on. You just want to concentrate on your cricket, because that is hard enough. So I heard about the decision much like the rest of the nation, when I woke up and turned on Sky Sports News on the morning of Saturday, 20 December 2014.

My reaction was to get in touch with Alastair to tell him I was sorry. Like any player who has just found out he is not going to a World Cup, he was absolutely gutted. In his case more so, because of what he had fought his way through the previous summer. It must have been draining dealing with all the questions and the constant speculation. When you play a team sport it is natural to grow close to your colleagues and you never want to see anybody suffer like that. But it was clear from our chat that he needed space and time to come to terms with what had happened.

In one way he had been a victim of our disproportionate scheduling. Certainly from my vantage point, over the previous eighteen months a much greater emphasis had been placed on Test cricket than on one-day cricket. For example, for the one-dayers at the end of our 2013–14

Ashes tour, a lot of the senior guys were either given a complete break, as in the cases of James Anderson and Kevin Pietersen, or left out for part of the series, like Stuart Broad. (Resting players after an Ashes series has become fairly common practice in recent years and I confess I was glad of the break at the end of the 2015 summer after missing just one international in the calendar year.)

However, while resting players gives new lads an opportunity to come into the international environment and step up a level, you can't develop the consistency that comes from the same guys regularly playing their intended roles in the side. From the time Ashley Giles began his spell as England's limited-overs coach, there was regular resting of the core members of the Test team, and it was hard to develop continuity in the team's play when, for instance, five changes were made for the 50-over series against Australia at the end of the 2013 Ashes in England.

Test cricket has retained its primacy in English thinking and that has proved hard for people to move away from, yet the one time under Giles we did get a full-strength side out, earlier that 2013 summer, we reached the final of the ICC Champions Trophy and should have won the tournament. Twelve months before the 2015 World Cup we went out to the Caribbean, and, because of the proximity of the tour to the World Twenty20, ended up playing a proportion of our 20-over specialists, such as Luke Wright and Michael Lumb, in the 50-over team.

Nothing against those who came in during that time –

they actually did well – but when you make changes in personnel like that it carries on through into your next series and it takes time for those returning to bed in. When you are developing any side, success is usually enhanced by continuity of selection, and it is almost impossible to build on performances when different players are shipped in and out.

Not that the task of selecting teams is easy. When you play as much cricket as we do in England, if you play all three forms of the game, you have no obvious rest periods. And those are important because otherwise you are going to get injured or mentally tired, and your performances are going to drop in standard. One of the hardest tasks for the management is managing player workloads and making sure that people get enough time away from the game. Of course, no player wants to miss matches. Everyone wants to play every game they feel fully fit for, so it falls to others to make sure that when you do play you are able to do so at your absolute best, or at least somewhere near it.

Successful one-day teams learn to work together. For example, batsmen develop an understanding of where their team-mates score their runs, how they complement each other, who is stronger against certain types of bowling and how to manipulate the strike accordingly. This requires the building of relationships within the team. It is not ideal to be developing these in the immediate build-up to a World Cup, and the departure of Cook meant changes in the batting order and a need to get a formula together in just six weeks.

* * *

I have never believed in playing for your place. You play to win. That means you play the situation in front of you, whether you're batting, bowling or captaining. And if that means you come in with five overs left, required to have a go, and hole out second ball, then so be it. But it is very much harder to stay faithful to that approach when there is a World Cup just around the corner and your place is on the line. Representing your country in a tournament like that is one of those boyhood dreams, isn't it? Every cricketer wants to be in that situation. And it certainly crept into my mind that I wanted to make sure I got myself into that squad. Whether securing their World Cup spots played on the minds of the rest of the squad as we departed for Colombo in mid-November, I cannot say. But selection was naturally cropping up in the media, and along with the debate of who was going and who was not comes a certain pressure.

In one regard, retaining that desperation to be selected is quite good preparation for a World Cup, because once you are picked it is in expectation of going on to win the silverware. If you aren't able to cope with the build-up of being picked in the squad, how are you expected to cope when the tournament proper begins?

To be honest, I didn't feel a settled member of the one-day side at this stage. Although I got off to a good start in one-day international cricket, I had not played a lot of white-ball stuff before appearing for England and what I had played was predominantly 40-over cricket, so it had been a case of learning on the job. During those first six months, from making my one-day debut in Rajkot in January 2013 to facing India in the Champions Trophy final in June, I averaged 53 and everything was fine. It was when I had a dip in form, passing 50 just twice in my next nineteen innings, that I learned some harsh lessons.

It was during this period that I decided to take more notice of those players around me who were being successful – of exactly how they were going about their business at training and in game situations. I have always been an advocate of doing what you can to eradicate problems that drift into your game as quickly as possible.

The big turning point came when, on the back of a good summer of Test form in 2014, I carried confidence into the one-day series against India that closed the international season. I do not know how close I was, and I never discussed it with anyone, but it certainly felt like I needed to make a score to retain my place in the side heading into the winter, so to make 113 in the final match of the series against the Indians at Headingley was a very pleasing way to finish off. Additionally, the aggressive manner in which I was able to play told me that I had addressed the issue of improving my strike rate.

There had been a period at the start of my one-day international career when I fitted well into the way the team played, and I was able to score at what I thought was a reasonable rate. It was copying the universally accepted formula of building an innings, then trying to help the team explode towards the back end of the 50 overs, having kept wickets in hand. Unfortunately, however, I was playing that way at a time when one-day cricket was moving on to another level in terms of scores.

To my mind, that Sri Lanka trip at the end of 2014 was the first evidence that my game was beginning to move with the times. Making that change was certainly hard, because for a substantial period of time I had played a certain way within the framework of a team that had, during 2013, risen to number one in the world rankings. All of a sudden, it almost felt like it was worthless to be playing in that manner. But the change of approach and a switch from number three to number four suited me.

I knew Sri Lanka would try and hit us with spin, so I was already asking myself how I was going to be most effective when confronted with it. What were the best options for scoring when the ball was turning away from me? What were the best options when the ball was turning into me? I planned to develop shots to get off strike and to ensure I scored off four or five balls an over. You would hope, of course, to include the odd boundary in these scoring shots and that being the case you are generally scoring at the right kind of rate. Once you've built a partnership with somebody, you can maybe look to be more expansive, and that was the sort of framework I was using for that tour.

There was also one significant technical change I made during the trip that was to prove beneficial for me across all formats. I did a lot of work with Jos Buttler over there on batting tempo and ball-striking, two things I have always admired in his game.

From a technical point of view, I tinkered a little bit with my backlift, finding that if I raised my hands higher in my stance I could get them back through the ball with greater velocity and therefore create a bit more power. This was done specifically with Asian conditions in mind, and it certainly helped me to hit down the ground more strongly, but I later found that it transferred into other conditions effectively too. I am not advocating trying to emulate every player you witness, but there is no harm in experimenting in the nets if you consider a change may enhance your performance.

The alterations I made proved seamless. Generally, when you are moving well with your feet, your hands tend to go in unison with them, almost moving at the same time to create a flowing motion, and the key to batting, I have found, is to keep it as rhythmical as possible. Conversely, when you are not playing well, it is often the case that your movements are not necessarily moving in sync. When you are out of nick, you are always trying to reconnect with that feeling of fluency.

One of the reasons I wanted to work with Jos was that I had noticed the ease with which he plays in batting power-plays. That is always something I have struggled with a little and I certainly cannot compete in terms of the distance he can strike the ball. So while I was not trying to match the same kind of strike rate, I was keen to at least develop the ability to go through the next gear. Jos has that ability to really press the accelerator because of the power in his game. Having spent a lot of time chatting things through with him, it was very nice to be in a position where we chased down a score together to pull the series back to 2–1 in Hambantota, our 84-run stand inside 11 overs sealing a five-wicket victory. He was also newly arrived at the crease shortly after I brought up my hundred in the other win on the tour, in the fifth match at Pallekele.

Tempo is one thing you can learn from watching Jos. Another feature of his batting is just how calm he remains under pressure – how, through his body language, he exudes composure. That's quite a signal to give off to the opposition, and it has a very positive effect on you as his fellow batsman at the other end. Without a doubt, increased composure of that kind is something I wanted to instil in my game, and not just for white-ball matches. These days you can take bits from all over the place and apply them to your general play. If you are able to give off that sense of calm at the crease when new partners arrive, it can take the tension out of a run chase.

Working with Jos did not radically alter my style – I've always felt that as a batsman I am at my best when I am just looking to time the ball and hit the gaps – it just opened up my eyes to slightly different possibilities. Even though he hits a long ball, he does not try to over-hit it, but allows his hands to follow through in the stroke. Similarly, Ben Stokes, who bludgeons the ball to all parts, does so effortlessly, looking as if he is hitting within himself as he dispatches the ball twenty rows back in the stands. I am not necessarily going to hit it as far as them but I worked on the theory that getting a more consistent strike on the ball would only increase my scoring rate. When I hit aerially, I don't tend to try to clear the rope, I just aim to hit one-bounce fours, and that way I have found you end up hitting the odd six.

That tour to Sri Lanka provided us with a good block of cricket leading up to the 2015 World Cup, and it was a good opportunity to spend a lot of time together, getting to know each other's roles within the team. Unfortunately, results-wise we didn't get what we would have liked. On a personal level, it was definitely a tour I took a lot from, because of the amount of runs I scored. To amass 367 runs across seven matches was pleasing.

For others it proved a defining trip for different reasons. It spawned devastating news for Alastair Cook and, after an equally fruitless adventure, for Ben Stokes. Ben was struggling with the ball, wasn't trusted with as many overs as he would have liked as a result, and batted low down in the order. He just wasn't putting in the displays that demanded selection for the World Cup. It must have been absolutely devastating to miss out. But in that situation you respond in one of two ways. It would have been easy for him to spend Christmas feeling bitter about the whole experience. Instead, he came home, accepted a chance to play in Australia's Big Bash League, did really well and used those big hands of his to grab every opportunity he has been given to play for England since. He is now an integral part of both our one-day and Test sides.

Some will say he was the victim – some may say we all were – of playing in conditions completely alien to those we were preparing for in Australia. But part of the challenge of international cricket is being able to adapt to different conditions, to go from place to place – from Sri Lanka to Australia, say – and perform. You can moan about the schedules all day long, but we do not control them and they are not there to be used as an excuse. We had seven opportunities to hone our one-day skills, both with the ball – bowling at the death, trying different skills, such as taking pace off or developing cutters – and with the bat, trying to dominate the opposition on slower pitches.

Say, for example, we were thrown into a World Cup match on a used pitch that might turn – skills developed in Sri Lanka could have been priceless. You can spend too much time assessing your prep but from a playing point of view you have to tell yourself it is all about how to work on development of individual and team skills. From a personal perspective, constantly changing my game to suit different conditions means that when I do come across a pitch that is not typically Australian or English, and I have to score runs at a certain rate, I can adapt to it. That was the way I viewed the trip.

As a collective, there were a lot of guys contributing in different games but not enough people backing up those individual performances. For example, in the opening match of the Sri Lanka series, we were bowled out for 292 with three overs unused chasing 318. Arguably, we should have restricted them to 280. Not using up our allocation of overs was a theme of the matches and our chief frustration was that we were just not quite able to patch all the elements of the game together. That was something that had proved hard to achieve in our one-day cricket for some time, and it often is a struggle for a team of young players. Unfortunately, it takes time to learn those lessons and we just did not have enough experience at that time. Ben Stokes had played just 21 ODIs and James Taylor, Alex Hales, Chris Woakes, Chris Jordan and Harry Gurney had all played fewer.

To my mind, it certainly wasn't the decisions of the coaches or their influence that stopped us from performing out there in Sri Lanka. We knew what we had to do; we just didn't deliver consistently as a team. And that went for all facets of the game: bowling, batting and fielding. We might do one of them well in one match, two of them well in another, but we rarely made it all three. These days if you have a bad display in one aspect of the game, you have to pay for it.

After Christmas, before the World Cup, we had the opportunity to form a new batting unit during the Carlton Mid triangular series in Australia. India had hammered us 3–1 in our own conditions the previous summer and so to beat them convincingly in this series on more than one occasion, and book a place in the final against Australia, gave us confidence that we were on the right track.

Nevertheless, some of our annoying traits from Sri Lanka travelled with us. For example, we made a good start against Australia at Hobart thanks to Ian Bell, recast as an opener in Cook's absence, playing out of his skin for 141. Unfortunately, after we had shot out of the blocks, our scoring rate went into reverse – which was very uncharacteristic of our middle order. Normally, you would associate it with being explosive and powerful, but it was nothing like that against the Australians and we ended up with 303. Once again, we had failed to back up a good individual performance, and then we were unable to defend a 300-plus target. In truth, it should have been 330.

In the final itself at Perth we felt as if we were bowling well when we got Australia in trouble at 60–4, only for Glenn Maxwell and Mitchell Marsh to take the game away from us. James Faulkner's late assault added to the size of our task and they blew us away by 112 runs. Only Jimmy Anderson came out of the match with any credit after taking a couple of wickets with the new ball and going at less than four runs per over. This merely extended the theme of impressive individual displays remaining isolated in matches throughout the winter. The tri-series had opened with Eoin Morgan scoring 121 at the SCG, his contribution more than 50 per cent of our team total, after he had arrived at the crease at 12–3. It was a problem that would stay with us into the World Cup, with so many pockets of brilliance, such as James Taylor's 98 against the Australians on 14 February in Melbourne, turning out to be the only significant contributions in an innings.

Make no mistake, we were desperate to do well at the World Cup, not least because the 1992 England team had reached the final on the previous occasion it had been played in Australasia. It was devastating not to be able to produce something similar.

Things could hardly have begun any worse, and without trying to offer excuses, our run of games did not help. To face Australia and New Zealand at the start, the two teams who turned out to be the two finalists, in their own back-yards, completely derailed us. When you are playing a global tournament you accept having to combat foreign condi-tions, but here we were facing the two pre-tournament favourites in their strongholds of Melbourne and Wellington.

In that opening Valentine's Day match against the Australians we could sense our opponents were nervous and there was a real 'what if' moment for us in the first over, after asking them to bat first in the day-nighter, when we missed a chance to dismiss Aaron Finch for nought second ball. Chris Woakes got his hands to a catch above his head but failed to hold on at midwicket. Finch made us pay by going on to score a hundred as, even though we got David Warner, Shane Watson and Steve Smith quickly, he dug them out of a tricky situation in tandem with George Bailey. The middle order of Maxwell, Marsh and Brad

Haddin then capitalised in the final ten overs and a score of 342–9 was Australia's highest ever at the MCG – but par for the course in the tournament.

In defence of their big total, they were able to force false shot after false shot, and it was only 'Titch' Taylor who stood up with that very good innings of 98 towards the end. It was annoying because on reflection there were so many little things that would have turned out differently if we had taken the half chances or executed our individual plans better. Unfortunately, spurning opportunities to dismiss opposition batsmen – the reprieved Finch could also have been run out before Eoin Morgan's decisive direct hit – and losing our own wickets in little clusters were to become features of our play.

I am sure that the more you experience situations like that, in pressure matches, the better you get at finding a way to turn them in your favour. You find that the more games you play together, the greater the number of guys who stand up and perform. But you tend not to take those chances when you are not performing to a high level, and being brutally honest, we were not. If you look at the make-up of our side during the tournament, there were a lot of young guys who had not won much previously. Winning is a habit, I believe. Unfortunately, so is losing.

Our next defeat happened in a flash. New Zealand simply blew us away the following weekend at Westpac Stadium. After winning the toss, we got our first taste of Brendon

McCullum's ultra-aggressive style of captaincy when he began with four slips in place for the new-ball spells of Tim Southee and Trent Boult and maintained at least three close catchers for the duration of our innings.

If this fresh approach of attacking fields took us by surprise, and it did, we reacted badly to it. Our response was to build cautiously, attempting to ride out their initial efforts in a bid to prosper later. Unfortunately, this never happened.

New Zealand sent down any number of good deliveries throughout our innings, which encouraged us to go into our shells. Sadly, we never re-emerged. We became so reserved in our approach to combatting them that the scoreboard just didn't move. It was no more than a survival exercise.

I arrived at the crease with the score on 36–2 in the seventh over, intent on soaking up the pressure, firstly alongside Gary Ballance, and then Eoin Morgan. However, there is no doubt that if I had that time again I would go completely the other way and be even more aggressive than usual. My aim would be to try to get Brendon McCullum's positive fields pushed back and transformed into more defensive ones. Because when you're batting in a situation with so many close fielders around you, there are huge gaps in front of the wicket. There were certainly vast expanses unoccupied down the ground because they had several slips and a gully, and against two new white balls on a good pitch you have to back yourself. If you do edge one and they catch it, you have to accept it. But if you just let the opposition bowl at you, you're more likely to face good balls in good areas because you have allowed them to settle into rhythm. In contrast, if you take the game to the opposition by being positive, that is when you create your opportunities to score. As we have seen since, doing so can knock bowlers off their line and length.

As it was, we were duped by McCullum's bravado. Having such field placings in a one-day international was certainly not something we had seen before, and perhaps that is why we reacted to it in a defensive manner. Typically, when Morgs did try to cast off the shackles against Daniel Vettori, he fell to a spectacular catch from Adam Milne, diving at long-on. It was the first of seven wickets to go down in 7.3 overs.

Every time a new batsman came out we spoke about building a partnership and taking a reassessment once we had been in together for a while, but it was all in vain, as Southee ran amok, bagging five of his seven wickets in a 20-ball spell. Finally, it was just myself and Jimmy Anderson, trying to recreate what we had done together in the Test match against India at Trent Bridge the previous summer when he had stuck around to help me to a hundred, and got close to celebrating one himself. In this game, there was so much time left to bat that it was possible to do something similar, but within a couple of minutes I was out attempting a pull off Milne.

To be all out for 123 in 33.2 overs was plain embarrassing, and things were about to get worse, thanks to McCullum's audacity with the bat. His fifty spanned a World Cup record

18 balls; he was dismissed from the first ball of the eighth over having contributed 77 of the 105-run total; ten more minutes of him would have finished the contest before the dinner break. As it was, they required just 74 balls to complete an eight-wicket win.

This contest highlighted a huge gulf between the teams on the day and a massive difference in approaches. Full credit to New Zealand, though, because the brand of cricket they played has since helped other sides, including ourselves, to develop more imaginative limited-overs styles, and the global game is better for it.

That Saturday, 20 February 2015, was reported as one of English cricket's lowest ebbs. 'It does not get any worse than this,' wrote Paul Newman in the *Daily Mail*. Unfortunately, it did for me.

Back in Wellington on 1 March, having breached the 300-run mark to register a first tournament win over Scotland six days earlier, we bettered that total by posting 309–6 against Sri Lanka. Statistically speaking, that sounds OK, and from a personal point of view, scoring a fourth one-day international hundred inside twelve months gave me immense pride. Later, however, after Sri Lanka cantered to a nine-wicket win with 16 balls to spare, it hit home that what I considered to be a good score in those conditions was not a good score at all. I was absolutely gutted trudging off the turf at the Westpac Stadium in the knowledge that I had misjudged it so badly.

During post-match analysis, I realised that we were 50 runs short of where we had needed to be. Perhaps 25 runs shy of being competitive. This may sound as if I am being hard on myself, but it was my job to judge what a good total was on that surface and so I scored at a certain rate until increasing the tempo with James Taylor during the batting powerplay. At the time, I thought I had paced the innings pretty well. Unfortunately, that pace was not good enough, and I reflected that despite finishing with a strike rate of 112 I had not been aggressive enough early in my innings. Just as in Leeds against India the previous summer, I had successfully addressed my old failing of getting in and getting out before I had caught up with the run-a-ball mark, and once joined by Jos Buttler, I had managed to get him on strike regularly, giving him the chance to hit an unbeaten 39 off 19 balls at the end. Yet the lingering frustration was that I had batted the majority of the innings – between overs 13 and 47 – in a match in which we were defeated with plenty of time to spare.

In old money, 121 off 108 deliveries and a team total in excess of 300 represented excellent returns, but other teams were now posting scores approaching 400 and appeared to be batting without limits. If it was a good batting surface, there was absolutely no stopping some sides. There was A.B. de Villiers's knock against West Indies in Sydney when, from a standing start, he crunched an unbeaten 162; then Chris Gayle scoring 215 against Zimbabwe in Canberra – these performances were truly amazing. The realisation that the game I was playing was still behind the times, despite having worked so hard to improve the tempo of scoring, really hurt.

That night represented the lowest point of the World Cup for me, because having gone through the stark disappointment of not performing against Australia and New Zealand on those first two weekends, to initially feel that we had performed, only to realise we had misjudged things was gutting. During the forty-five-minute interval between innings, my assessment was that I'd played really well, and I thought that if we got a couple of early wickets we would be on course to win the game. Unfortunately, we got an absolute batting masterclass from Kumar Sangakkara, who was in the purplest patch of his or anyone else's career. His unbeaten 117 was the second of four consecutive hundreds for him in the tournament, representing the best individual sequence in World Cup history. To show that kind of consistency is extraordinary.

For any neutral or Sri Lankan fan it must have been a joy to watch, but for English eyes it made for painful viewing, and it wasn't much fun having to keep throwing the ball back from deep midwicket, or wherever else Kumar chose to hit it to. It became apparent very quickly that my mid-match musings required reassessment; we needed a clutch of quick wickets or we were going to be on the end of something utterly deflating.

If it was the batsmen refusing to set limits on what was possible in an innings who were prospering in the tournament, and they truly were, the best bowlers were generally the ones who hunted for wickets rather than those who tried to dry up the runs. Dismissing batsmen has always been viewed as the best way to slow down the opposition's scoring and perhaps we were not proactive enough in this regard. The containment game, of sitting back after posting a good score, seemed a little outdated.

Our established one-day pace attack of Jimmy Anderson and Stuart Broad have always been at their best when they can get the ball to move laterally, but the conditions we encountered did not aid traditional seam movement. So if they were able to create chances, it was important we slip fielders took them. Not taking the conventional opportunity we created with the new ball – when Broad found the edge of Lahiru Thirimanne's bat before Sri Lanka had made it into double figures and I failed to pouch the catch at first slip – was to cost us. Like Sangakkara, Thirimanne went on to score an undefeated hundred.

I came off the field absolutely devastated and headed to the post-match press conference with a bit of a bulge in my throat. This was our third heavy loss in the competition and I felt culpable for the part I'd played in our downfall. Usually, after a one-day international you feel exhausted but when I got back to my hotel room that night I felt slightly different. After our two previous heavy defeats, we had reconvened for dinner as a team, but on this occasion I could not face that. I just wanted to be on my own. I certainly didn't want to be miserable around the other lads, so I decided, as I was absolutely knackered, to go to bed. But I just could not sleep as my mind tripped through every scenario the match had thrown up.

Generally I speak to my agent Neil Fairbrother after most games, and certainly after one-day games, because he has bags of experience and was an integral part of the England team that got to the World Cup final in 1992. He had sent me a text from the UK to ask if I wanted a chat – as he had done after the defeat to New Zealand – so I took him up on the offer. Later, he told me that throughout a conversation in which I expressed some disbelief at what had gone on in the preceding few hours, my voice seemed so different, so withdrawn and quiet, that he thought I had been talking to him with my head under a pillow.

I certainly needed a bit of a lift after that game and I have made a habit of ringing three old schoolmates, James, Tom and Tom, whenever I am at my lowest. I also try to check in with my girlfriend, Carrie, brother Bill and Mum and Dad after most games, particularly if I am away from home. It is not so much 'poor me', because I consider travelling the world playing cricket the best job I could possibly have. It's just nice to hear comforting voices from home when you're on the road. The people that are really important to you can make you feel good about yourself again, and with proper mates you cop a bit of well-intended stick too. You can't overestimate the recuperative powers of having the mickey taken out of you by those who know you best. It makes you feel human again, not just a robot that plays cricket.

There are times as a cricketer when I do take things very personally. We are extremely lucky to represent England and wear those three lions on our chests and on our caps, and we understand how great a privilege it is because we are all massive cricket fans, as much fans as anyone out there watching in the stands or at home. So contemplating that you are the ones putting in the performances to lose your team the game hurts all the more. That in turn means that at times like this you need those close to you to remind you that it is only a game. It's as much a self-preservation tactic as anything else.

Time proved to be a bit of an enemy out there as well. With six- to eight-day gaps between matches it meant the desperation to put things right festered during day after day of nets and hanging around the team hotels. On a normal tour you get the chance to put a bad limited-overs performance behind you within seventy-two hours, but the World Cup scheduling simply elongated our sense of suffering. Heading back into the nets is one thing, but you can never really replicate a true match scenario.

Perhaps until the penultimate match of the group stage we didn't get the balance of our side right. It's easy to say that with hindsight, but someone like Alex Hales is a very exciting player and one look at other sides out there told you they were basing their one-day formula around

Twenty20 cricket. Australia had Aaron Finch and David Warner as an opening pair; New Zealand partnered Brendon McCullum with Martin Guptill; India went with Rohit Sharma and Shikhar Dhawan. We were almost the other way around and based ourselves a bit too much on our Test cricket, with Ian Bell, Moeen Ali and Gary Ballance forming our top three.

They are all fine players but ones that tend to rely on finesse and timing rather than physique and power to get the ball to the boundary. The problem with playing that way, and not possessing a more muscular ball-striker at the top of the order, is that if you don't get off to an explosive start and instead bat in a more conservative manner, you have to ensure that you do go on deep into the innings and make big scores. Otherwise all you are doing is wasting time. It certainly took me some time to work that out on a personal level and I think it's fair to say the same for other members of the team. Losing those first three games as we did made it very hard to then try to switch tactics. We were already low on confidence and under increasing pressure with each game we played.

We limited ourselves as to what good scores were. Instead of getting off to flyers and maintaining the pace, it was more about getting to a certain position in order to get to 300–330, a range we viewed as being good. But we rarely got into positions where we could emulate anything like the kind of tallies other teams were making. We were not even in the same ballpark as the big teams, and at no stage did we play the batting powerplays well, apart from that one game against Sri Lanka when we managed 42 runs across five overs without losing a wicket.

Maybe we looked at statistics a little bit too much, but don't for one minute think we sat studying them for hours. I know in the aftermath of our elimination, confirmation of which came via our defeat to Bangladesh in Adelaide on 8 March, there was a furore over Peter Moores's apparent reliance on it, but the bottom line was that we're unable to perform to the standards we wanted to both individually and as a team.

Of course, we did discuss things such as bowling a certain number of balls in good areas being our best chance of taking wickets based on statistical evidence of previous matches in Australian conditions, and general scoring trends – you would expect all international teams' management to examine previous matches on each ground – but to suggest it was the main focus of our attention would be wrong. From a batting point of view, we didn't look at games overly statistically, relying instead on our instincts as to what good scores were when building a platform and what positions we required to get into when chasing. We were just not able to do either discipline well.

Further humiliating evidence of this came after Eoin Morgan asked Bangladesh to bat first in the day-night encounter at the Adelaide Oval. After we took a couple of early wickets, Mahmudullah played brilliantly under pressure to stabilise things on his way to his country's first ever

World Cup hundred. Bangladesh kept wickets in hand and he mastered the pace of their innings before his fifth-wicket partnership with Mushfiqur Rahim forced us to leak a few too many runs towards the death. We bowled pretty well throughout but they suddenly got away from us a little by scoring 115 from their final 15 overs.

Even then, a target of 276 was still one we would expect to chase down, and during our pursuit it felt like we were in control of the situation. But critically we followed the loss of our second wicket, that of Hales with the scoreboard on 97 in the 20th over, with two more in an over not long after – those of Bell and Morgan – and suddenly they were all over us. Low on confidence, we didn't respond well under pressure and they focused their energies on making it hard for the new batsmen coming in.

The way to win games of one-day cricket will always be to build partnerships and we were just unable to do so. But every time we got one together we lost another wicket, mine included. For a while, watching on from the balcony, it seemed that Jos Buttler was going to do what he had made a habit of in recent times and haul us out of trouble and over the line, but we were just not good enough to support him and the loss of confidence from the previous games was all too evident in our play. The heavy defeats at the start of the tournament had taken their toll.

That evening in Adelaide was horrible. Again, there was a feeling of sheer embarrassment, not because we had lost to Bangladesh – that would certainly be doing them a disservice – but because we had bombed out of the World Cup in the group stages. There was no doubt in our minds that we should have got to the quarter-finals as a bare minimum. We were certainly a better side than we had shown out there. Our performances were nowhere near up to scratch. A year that we had all so looked forward to had begun disastrously.

4 A CARIBBEAN COMING TOGETHER

THE team spirit that kept us tight in testing moments in the height of summer in 2015 had been fostered in the Caribbean spring. The tour might not have delivered the expected results, but it should be remembered as where things started coming together for an emerging England team. The players within the group dispatched on that three-Test trip all enjoy each other's company and that is a very rare commodity in international teams. Most suffer from squabbles and arguments from time to time – it is only to be expected between individuals competing for places in a professional environment – yet there was not really any of that stuff throughout our month away.

Perhaps we had bottomed out with what happened at the World Cup and everyone involved had taken their own decision to completely forget about what had gone before, chill out and take refuge in a destination that promoted a laid-back vibe. Perhaps the influx of fresh faces helped everyone see things differently. Perhaps it was just that after recent results, admittedly in another format, feeling as though we were playing better cricket simply felt good again. What I do know is that from a personal perspective the West Indies experience helped me enjoy playing once more. The people of the Caribbean love it if you have a good time and embrace their culture, and that is what I immersed myself in.

Preparation for the series was very low key and despite some questions about the standard of the opposition in St Kitts, the venue for our first warm-up games, from a selfish perspective I felt well prepared, having faced our own bowling attack after being one of those chosen to strengthen the hosts in the second of two two-day matches. It was certainly better to be out in Caribbean conditions, adapting to the pace of the pitches and the heat, rather than back indoors at Loughborough.

With the onus on us to bounce back after a substandard winter away, we were boosted by the return of Ottis Gibson to our set-up as bowling coach. As he had been in charge of West Indies only a matter of months earlier, there was no one better to give us the low-down on what to expect from a new-look home team. For our part, we were in a good place heading into the first Test in Antigua on 13 April, just as we had been the last time we had played the format, eight months earlier. Albeit in different conditions, we had smashed India, with a lot of young players putting in very strong performances at the start of their international careers.

Ironically, having prepared in expectation of typically slow, low pitches, the one served up in Antigua was almost like an English seamer. It was quite a green pitch and the West Indies bowlers made the best use of it to reduce us to 34–3 in the 17th over at the Sir Vivian Richards Stadium on the first morning, leaving Ian Bell and myself to redress the balance.

I certainly felt the benefit of playing a lot of one-day cricket that winter. Of course it was a different format, but seeing the way the scores in the World Cup had mushroomed, and listening to our bowlers talking about going out of the park if they missed their lengths slightly, had made me re-evaluate my approach. What was the difference, I asked myself, between Test cricket and one-day cricket? There are obvious contrasts such as the fact that the red ball swings more, and does so for longer, but why not try to put Test bowlers under pressure with greater intent? When I considered both my Test and one-day games, I concluded they were fairly similar. All I kept thinking was how I wanted to put pressure back on the opposition bowlers – rotate the strike, knock them off their lengths, create scoring opportunities for both myself and my partner.

When discussing the state of the game a little over an hour into the series, Ian Bell was of the same opinion, and by the end of the day, after trying to be positive, we found ourselves in a really good position. Changing the game situation as quickly as possible has become my favoured option and by sharing 177 runs at 3.76 an over we altered the match's momentum. Bell's was a brilliant hundred and the only frustration with my innings was that I chopped on to Jerome Taylor when 83 and well set.

Whenever I travel abroad I like to get mentally prepared for the different surfaces and types of bowling likely to be encountered. For example, in the Caribbean you are generally tested more with reverse swing and bowlers tend to bowl a little bit more wicket to wicket, with fielders in front of the bat rather than behind it. The pitches are generally slower and that means you have to find slightly different scoring areas to get off strike. The ball gets softer and although it doesn't tend to go sideways off the pitch it is hard to get away.

You only have to study the West Indies batsmen to see how differently they go about things. Look at someone like Jermaine Blackwood, whose unbeaten hundred in response highlighted his penchant for hitting the opening bowlers back over long-on for six. He appears to do this almost randomly, from out of nowhere – tactically, it is a ploy to force men back and create new areas to score singles. Scoring square of the wicket can be hard work, so whenever you get any width it is important that you strike the ball with everything you've got. Having been successful on a one-day tour there previously, I believed that their spin bowlers were guys that we could really dominate. If we were able to do so, it would give Denesh Ramdin, the West Indies captain, the problem of bowling his pacemen for five or six overs a day more than he would want.

Yet here we were in Antigua combating fast bowlers with a full slip cordon. That meant there were gaps around and I always think that when bowlers are searching for wickets, they get greedy, and that is the best time to capitalise with scoring shots. We immediately discovered that despite missing half a dozen players due to the clash with the Indian Premier League, they still possessed some very skilful bowlers. Jason Holder was always hard work to face, banging away consistently on a good length, while at the other end Jerome Taylor showed ability to swing the new ball with good pace and control.

That drawn match nevertheless provided an eventful end when Jimmy Anderson marked his 100th Test appearance by equalling and then passing Sir Ian Botham's England record wicket haul. He'd flown his entire family out to Antigua in expectation of doing it there and in a way that put more pressure on him. He had so wanted his daughters, Lola and Ruby, to be there to witness it, and didn't want them to be off school for another week, so we were all made up for him when the moment came. It was fitting that Alastair Cook held the catch at slip that dismissed Denesh Ramdin and took the Anderson tally to 384 as we pushed for victory on the final evening. As they have played so many Test matches together, I am sure it was an extremely special moment for both of them.

When you look at all the guys Jimmy has passed to get to the top of the list – what people say about Botham, Fred

Trueman and Bob Willis, some of the greats of the game – it puts his achievement in perspective. Jimmy will never be called a great until he retires but in my eyes he already is one. In fact, he's the greatest of them all in terms of England's fast bowlers. What he brings to our team is outstanding. The control he offers, swinging the ball both ways at the pace he does, in addition to the wobble-seam delivery that gives left-handers nightmares. When you think that he also has the skill to be successful on the subcontinent with his reverse swing, it shows you he is the complete fast bowler. His contributions to team meetings are also invaluable. Generally he doesn't say too much, but when he does you listen because of what he's achieved.

Jimmy is a modest man and would never speak highly of himself, but I am sure that will go down as one of the proudest days in his life.

Not that I've always admired him. When we played a Roses match against Lancashire at Liverpool in 2011 he left me thinking, 'Who does this guy think he is?' His aggressive behaviour had shocked a new kid on the block like me. I have since come to acknowledge that his abrupt on-field nature is purely designed to get the best out of himself. On this particular occasion, our opening batsman Joe Sayers had got him in a flap late on the third evening when surviving an appeal for caught behind. I didn't agree with the way Jimmy performed subsequently – he gave Joe a verbal barrage, with plenty of expletives. He then walked down the wicket to me and told me to give Joe a batting lesson after play, to show him what to do. I took this as an inverse compliment. His words suggested that despite it only being my sixth County Championship game, he thought I could bat. However, it took only a few more balls for me to realise his comments were no reflection on me at all. I was getting a serve too.

All I can say is that he is totally different off the field and it is as if a switch flicks in his head when he crosses the white line at the start of play. At the end of the day, it takes him about half an hour to cool down and you recognise a completely different character. It's almost as if he is two different characters. One is very quiet and shy, albeit with a very dry sense of humour; the other one, the grumpy fast bowler, can be hard work and turns into a snarling beast.

Earlier in the day, Jimmy had drawn level with Sir Ian – who provided a nice touch by offering his personal congratulations as soon as we left the field that evening – when Marlon Samuels drove to gully. It came during a period of play in which we had started to really wind Marlon up, actions for which there were to be consequences for Ben Stokes. When he'd arrived at the crease it looked like we were massive favourites to win the game. West Indies had nevertheless only lost two wickets in the opening 34 overs and we knew he was a batsman capable of occupying the crease for lengthy periods.

So we tried to play on his ego a bit, encouraging him to take on a few of the bowlers with some extravagant shots.

Within earshot we started talking about how previous guys representing West Indies would have played big shots already, wondering out loud why he was biding his time. One suggestion being offered during this prolonged teasing session was that his slow scoring was the reason he had not been picked up for the IPL. As he'd taken 41 balls to compile half a dozen runs, we appeared to have got under his skin when he hit a couple of sixes using his feet against James Tredwell's off-spin. Soon afterwards, a lack of foot-work cost him when he took a liberty against Jimmy.

In the next game, in Grenada, the goading had no effect at all and he went on to get a first-innings hundred. So when it was our turn to bat, Stokes, the front man for our wise words, copped a bit and then some. There were several players on our side, myself included, willing to chirp at Marlon and he is not averse to giving it back. I actually respect him for it and when you look back at tours, confrontations like that stick in your mind. The moment Marlon mimicked Ben is something I will never forget. No one got a better view of it than me at the non-striker's end.

There were half a dozen overs left on the third evening when Ben hauled a short ball from the leg-spinner Devendra Bishoo straight down deep square leg's throat. As it was late in the day, he would already have been asking himself whether we really needed that kind of shot, so he didn't need anyone rubbing it in. I was standing in the middle of the pitch, focused on one of the lads running out to me with a drink, when I noticed out of the corner of my eye one of the West Indies fielders holding his cap across his chest and giving a farewell salute. He must have held the position for thirty seconds before signing off with a flourish.

It wasn't necessarily the act itself that infuriated Ben – and you could see he was seething – it would have been the fact that all the other West Indies players were laughing. He was still fuming in the dressing room at the end of the day's play, but to be fair to Ben, when we got back to the team hotel, he had calmed down and could see the funny side of things. The good thing about him is that while he is more than happy to dish stuff out, he can also take a joke. You want to see some humour in Test cricket and you want to see the human element of blokes going up against each other and showing no mercy. The sport needs its characters and I was just glad it was not me at the wrong end of it. Marlon's obviously a feisty competitor. The fact that we tried to egg him on shows what we think of him as a player. You don't tend to bother trying to upset players who are easy to dismiss. There's no point.

That hilarious on-field spat was part of a tour that put the fun back into our cricket. Characters like first-time tourist Mark Wood make you laugh all the time. A teetotaller with bundles of energy – some of the stuff he comes out with makes you wonder what he'd be like if he ever had a drink. He's an infectious kind of guy who fitted perfectly into our environment, which was full of pranks. A feature of that tour was players donning the Albert Einstein mask that was to get greater attention during the Ashes campaign, then jumping out of hotel wardrobes and from behind dressing-room doors to spook unsuspecting team-mates. Being able to laugh when the joke is on you, and being relaxed enough to poke fun at a serious subject matter, are key ingredients to a convivial environment. They were put to the test on this tour when Ben Stokes' locker was strapped up with padding (for his own protection!). And it's a good job we Yorkshire lads are able to take a joke, the five of us having been forced to put our hands in our pockets to test our inherent tightness by buying extra players when it came to our golf sweepstake for the Masters.

Never do we enjoy each other's company more, however, than in the situation we found ourselves in at the end of the match in Grenada. Being able to celebrate Test victories is pretty special and we had not had the chance to do so for quite some time. Toasting them has always been a special thing for me and I never take winning a Test lightly. It is true that it is difficult to have a laugh when you are losing, but the mood in the Caribbean certainly proved a nice contrast to that which had dominated our time in Australia. It might be because we were winning that it stands out, but I would like to think that the atmosphere in the dressing room at St George's was more representative of what it has been like to be a part of this England team: playing drinking games, reflecting on fine performances and enjoying collective success.

This nine-wicket win was all the more special to me as it

featured my first Test hundred overseas. Registering it was something of a relief because I had played quite a lot of cricket for England by this stage and to finally get one away from home took the monkey off my back. I never doubted that I could do it – after all, I had scored several hundreds abroad in one-day internationals – but to prove it was good for my mind, particularly after twice throwing my wicket away after passing 50 in the opening match. It's as frustrating as it gets for a batsman when you break the back of an innings and then get out when set. Afterwards, I had vowed that if I got the opportunity again I would nail it, and this unbeaten 182 suggested I'd learned from my mistakes. Secondly, I had travelled to the West Indies no longer feeling like a young pup when it came to international cricket. With seniority comes greater responsibility and that change in status drove me on towards compiling bigger scores.

Again, the pitch in Grenada looked as if it was going to seam all over the place, encouraging Alastair Cook to bowl first. During that first morning it certainly felt like we were playing in our own conditions. However, the early juice in the pitch dried relatively quickly, even though there were a few rain showers across those first two overcast days. On the third day, with the platform laid by the openers Cook and Jonathan Trott, it gave me and Gary Ballance the opportunity to cash in. We did so with a stand of 165 inside 42 overs. I felt at ease in turning a sixth consecutive Test 50 into a sixth Test hundred, my policy of taking on their recalled leg-spinner Devendra Bishoo richly rewarded.

Unbeaten on 118 overnight, and left with just the tail for company when Jos Buttler was dismissed in the fourth over of the fourth morning, I farmed the strike as much as I could, trying to hit a boundary an over before taking a single. Obviously, it doesn't always work as perfectly as that, but I have found that if you give the bowlers a simple task of facing just a couple of balls an over, it can help them focus better on their batting. They then lock in to those couple of balls rather than think too much about staying out there for a certain amount of time. As the batsman, your job is to make sure they are not facing the first ball of an over too often. I knew I could manage that kind of situation because I had done it successfully with Jimmy Anderson against India at Trent Bridge the previous summer. This time, Jimmy and I managed to share 33 runs before he was run out going for a second from the first ball of a Jason Holder over.

That innings earned me a new nickname from Alastair Cook. Thankfully, though, I was only called 'Geoffrey' temporarily. Much as I admire my fellow Yorkshireman Geoffrey Boycott, I was not all that keen on being compared to him for my running between the wickets. I was involved in three run-outs in our 464 all out, although it seemed unfair to share any of the blame for Jimmy's in particular. Even he admitted to being a bit dozy, in not running his bat in properly at the bowler's end when, had he done so, he would have been in comfortably. The reason I slammed my bat on the floor in the immediate aftermath was that until I saw the TV replays I thought I was culpable and that he would be mad at me.

Instead, he channelled all his aggression into a typically stunning bowling performance twenty-four hours later to set up a hunt for victory out of nothing. By the fourth day, the pitch was as flat as anything, as signified by West Indies closing the day on 202–2. Not for the first time, Jimmy showed his skill on flat pitches to inspire a clatter of eight wickets for 83 runs. This was a prime example of him being able to turn it on despite there being no swing, getting something out of an unresponsive wicket to account for centurion Kraigg Brathwaite, veteran Shivnarine Chanderpaul and Marlon Samuels, who had hit a hundred in the first innings, in an intoxicating second-new-ball spell of three for one that flipped the game on its head.

When we got to the ground that Saturday morning and spoke in the dressing room, I don't think any of us could have expected things to happen as quickly as they did. Yes, we knew the new ball was only five overs away, but Jimmy's display with the ball and a run-out were backed up by the team performance – Cook's slip catch to remove Chanderpaul, Moeen Ali nipping in with three wickets to clean up the tail, Gary Ballance seeing us home with an unbeaten half-century that also made him the fastest England batsman to 1,000 runs in terms of innings since the Second World War.

It was a match that highlighted the promise of this developing team. It was also one of firsts. For Ben Stokes, it represented a first Test win anywhere. For a good number of others among us, it was our first Test win outside England.

Unfortunately, a team learning on the job also makes mistakes and a bad hour at the start of our second innings of the final match in Barbados cost us that Test series. It was a harsh lesson for us all. Alastair Cook played out of his skin to end a twenty-three-month wait for a Test hundred. Throughout the tour he played like a man with a point to prove after being left out of the World Cup squad, and he deserved more for his effort than being on the losing side. Quite simply, no one backed him up and showed the kind of determination he did. For 18 wickets to go down in a day was quite incredible. But unless you maintain your focus, you can get hurt in Test cricket. We just weren't ruthless enough and West Indies took advantage.

After Jimmy Anderson claimed 6–42 to help us take a 68-run lead on first innings, we lost half our side in a 15-over spell at the start of our second innings. Even though we have genuinely been successful over this past year, when we've got things wrong we've got them spectacularly wrong. Like losing wickets in clusters. As a side we need to get away from that and learn how to avoid falling into similar traps. One bad hour ruined the whole tour. Having been dismissed in a soft manner in the first innings, feathering a catch behind trying to guide one through backward point off the left-arm spinner Veerasammy Permaul, I nicked off to Jason Holder in the second.

To slip to 39–5 on the second evening let West Indies

– a team we had dominated for almost all of the dozen days in the series – back in and gave them a chance of squaring the scoreline. We were dismissed for 123 when, had we got another 100 runs as we should have, they would have come nowhere close. The pitch, containing none of the pace and bounce traditionally associated with the Kensington Oval, deteriorated very quickly. The ball spun a lot and we just did not adapt to the conditions very well at the start of that second innings. It sounds strange, but you find that in the longest form of the game the worse you are in shorter periods, the more it can hurt you. If you have a bad twenty minutes in Twenty20 you can sometimes get away with it, but in Test cricket if you have a bad twenty minutes, because the game is so long, you have ceded advantage to the opposition. They have plenty of time to take advantage and turn the tables on you.

Accusations of us taking our eye off the ball were not accurate. Complacency is something associated with established teams and our problem was the product of being predominantly young and inexperienced. We are certainly not immune from making mistakes in future, but I would hope that when we come across similar periods we will find ways of dealing with them better.

Only once West Indies had completed their chase did I become aware of the comments made by Colin Graves, the England and Wales Cricket Board's new chairman, prior to us flying over to the Caribbean.

'I'd certainly be disappointed if we don't win the West Indies series, because I am pretty sure the West Indies are going to have a mediocre team,' Graves had said.

'A lot of their stars are going to be playing in the Indian Premier League anyway, not in the Tests, so we should win that series. If we don't win, I can tell you now there will be some enquiries of why we haven't.'

I know Colin well from his time at Yorkshire, where I became accustomed to his public demands of the team. He's always been a chairman to speak his mind and I am convinced he did not mean it as a dig at the West Indies, just a way of showing what he expected from the England team on his watch. He wanted us to start his term as we meant to go on. He sets high standards. Of course, as players we do the same and regardless of the opposition West Indies put out – a lot was made of them being ranked eighth in the world – you have to beat the opposition you are pitted against.

Those England players not aware of Graves's words were made so immediately after the series was over when someone from the West Indies team stuck a cutting of a newspaper article containing them on their dressing-room door. One suspects that clipping had spent the previous three weeks on the inside as motivation. I can imagine it upset a few of them.

That defeat in Barbados also had repercussions in our dressing room. For it was there that Jonathan Trott announced to us after the match that he would be retiring from international cricket. Welcoming him back into the group before the series had proved an easy transition. Anyone who has been fortunate enough to call him a team-mate would tell you that he is one of a kind. You would get that from the idiosyncrasies he displays at the crease. He not only enjoyed playing cricket but enjoyed the dressing-room vibe; he's someone who liked the banter that goes around a group trekking the world for a living.

To hear him announce that he had reached the end of this journey was obviously a very sad moment, coming only three matches back into a return following eighteen months away. After his breakdown during the 2013–14 Ashes, he needed to give international cricket another crack for his own peace of mind. I cannot imagine there being any worse feeling, in his circumstances, than thinking 'what if?' for the rest of your life. He'd worked so hard to get picked again, and did so on merit not reputation, having scored runs with Warwickshire and then again earlier in the winter with England Lions. So it was a shame he was unable to go on and produce some of his customary big scores.

I am not sure why things didn't work out on his return – whether it was a mental or technical problem that caused him to quit – but he just didn't look quite right and a collection of five single-figure scores was not up to his meticulously high standards. Once back in the team, his performances were always going to come under close scrutiny. Questions like whether he was the right man or whether someone else should have been picked to play at the top of the order were a feature of the tour, so, after what he had been through, it took a lot of guts for him to put himself back in that environment.

Naturally, after fifty-two Test appearances and sixty-eight in one-day internationals, he was very emotional when he announced his news. But afterwards, the chance to give him a proper send-off in a private room at the team hotel, with all our families in tow, helped improve our mood. It was a career deserving of a celebration and the bigger picture of what he accomplished for English cricket helped lift the gloom after what had been a pretty disappointing result at the Kensington Oval. A lot of people will remember Trotty for the tough times he's been through, not necessarily for the great things he's done for England as a batsman. In the immediate aftermath of his decision, we wanted to show him that as team-mates we appreciated how invaluable his contributions, such as his match-winning hundred on his debut in the 2009 Ashes, had been to English cricket.

To provide symmetry, the tour had begun with a departure too. At lunch on the first day in the second of two practice games at Warner Park, we were called into a team meeting and informed that Paul Downton, the England managing director, no longer occupied that position. As one of the younger members of the team during his two-year office, my interactions with him had been few and far between, and I only became aware of what his job entailed throughout the ongoing selection issue regarding Kevin Pietersen.

The Root family. Clockwise from top: my dad Matt, me, my mum Helen and brother Bill.

A family skiing holiday to Canada. We were always into any sport going.

My dad Matt and grandpa Don in familiar surroundings – a cricket ground!

With my younger brother Bill at Lord's. He's been England 12th man on several occasions.

My first ever net session with Kevin Shar as a 12-year-old in Headingley's indoor school.

Graham Thorpe, the England Lions coach, instrumental in handing me international recognition versus Sri Lanka A, Scarborough, August 2011.

en Stokes celebrating a West Indies wicket at
e Under-19 World Cup, January 2010. Azeem
afiq, the England captain and my ex-Yorkshire
am-mate, is behind.

Jos Buttler during the Under-19 World Cup
quarter-final against West Indies, Rangiora,
New Zealand, January 2010. Jos and I have
been team-mates for years.

atting against Sri Lanka Under-19s at Fenner's, Cambridge, August 2010.

Craig White, a Yorkshire cricketer that played for England, was a hero of mine growing up.

Kevin Pietersen. The man stood at the non-striker's end when I walked into bat on Test debut, Nagpur, December 2012.

Michael Vaughan celebrating a third-Test hundred during the 2005 Ashes. I modeled my game on his.

Sachin Tendulkar. I was not born when he made his Test debut. He played in mine.

This post-match picture at the Premadasa Stadium sums up the mood after a 5–2 defeat on the 2014–15 tour of Sri Lanka.

There was a sense of humiliation about the defeat to Bangladesh – not because of the identity of the opposition but how badly we played.

Marlon Samuels gives Ben Stokes a special send-off, Grenada, April 2015.

My own take on the Samuels salute, acknowledging a Stokes Test hundred against New Zealand at Lord's, May 2015.

Kane Williamson, a Yorkshire team-mate, and the rock of New Zealand's batting at number three.

Brendon McCullum, the New Zealand captain, whose aggressive tactics changed attitudes towards playing the game around the world.

Paul Farbrace reintroduced our daily kickabouts during his time as England caretaker coach.

Paul Farbrace's calm dressing room presence smoothed the transition between England coaching appointments.

There was a relaxed vibe about our cricket under Trevor Bayliss, the newly-appointed England coach, throughout the 2015 summer.

Conditions meant I got a rare bowl, and a couple of Australian wickets to show for my efforts, this one Mitchell Johnson, Cardiff, July 2015.

All the talk about Pietersen and whether there was a chance of him returning to the England team was taking place back home – Colin Graves had suggested in March that what had happened in the past was history and that KP could only be considered if he was performing in county cricket: 'If he does that and then comes out and scores a lot of runs they can't ignore him, I would have thought, but that is up to him.' But it was not an issue discussed by those of us holding a place on the tour. In fact, the first time I recall the subject coming up was at the start of the New Zealand series in May 2015, when it was already too late for him.

On a purely personal note, I found the lobbying for Pietersen irrelevant. As an England player you are under pressure to keep your place with good performances and it goes with the territory that if someone has an outstanding season – scoring more runs or as many runs but in a better fashion than you – they could force themselves into the England team at your expense. That is something that you accept as an international cricketer. I knew that I was playing well, scoring the weight of runs required of me, and I wasn't worried about selection.

From Kevin's perspective he obviously jumped on Colin Graves's words in that initial BBC radio interview when he suggested all future England selections would be based solely on runs and wickets. But my opinion is that Kevin wouldn't have gone about things the way he did if he had been truly desperate to play for England again. If that had been the case, he wouldn't have written a book slating the England dressing room, slating the management and slating his peers around the country. That dressing room is sacred to the team and once you speak badly of people who inhabit a space within those four walls it is very hard to regain trust.

Just a few months later, he was asking for a clean slate, having commited playing County Championship cricket for Surrey once more, and some of his influential friends appeared to be trying to railroad him back into the team. A Twitter campaign by his supporters homed in on the failures of rivals at any opportunity and lobbied for his inclusion.

It was a shame he could not have done all his talking through performances from the start. The most disappointing thing for me is that he is such a good player. Special talents like him don't come around very often and they are invaluable to any side. If he just concentrated on playing cricket, he would walk into any team in the world. Of course, I do not believe that you should exclude individuals from teams just because they have slightly different characters to the rest of the group, but one of the reasons I believe in what we are developing right now is the great team unity. Whenever things get really tough, we get tighter. You need individual brilliance, but it doesn't weigh heavier than the team. The powers that be made the decision not to gamble on one man but invest in the ones chosen in his absence. It was a decision that has delivered huge rewards, including our exciting, futuristic one-day cricket and seeing cricket's most famous return to our shores. This is not to say if Kevin had played it would not have been the case, but without him we have developed a group of youthful individuals who are full of beans regarding their own games.

When I first became a member of the England set-up as a young lad, Kevin helped my game no end. Especially on my first tour, the work he put into teaching me and others how to combat spin in India conditions was invaluable. Jos Buttler, I am sure, would tell you the same story. He spent hours helping us, giving us his insights into how to play different situations and different conditions. I cannot deny how positive an influence he was on my development as a batsman. One of the things he taught me was to look to play the spinners through the off-side as often as possible. Guys like Rahul Dravid and Virat Kohli have been masters of this over the years – regardless of whether the ball is spinning or not, their first thought is to try to pierce the gaps in the covers. Doing so effectively forces fielders to be moved across, opening up gaps to leg, and the chance for easier singles.

As well as tactical advice like that, he helped me understand the need for precision with my footwork; to use the depth of my crease to its full potential. Doing so – going right up against the stumps when playing off the back foot and down the pitch off the front – provides better options to score on both sides of the wicket. It was a privilege to watch him put all this into practise on that tour. The way that he and Alastair Cook complemented each other, with their different approaches to batting, fascinated me. They worked so well together in partnerships with their contrasting styles, it is ironic their relationship deteriorated later.

Our return home coincided with news that I found disappointing on two levels. Within hours, Peter Moores was sacked as England coach, and he did not find out in good circumstances, with the news leaking out twenty-four hours before it became official. That was not nice to discover. He deserved better than that, having hot-footed over to Ireland for a one-day international that saw several players, including myself, rested. We were aware as a group that there had been talk about his future, but it still remained a shock to us all when he went.

The fact was I really enjoyed working with Pete and I had reaped the benefit of the hard work he put into the technical side of my game. He really helped me improve as a player, and over the thirteen months of his second spell in charge of the national team I had results to be proud of. In ten Test matches, I scored 1,135 runs at an average of 94.58 and was almost in four figures in one-day internationals too, with an average of 41.26.

His influence was a vitally important component of why I had become more successful in all formats of the game. I found him to be a very good coach, someone whose best work was in the fine-tuning of individual techniques, recognising how one player's differed slightly from the next. His bespoke work dovetailed perfectly with that of assistant coach Paul Farbrace, who reinforced confidence. Between them, they helped me understand, enjoy and take greater responsibility for my own game.

Circumstances aside, what happened immediately after that tour of the Caribbean was rather reminiscent of modern-day football in that the new big bosses decided they wanted their own men in the coaching positions. Andrew Strauss, as the incoming director of cricket, wanted his own appointment to be responsible for the England team performance. With hindsight, if you look back at the way the 2015 summer panned out, as much as I enjoyed working with Pete, it is hard to question the decisions taken in May.

Of course, you never want to see anyone you like working with lose their job, but in any sport things do not remain the same for ever and there are always going to be new coaches and new players brought into any side. Your job as a player is finding ways of dealing with that change, because if you don't you could well be the one next in line to get the boot. That's the ruthlessness of it all.

I also know I was not the only one who enjoyed working under Pete and for that reason he should take credit for a proportion of the individual improvements shown in 2015.

5 RIGHT HAND MAN

'IT's the right time for Joe Root to take more of a leadership position and I've asked him to be the new vice-captain of the team. He's got outstanding leadership capabilities and we need him to start thinking more as a captain. It's in no way a reflection on the job Ian Bell has done – he has been excellent in that role by all accounts – but it's time for Joe to step up in that regard.'

These were the words of Andrew Strauss during a televised press conference on 12 May 2015, to mark his appointment as England's new director of cricket. It had been a proud moment for me when, forty-eight hours earlier, he'd conveyed the same message during a telephone conversation while I was driving from Leeds back to my house in Sheffield. I was passing the Meadowhall shopping centre on the M1 when an unnamed caller rang on my car phone. The voice on the other end belonged to Strauss.

He began our chat by outlining his new role at the ECB, and how he envisaged the England teams moving forward. He explained that he wanted me to be more involved in that process as someone he'd identified as part of the Test side's future. My brief from the start of the international summer of 2015 was to learn as much from Alastair Cook as possible, and offer advice where I thought it might be appropriate. I was asked, from that moment forward, whenever stepping onto the field to represent England, to put myself into Cook's shoes and think about what I would do in any given situation. Before that conversation, it is fair to say that I did think about the bigger picture, and viewed things from a team perspective, from time to time. I have since found that I am thinking about the whole game the whole of the time. It has definitely helped my individual performances, I feel, because I have a more rounded view of what is going on.

Some people in the media had already dubbed me as the latest future England captain, but the 'FEC' nickname is not one I have ever coveted. Although I quite enjoyed captaincy, having done a little through school and junior cricket with Sheffield Collegiate, when the best player tends to be given the honour, as well as regional representative sides and the Yorkshire academy, my experience at senior level has remained rather limited.

The extra responsibility certainly had a positive rather than negative effect on my batting in May 2013 when I was asked to lead England Lions against the New Zealanders at Grace Road, a game restricted to an innings apiece due to wet weather, in which I contributed 179. However, my first experience of captaining Yorkshire did not go so well the following April when, with full availability causing selection headaches, captain Andrew Gale decided to leave himself out of a County Championship match against Middlesex at Lord's. I am not sure he will be doing that again, as it was the club's only defeat in the first season of our back-to-back title wins.

Although things got off to a bad start in that game when we were inserted, we actually combated the conditions admirably, as it was doing all sorts on that first morning. So, having battled really well through that initial period, losing just one wicket in the first hour, it was disappointing when the team was dismissed for 178. Even then, the bowlers performed brilliantly when they got a chance, to secure a healthy 55-run lead on first innings.

With the pitch flattening out, our top four made a better fist of things second time around, all contributing towards a score of 194–3, at which point Gary Ballance walked in to hit a brilliant 130. So commanding was our advantage, in fact, that on the third morning it actually became plausible that I could declare. As lunch approached, I discussed the situation with our coach Jason Gillespie and told him, 'I think we are close to having enough now, Dizzy.'

With so much time remaining in the contest, however, that was deemed unnecessary and I allowed the innings to take its full course, with Gary last out following a blaze of sixes. The bowlers had bags of time to take the ten wickets required and a 472-run target to defend. Given our quality of attack, there could only be one result. Or so we thought.

To be fair, Chris Rogers and Sam Robson played out of their skins, but equally we bowled atrociously. It was most uncharacteristic for us to be offering the kind of width we did and they were only too willing to latch on to anything loose to race out of the blocks. By the close, they had wiped 230 off the requirement for the loss of Robson. Suddenly, an away victory was not such a formality. I acknowledged as much deep into that evening session when, having left the field for a wee, I looked across at Dizzy in the dressing room, failing to disguise a concerned look.

'Keep going, skip,' he said.

Of course, that match would go down in county cricket folklore as the third-highest successful run chase in more than a hundred years of the Championship – by seven wickets, before tea on day four, and it happened on my watch. I could hardly believe it. My only defence was that Rogers's unbeaten double hundred was a truly outstanding innings, and it extended the habit of him scoring lots and lots of runs whenever I am in the opposition. For a while, it earned me a new nickname from my Sheffield mates. To them, even after resuming the role for the title-deciding victory at Trent Bridge in September – when Gale was serving an ECB ban – I was now universally known as 'craptain'.

During his first media address, Strauss confirmed various other things, chiefly his faith in Cook and Eoin Morgan as Test and one-day captains respectively, and confirmation that Kevin Pietersen would not be considered in the short term due to 'trust' issues between the pair of them. We were about to see all those decisions vindicated.

To witness first-hand how Cook developed as a captain over the summer was the biggest eye-opener for me. It is fair to say stubbornness is a trait we share and it must have been incredibly difficult for an established captain, set in his ways, to change. But he undoubtedly became more free-spirited with his decisions over the following six months – operating much more on instinct than in the past, for instance when declaring at Trent Bridge to catch the Australian opening batsmen David Warner and Chris Rogers unawares. Credit to him for doing that, because the side has certainly benefited from a more proactive approach.

Wearing the deputy's badge has not altered things much for me, but it does mean Alastair and I tend to have little chats before each match, when he will ask my opinions on certain things and I will offer whatever comes into my head. Since my early days in the Yorkshire dressing room, I have been of the belief that an idea is no good unless you share it. If I have ten ideas in my head and he accepts one, implements it and it works for the team, that can only be for the better. Pleasingly, though, we tend to bring up ideas the other has already considered.

I view captaincy as something for the future, and certainly not the near future. I know Alastair revealed he considered his position on more than one occasion in 2015, but I feel it is important that he carries on. There has been a lot of change over the past eighteen months and he has helped get us through some difficult times by unearthing a formula that can be successful for this emerging team – undoubtedly one that has got us moving in the right direction. I just hope he continues to find fulfilment out of leading it forward and not find it a chore, because I recognise that he has thoroughly enjoyed doing so over recent months and should be extremely proud of the role he has played in its development thus far.

The mood began to pick up from the moment Ben Stokes joined me at the crease in the first Test against New Zealand at Lord's in May. We were in all kinds of trouble at 30–4, and not for the first time my mind went back to the World Cup and how I'd pledged to always be positive when encountering choices in the future. If I found myself in a similar scenario to the one which I experienced in Wellington that shell-shocked Saturday afternoon, I had vowed to come out fighting, and at Lord's I saw that the gaps left by their attacking fields meant a successful counter-attack would be heavily rewarded. As Ben never thinks any other way than positively, he was the perfect partner to put my theory into practice.

Of course, when it worked so spectacularly, there were lots of column inches devoted to how we were copying Brendon McCullum's formula. This was New England v New Zealand, some wrote. That wasn't necessarily true. It wasn't as simple as emulating their template for success. What was true, however, was that Brendon's own attacking style forced us into playing in a more expansive style. His actions kick-started our summer.

By setting his attack-minded fields, he allowed us to score at a rate of five runs per over and we simply ran with the momentum. With huge gaps created by a heavily peopled slip cordon, there was no choice but to score quickly, because whenever you got bat on ball there were runs to be had. Such was his desire for wickets that he was prepared for his bowlers to sacrifice their economy rates. His theory was that one of us would nick one eventually and that we could score as many runs as we wanted, because his attack were good enough to send us packing. Only if we batted for a lengthy period of time would this backfire on him.

Thankfully, Ben and I were able to counter this positive intent, sharing 161 runs inside 32 overs, which is a decent lick by anyone's standards and felt quite remarkable from the position that we had been in. Ironically, it concluded when Ben, someone you associate with being caught on the boundary at long-off or fine leg, was bowled leaving off-spinner Mark Craig's arm-ball. It was a shame he missed out on that hundred, but it was nevertheless a breakthrough innings for a resurgent cricketer.

Credit had to go to Paul Farbrace, the caretaker coach, for this transformation, because immediately prior to this series Ben had been batting at number seven. He was insistent that Ben was the sort of player who responded to responsibility – as in the more you give him, the more you get out of him. To my mind, he remains a batsman who bowls rather than a bowler who bats. Putting greater emphasis on his bowling has never suited him, in my opinion.

The fact Ben delivered the goods at the first time of asking set him up for the whole summer. Knowing you have a quality all-rounder on your side gives the rest of a team a lot of confidence. In this match, it was the all-rounder that did most to get the 2015 international fixtures off to a winning start, quickly overcoming his first-innings disappointment with a second-innings hundred and then taking two vital wickets in dismissing New Zealand on the final day.

I've played a lot of cricket with Ben and he has become a good friend as well as team-mate. In fact, the two of us and Jos Buttler have played with and against each other since we were 15, and that is another reason why as a team we all get on so well. We only finished eighth at the Under-19 World Cup in 2010, but that did not do justice to how strong a year group we were. Nearly everyone in that side went on to establish themselves in county cricket and that's unusual when compared to other Under-19 intakes.

From my perspective, it is great to see my peers prospering. Ben would be the first to admit he has done some daft stuff since making his international debut, such as punching that locker in the Caribbean, which put him out for several weeks after the World Twenty20. Then he got into the team for a couple of Tests against India before being left out for the rest of the series, not quite able to establish himself. That was followed by further disappointment in one-day cricket when he struggled in Sri Lanka before Christmas, leading to his failure to make the World Cup squad.

To be fair, he has not looked back since, so when he made it to three figures in that match at Lord's I wanted to revel in the moment. For a while I had been thinking about revisiting that Marlon Samuels salute from earlier in the year by bringing it into our own celebrations. This seemed to be the perfect opportunity. I planted the seed with some of the other lads and we decided that if he made it, we would honour his landmark with a reprise of that Grenada moment. On the balcony, I talked with Adam Lyth about doing the salute together and he seemed enthusiastic enough. But when the time came, I stood up, gave it the rigid elbow and flourish – and found I was on my own. Lyth was with the rest of the lads clapping. Too late. When I realised he had not come with me, I just stuck with it. Thankfully, it was well received by Ben, at least.

That was reflective of the England environment at the start of the summer. There was a huge emphasis placed on the enjoyment factor when Paul Farbrace took over, and the first thing he did to improve the mood came at our first training session when he strolled over to the practice area with a football tucked under his arm. For the first time in a couple of years, we had a proper kickabout and, quite frankly, it was brilliant. International sportsmen are madly competitive beasts and want to win whatever the challenge, but for cricketers this especially applies to football. A number of us found that warming up that way allowed you a break from solid cricket but retained the competitive edge ahead of getting into the nets.

We retained that positive spirit throughout the entire match, not just during the first-innings recovery. After conceding a 134-run lead, we once again remained undeterred by the loss of early wickets when we batted for a second time. Transferring my own form from the West Indies series was pleasing, although scores of 98 and 84 carried with them a deal of frustration. To get two chances and convert neither irked me.

That second-innings effort came in tandem with Alastair Cook, who did manage to convert his start into three figures. Ben simply took on the mantle, and his 85-ball hundred, the fastest ever in a Test match at Lord's, was worthy of that salute. Seizing on his promotion in the order, he changed the momentum of both innings, and then turned a match most would have given us no chance of winning forty-eight hours earlier by claiming the key wickets of Kane Williamson and Brendon McCullum in consecutive balls. That reduced New Zealand to 61–5 and drew deafening cheers on a glorious final day on which 25,000 people turned up. As England players, we love playing in front of big crowds and getting the kind of overwhelming support we did that day, but it also represented a huge compliment to the New Zealanders from the cricket-loving British public.

Even though we get great crowds over here for Test cricket, you do occasionally have gaps in the stands, particularly on the fifth day – even when the game is going in England's favour, you might see only half the ground full and sometimes very few people turn up at all if it is meandering towards a stalemate. So to arrive on that final morning and witness people swarming towards the entrance as I drove along St John's Wood Road was a real buzz. That is the kind of crowd you want to play in front of and the exciting nature of the cricket promoted throughout the previous four days clearly sold it. Full credit to New Zealand for attracting the kind of attendance we have come to expect for Ashes cricket. It was because they played in such an exciting manner that people wanted to come and see how we responded.

That victory, by 124 runs, was a truly stunning one, our triumph completed in exactly the kind of style that we want to become associated with our play. There is an omnipresent hum around a Lord's Test match but that day's buzz still resonates. I don't think people could quite get their heads around the magnitude of that win. New Zealand's first innings of 523 was the ninth-highest score by a side to lose a Test match. We had been four wickets down inside the first hour of the match. It was so thrilling to be a part of it.

Part of that thrill was sharing the experience with Adam Lyth. What a match in which to make your international debut. It was so refreshing to see how excited he was in the build-up to playing; it took me back to my second XI debut opening the batting together at Abbeydale. I told him that if there was anything he wanted to talk about, any advice I could give him, then he knew where I was. At the same time, I didn't want to bombard him with my thoughts. One advantage for Adam was that he had already been on tour with us in the Caribbean, so by the time this match came around he probably already felt like an England player. Plus, he had played a lot of first-class cricket by this point and had his own way of preparing. He showed no signs of nerves whatsoever.

I know from experience what it is like to manage what Adam achieved in his second match the following week – scoring a maiden hundred at Headingley – because I had done the same two years previously. To score a hundred on your home ground is the best feeling you can get in international cricket. Having the local crowd spur you on, achieving something like that in front of all your family and friends, is so special.

Unfortunately, it was to come in a losing cause as New Zealand prospered from sticking to their all-out-attack policy. If our comeback at Lord's had been improbable, so was theirs in Leeds. Not that we weren't warned. When you are up against Brendon McCullum's team in any format you know they are going to throw everything at you from the start. They are looking to make inroads at the beginning of each innings. Whether it be with bat or with ball, New Zealand are always looking at getting ahead of the game. That means Trent Boult and Tim Southee hunting for new-ball wickets or Martin Guptill altering opponents' game plans with fearless ball-striking. Brendon demands that his bowlers should not fear going for runs; nor should his batsmen fear getting out.

Whether it works or not for the Kiwis on the day, what you are guaranteed with them as opponents is a result in any particular game. As a bowling unit, their modus operandi is to get as many balls in good areas as possible, and on responsive surfaces they get their rewards. Whether it was with the first new ball or the second, they posed a threat against us in each of the two Tests.

At Lord's they did their major damage on the opening morning when conditions were conducive to swing and seam bowling. At Headingley it was with the second new ball when the floodlights were on that they turned the contest on its head. Until then it had looked as if we were going to build a big first-innings lead, in response to New Zealand's 350 all out. Our first wicket was worth 177 runs, and yet we only achieved parity.

It was some sloppy cricket on our part, including the run-out of Lyth with the scoreboard reading 215–1, shortly after he had celebrated three figures and within five overs of the second new ball becoming available. Without blaming Adam – it wasn't necessarily his fault – that was exactly the time we didn't need to lose a wicket. For two new batsmen to be subjected to those overcast conditions with two world-class bowlers operating in tandem was extremely difficult. The two-hour period that followed represented the essence of Test cricket. New Zealand grabbed the initiative and ran with it for the rest of the Test match.

Brendon had been quite conservative for a while, certainly by his standards, but when he saw his opportunity he went for the jugular. If this match showed us anything, it was that when you are able to get on top in a Test match it is important to ram that advantage home. New Zealand take the game forward at pace and leave the opposition trailing in their wake. They showed how, with concentrated aggression, you can leave the other team in an extremely compromised position. If they are allowed to maintain their dominance for a full session, the game can have gone, and they had done it to a number of teams before they met us. The year of 2014 was New Zealand's best ever in Tests and they arrived on our shores unbeaten in six series, winning four.

Since the 2015 World Cup, there seemed to be an acceptance that even Test cricket would be played at a higher tempo. It might not be a trend that lasts, but the fashion should prove exciting for people to watch. Run rates tend to be hovering around the four mark as a matter of course, and the challenge for us is to find the balance between scoring at that kind of rate and posting the size of scores to put opponents under pressure.

New Zealand hit fifteen sixes in a match in which their overall scoring rate touched five. It allowed them to declare with plenty of overs in the bank to dismiss us, despite wet weather lurking in the vicinity. On the fourth evening, after Cook and Lyth had wiped off 44 runs of the 455-run target, I promoted our chances of winning at the end-of-play press conference. Certainly on the evidence of what had gone before in the series, you could not have totally written that off, although I admit that even accounting for the modern scoring phenomenon it may have been over-ambitious.

Nevertheless, the comment was in keeping with our preferred style of cricket, and in my opinion retaining a positive attitude actually gives you a better chance of saving a game like that. If you play just to survive, there is every chance a ball has your name on it, because you are letting the bowlers settle into a rhythm. Playing shots can throw them off it. Things didn't materialise for us on that day, but that is the way you can expect this England team to play in the future. If you want to get your feet going, and your batting in rhythm, it is better to play some strokes than poke about. We got to within one hour of the finish line that evening but were ultimately undone by the six wickets shared between Kane Williamson and Mark Craig, a pair of off-spinners. The challenge, if we want to achieve our objective of becoming the number one Test team in the world, is to get over that line.

Between the two New Zealand Tests it was revealed that the man tasked with getting us there was Trevor Bayliss. On the eve of the first match, the playing squad and support staff had been called into a meeting with Andrew Strauss at the Langham Hotel, central London, and informed that the ECB was down to two candidates for the position of England coach.

It was anticipated that for the first time in English cricket history an Australian would be named coach of the national team. To be going into an Ashes series with two Australians as the front runners for the vacant job was not something you would have envisaged. But, ahead of the announcement on 26 May that the chosen individual was Bayliss, a lot of the talk was of Jason Gillespie, my coach at Yorkshire, getting the job. You only had to hear what the Yorkshire lads were saying in public to realise their concerns about losing him. And the fact they were so worried showed what an impact he has made at our club.

It is credit to the way he coaches that he has managed to get so much respect and admiration from the players in the dressing room. He's a very calm, laid-back coach, with a very similar style to Trevor. He encourages aggressive cricket to be played with a very simple outlook. From a bowling point of view, he asks the bowlers to bowl their best ball as consistently as possible and encourages the batsmen to focus on building partnerships. When he arrived in the winter of 2011–12, we had some young talent in the Yorkshire squad mixed with older heads. He galvanised the side, earning immediate promotion and transforming the place into a very comfortable but ultimately successful environment. Two County Championship pennants in consecutive years have shown that what he has put in place is sustainable. The improvement has been undeniable. As well as securing a return to Division One in 2012, there was the club's maiden trip to Twenty20 Finals Day. In 2013, we were pipped to the title by Durham, since when there have been two first places. There is also a deep desire to be successful in one-day cricket.

To some it would have been a surprise that Trevor was chosen, though it shouldn't have been when you consider what he had achieved previously, his record in limited-overs cricket with New South Wales, Sydney Sixers and Kolkata Knight Riders being exceptional. A fortnight earlier, Strauss had made it clear that there would be greater focus on white-ball progress. Not that Trevor was just a specialist, though. His spell with Sri Lanka, two years of which was with Paul Farbrace as his assistant, proved successful across the board. He has also won Sheffield Shields as a coach.

I'd only met Trevor once previously when, on the 2013–14 Ashes tour, we had a training session that immediately followed on from a Sydney Sixers session at the SCG. I didn't know his background in depth at that point, but I introduced myself as we crossed paths on the outfield.

After the announcement, because of their history, Farby was able to guide us on how the new coaching dynamic would work. They obviously enjoy working alongside each other and they had talked about how they wanted us to play ahead of the one-day series against the New Zealanders.

'We've chatted a lot. He's had an influence on selection and quite an input into how he would like to see us working, even though he will not be here,' Farbrace revealed in a press conference ahead of the series. 'The message will be "You've been selected because of the way you play at county level. You have to go and do exactly the same at international level." The players who have the guts to do that will be the ones who make a success of it. I want them to go and enjoy playing international cricket and express their skills.'

Eoin Morgan had similarly strong views on our approach. Having played alongside Brendon McCullum, and indeed under Bayliss, at the Knight Riders in the Indian Premier League, he knew what to expect from New Zealand and wanted us to fight fire with fire. We had seen how they were driving one-day cricket forward at the World Cup, encouraging a no-fear approach, especially with regard to batting. When we gathered in Birmingham ahead of those five matches, he spoke about a refusal to relent, particularly if we got off to good starts. From that moment on, the England one-day side would always reject periods of consolidation in favour of backing one's individual talent.

*   *   *

There was certainly a mood for change. As attention shifted to the first run-out against top-class opposition in white-ball cricket since the abomination of a World Cup, Paul Collingwood, the only England captain to have lifted a global trophy, dubbed our one-day cricket prehistoric.

Because we were so behind the times, there was an expectation on us to try something different. In one way, this made things easier. The public wanted us to embrace a new start; we had new faces, a new coach on the way and New Zealand, World Cup finalists who were expected to beat us, as opponents. This combination decreased the pressure to get things right immediately as we headed into that first day-night game at Edgbaston on 9 June. It was as if we were all taking part in one big experiment.

For a long time one-day cricket had been secondary for England. It seemed to be a bit of an afterthought once the planning for Test cricket had been done. We wanted to show that we could excite crowds just as the New Zealanders and Australians had done – to make people love English cricket again. We wanted them to be excited by what we could produce and how far we could push the boundaries of our games, not anticipate the same old safety-first approach we had gained a reputation for.

Eoin demanded freedom of expression from us. That was brave from him, because results go against a captain's name. But we were soon to see that he put into practice exactly what he preached and that brought home to everyone exactly what was expected. The product of all this was the most spectacular start imaginable and a team performance that set the tone for the whole series.

Our first innings of this new era all happened in a bit of a hurry. Indeed, the speed of it caught me on the hop. After Brendon McCullum asked us to bat first, I was still putting my pads on when Jason Roy was dismissed first ball, and I rushed to the crease still adjusting my thigh pad. I normally like to have a cup of tea before going out to bat, but this scuppered my usual routine. Alex Hales was waiting for me in the middle and immediately took the mickey out of the way I had waddled out.

This might sound stupid, but Jason getting out in the fashion he did – slicing the ball to point, looking to be aggressive from the very first ball of the game – helped me out. It set the tempo for how we should be playing, and it only took a few deliveries to realise that the pitch was a brilliant one for one-day cricket. Off the mark first ball, every time I found the middle of the bat, the ball seemed to thread its way through a gap in the field. It's rare you have days like this, but it helped get the scoreboard moving and with Alex doing something similar we raced into the 30s in no time, offsetting the loss of that early wicket.

The real turning point in our play as a limited-overs team came once we had pushed the attacking New Zealand field back and recognised that the next period of play should not be one of consolidation, just knocking the ball around, as we had done in the past. Instead, any opportunities to hit boundaries – and a bowler out of the attack – had to be taken.

During that innings we did that a couple of times. Morgs promotes this disruption of an opposition captain's plans as a key limited-overs tactic and the flurry of boundaries struck by myself and Hales led to McCullum bringing on his brother Nathan McCullum for some off-spin as early as the fifth over, with the scoreboard at 32–1. Sustaining the approach meant that, despite New Zealand possessing a five-man attack, he was forced to put on another bowler he wouldn't normally have brought in for the 18th over of an innings, in the shape of medium-pacer Grant Elliott. That is what can happen when you maintain a run rate at over seven runs an over despite the loss of wickets. It puts the opposite captain under pressure to do something different. A fielding team always begins with a set of plans, and although plans B and C have also been discussed, if your opponents continue to play in such an expansive way it can really throw you. If you are scheming Plan D on the job, juggling bowlers who don't always bowl, you are not where you wanted to be.

As a fielding captain, you are looking to exert control for the middle period of the game, but Morgs showed his intent when he greeted the return of Nathan McCullum into the attack for the second over outside the initial power-play by pumping the ball back over the bowler's head and into the stands. It gave me confidence to try to do a similar thing. Luck was certainly on my side when, the ball after hauling him from outside off-stump over midwicket for six, I tried a repeat and was dropped by a sprawling Ross Taylor at wide long-on. Living on my fortune was something I tried to embrace. Previously, I would never have attempted to follow a six by trying to hit another one, but this positivity was infectious. It was more important for me to try to take McCullum down, and put New Zealand under pressure, than worry about my individual return.

And it was during this passage of play that my attitude was given its sternest examination. The departure of Morgan – immediately before I brought up my hundred off 71 balls – sparked a collapse from 171–2 to 202–6. Normally that would be a signal for doom and gloom. However, we were about to witness the beauty of the new regime. In this England one-day team, everyone just keeps coming at you.

Adil Rashid possesses a fine record as a batsman in first-class cricket and Jos Buttler's destructive ability had regularly returned devastating results in the highest company, so we knew we weren't finished. On the other hand, it is fair to say that we didn't anticipate a world-record stand for the seventh wicket in one-day international history. I held the record of England's third-fastest hundred in one-day internationals for less than two hours, thanks to a typical contribution from Jos. It was a pleasure to watch.

In our pre-match discussions, Eoin Morgan insisted being dismissed without seeing out our allocation of 50 overs was irrelevant. 'I want to see what we can achieve,' he said. This meant leaving the old-school methodology of having certain target scores for certain over milestones in the past. When we encountered a good pitch, the challenge, he told us, was to make as many as we could. Of course, he wasn't promoting being bowled out, but consider which score you would take: 330 all out in 48 overs or 303–6?

Adil is the kind of cricketer who thrives if you allow him to play with a carefree attitude and these words of Eoin were clearly reflected in the way he played. When talented players like him and Jos come in with a platform underneath them they can be very hard to stop. To score an England record 408–9 after that collapse highlighted great potential, but the challenge was whether we could back it up.

Ahead of the second ODI, at the Kia Oval, I made this clear in a pre-match press conference. 'It's something we want to replicate,' I said. 'We want to go out there with a similar frame of mind but not be naive enough to think that they won't come back hard at us – because they are a great one-day side, and have been for some time. We know we will have to play extremely well if we want to get another win under our belts.'

We kept that hope alive all the way to the death, despite New Zealand posting another monster score. Kane Williamson, the rock of their batting across all three formats, and Ross Taylor both played extremely well to construct another sturdy base and that allowed them to put on the board a score similar to the one we achieved in Birmingham. Their total of 398 was their highest against a Test-playing nation and second only to the 402–2 they managed against Ireland in 2008.

Eoin Morgan was unbelievable in the way he kept us in the chase that evening, after we lost three quick wickets to the spinners to slip to 100–3 after 16 overs. We seemed miles behind the game at that point but in the next 16 overs he shared 159 runs in partnerships with Ben Stokes and Jos Buttler. So even when all three had been dismissed, the feeling in our dressing room remained that we were going to win. Only a few weeks earlier, that would have seemed raving mad, but despite New Zealand being favourites we knew that the calibre of player we had down the bottom of our order gave us a genuine chance.

Only wet weather – and Duckworth-Lewis – stopped us having the opportunity to complete something special. We will never know, of course, but without the rain we felt we were destined to chase them down. It was gutting that the equation swung the balance firmly back in New Zealand's favour. With Adil Rashid and Liam Plunkett together, we actually felt in control. It was our game to lose, not theirs. To go from a requirement of 54 runs off 37 balls to 34 from 13 when the contest recommenced after the stoppage, from needing under nine runs an over to nearly 16, was devastating. We had been behind the eight ball at the start of the innings but fought our way to a position modern teams are comfortable with. Going off the field at the point we did, and having to start again twenty minutes later, took all the momentum out of our innings.

If this episode showed one thing, it was that Duckworth-Lewis needs addressing. With evidence that teams can now chase down scores of 350 and greater, I am not sure that adjusted targets such as we faced represent a fair reflection of what is possible nowadays. There is now a lot more confidence in numbers eight, nine and ten contributing significant scores and being unflustered at having to score at ten runs an over at the back end of an innings. With sides batting deeper and players able to make scores of 30 off ten balls more consistently now, this will surely have to evolve. Let's face facts – the game has changed massively since the Duckworth-Lewis method of revising chases first came in. The recalculation of our target suggested New Zealand were heavily on top, and we didn't feel that was the case.

Even then, we weren't completely out of it and the fine margins involved were emphasised when Tim Southee and Trent Boult combined for a stunning catch on the long-on rope to dismiss Rashid with 24 runs needed off seven deliveries. Had the ball gone for a new England record fifteenth six in an innings, and it was three inches off doing so, you never know. However, even though we didn't quite make it, the confidence we took from that match was incredible. I don't think I could ever have imagined a team feeling so empowered after a loss.

Suddenly, it felt like anything was truly possible at any

given stage of a match, and that's exciting for players and spectators alike. From that first match on, no one knew which way games were going to go. To the extent that when we got things slightly wrong at the Rose Bowl in the next match and slumped from 194–3 in the 33rd over to 302 all out with 28 balls unused, people were still backing us. This was telling deep into a game that New Zealand appeared to have under control at 242–2 in the 39th over of their reply. All of a sudden, from out of nowhere, the crowd came alive. There was no particular incident to spark them. It was almost as if they knew we needed a break-through and wanted to play their part. We duly took Williamson's wicket, then ended the powerplay with another and clawed our way back to a position where we had a semblance of a chance, before losing by three wickets.

What happened next, in the fourth ODI at Trent Bridge, showed that this England one-day team was indisputably heading in the right direction. To not only chase down a target of 350 but to do it with 36 balls to spare to square the series at 2–2 was a real statement about our quality. It was only England's third successful chase of over 300 in forty-four years of one-day internationals, and thanks to our new approach we had smashed it down. Rather than apply any conservativism in the chase, we managed to develop a smarter way of executing in a must-win scenario. It showed how rapidly things were turning around.

The openers Jason Roy and Alex Hales broke the back

of it by taking us into three figures before being parted. Hales is someone I have a lot of time for, so it was pleasing to see his talent flourish when under scrutiny. He's a relaxed kind of character, bordering on dippy occasionally, and he has a tendency to say things before he thinks, providing no end of amusement for the rest of us.

Back in our England Lions days, on a one-day tour of Sri Lanka, Baz, as he is known, had one of his moments at a net session at the Premadasa Stadium in Colombo. A local spinner with an unconventional action had wandered over for a bowl, and Hales greeted his introduction by hauling him out of the net and high over midwicket.

'Who does this Tom Noddy think he is? Muralitharan?' he quipped.

Only when he charged down the track and was stuffed by Tom Noddy's next ball, a deadly doosra, was he to discover the embarrassing truth. It was Murali. Graham Thorpe, our coach, obviously knew him well and had invited him down to our session as it was mutually beneficial. On one hand, it would aid our preparations, on the other, it would provide him with some bowling ahead of his Big Bash League commitments in Australia after Christmas.

Baz may not be the sharpest at times but his ball-striking can be and our opening pair arguably did not get the credit they deserved for their part in this momentous victory. As one of two centurions in that chase, I did, and what I will say is that the work of Roy and Hales was crucial, even though they departed in quick succession. Knocking off

250 from 40 overs, as opposed to 350 from 50, made it a totally different game. Sometimes a pitch can get a bit tacky under floodlights, at others it can just offer a little bit more off the seam for the quicker bowlers, but on this occasion the ball skidded on nicely and Alex, in particular, with 67 off just 42 deliveries, made the most of it.

It might sound like false modesty on my behalf, given how pleased I was with my own form, and naturally I was delighted to score a second hundred in four matches, but Eoin Morgan's influence then helped me through our pursuit. He has this remarkable way of keeping you at your ease when he's stood 22 yards away from you. Immediately after overs when you only manage a couple of runs and cannot do anything else because the bowler has bowled exceptionally well, he will get on strike and deposit a ball for six, follow up with another boundary and before you've blinked you're ahead of the game, despite contrary feelings only moments earlier. The way he batted in those post-World Cup ODIs was to make his 50-over game an extension of his Twenty20 game, and it worked a treat.

He had been under a lot of pressure as captain at the World Cup in Australia and not got the scores he would have liked. Now, having told the guys what he wanted, he delivered the goods himself. In this game, he had been back in the dressing room a full half-hour when we won, but his was the match-winning hundred, greeted with a shout of 'you beauty'. More than anything, that stand between us, worth 198, was fun; part of a series that made you want to be out there, doing it all again, day after day.

The real beauty of the team was yet to show itself, however. That came in the final match of five in the Royal London Series, the winner-takes-all finale on 20 June at Chester-le-Street, when players on the periphery came in and performed from the outset. We had been given some brilliant one-day surfaces, which played a huge part in making the series such an entertaining spectacle, and by far the spiciest pitch had been kept until last.

David Willey bowled well with the new ball on debut in New Zealand's 283–9, a total that was re-evaluated as 192 from 26 overs after a lengthy rain delay. After we were reduced to 45–5, our hopes were fading. At that stage, we genuinely thought the series was gone. The top order had all found ways to get out and the last of our top six batsmen standing, Jonny Bairstow, had only been called up twenty-four hours earlier after Jos Buttler split the webbing in his right hand.

Jonny is someone I've known for a long time and in the past twelve months he has definitely been a lot more relaxed and at peace with himself. One of his previous weaknesses was to place too high an expectation on himself. These days he seems to be more comfortable with what he is trying to achieve and appears to have a better understanding of his game. That has been evident in his consistency. He's had the confidence to play every ball as he's seen it and take the opposition on when merited.

That is what he did on this occasion and, well supported by Sam Billings and then Adil Rashid, he got us into the position of favourites as the match hit the home straight. It was a really skilful knock, against the spinners especially, but even though he seemed to have everything under control, it didn't stop Mark Wood looking absolutely terrified in the dressing room. He had all his kit on, praying we would get across the line without the need for him to bat, unable to control his nerves. Similarly, Paul Farbrace, normally the embodiment of calm, was flapping around, excitable and emotional. You could see how much it meant to him when Jonny sliced the ball behind backward point for two to finish on 83 not out and complete a 3–2 win.

This was something worth celebrating, and although the majority of the lads headed out to Newcastle afterwards, I did not feel it was appropriate for me to do so. A few days earlier, after the win at Trent Bridge, we had gone for a few victory drinks and ended up at the Crisis all-nighter at Rock City in Nottingham. Within a few hours, news of our revelry had been published in the *Tab* student newspaper, the same publication that exposed Gary Ballance for baring his chest at another Nottingham nightspot a year earlier.

This time their headline revealed that I was 'absolutely smashed'. It was actually quite a funny article, reporting how appropriate it had been that I'd been dancing to

'Cotton-Eyed Joe' before leaving in the early hours. I had come off the field buzzing after scoring a hundred in a great win and because it was a day-nighter we didn't have our first drink until around 11 p.m. I've always enjoyed celebrating wins with the rest of the lads, away from the game, but I was very conscious of the fact that our celebrations had subsequently been picked up by the national newspapers. With the Ashes being so close, I was wary of creating the wrong kind of public image and decided on this occasion to keep a low profile.

6 PREPARING FOR BATTLE

AN Ashes series is not something that creeps up on you overnight. If you are an England cricketer, preparation begins a long time before the meet-up date for the first Test is marked in your diary. In my case, the planning had begun a good couple of months before I first spoke about what I considered my one career failure.

The confession that my record against Australia was the one blot on my international cricket CV came on a walk with Carrie in the Peak District immediately after the one-day series against New Zealand. Taking in the stunning scenery from Stanage Edge, I told her that while I'd had a really good year in Test cricket, I was desperate to prove to myself that I could do it against the Australians. I didn't want to prove it to anybody else. Just myself.

Yes, I'd had good series in the West Indies, against India and Sri Lanka, but I didn't feel I'd hacked it at Ashes cricket. I really wanted to get into a position where I could say I had accomplished something. As international cricketers, we are all aware of our statistics, and if you are going to be a consistent performer – because England play Australia more than anyone else – you have to be successful in these matches. To finish with the kind of career numbers that suggest you are a top batsman, you have to score runs against them.

The pair of us don't talk about cricket too often but when we do I always find Carrie a good sounding board. She allows me to get things off my chest, and understands my drive to succeed from a different angle to that a team-mate or a coach might have. I find in this kind of environment, hearing your own thoughts out loud can actually reinforce ambition in a positive way. From a mental perspective, I was getting myself ready for the challenge.

From a physical point of new, I had been preparing for the Australians as far back as our tour of the Caribbean in the spring. Because of the extra pace I knew Australia were going to bring to our encounters, I spent numerous sessions there facing bucketloads of yellow indoor cricket balls – which are lighter than the outdoor variety, and thankfully don't tend to break bones when they hit you – hurled at me at breakneck speed by Mark Ramprakash, our batting coach, from the side-arm contraption modern coaching features heavily. You might recognise it as the ball-thrower that dog-owners use.

Those indoor balls do not possess as much weight but it's still not much fun being peppered – believe me, it stings – so that kind of session certainly sharpens the reflexes. The idea was that having that intensive work behind me would also give me confidence that I was prepared for the extra speed of fast bowlers like Mitchell Johnson. Ramps would position himself to recreate the left-arm angle, specifically with Johnson in mind.

From experience, I had formed an idea of how Australia, and Johnson in particular, were going to attack me. Initially, I suspected they would plump for a very full length at me, with the odd short ball thrown in. Almost a two-length plan, if you like. This seemed pretty obvious to me, considering what had happened the last time I had faced them, in the 2013–14 Ashes. On the evidence of that series, it was exactly the kind of strategy I would have been devising if I had been orchestrating a bowling attack against a virtual me.

However, I reckoned that if they did, they would be playing straight into my hands. Since the last time I'd faced them, my front-foot game had improved a hell of a lot and I'd developed much more clarity about playing and leaving outside off-stump. Equally, if Johnson was going to bowl short at me, I felt much better prepared. One of my failings in that series in Australia had been getting stuck at times – unable to get out of the way or play an attacking shot. The ball seemed to follow me and I had nowhere to go, meaning I was trying to fend balls off my body with two men positioned around the corner. Even when I managed to get through those periods, it always felt like just a matter of time before there was an unplayable delivery coming my way.

So I felt it prudent to practise taking on the short ball,

rather than just trying to duck and sway. With an attacking option in my game, I believed I could get a few boundaries away and put the pressure back on him. Also, if I was able to counter his bouncer in this way, he might think twice about bowling it to me.

Fortunately, this was where one of the alterations I had made to my batting while working with Jos came in useful – increasing my backlift to enable me to get my hands at the ball quicker. When the speed of the ball is over 90 miles per hour you have to give yourself every opportunity to hit it by shortening your arm movements. Because my hands were previously so low, there just wasn't time to get them up and back out front again to get them over the top of the ball. That is why all I seemed able to do was fend it upwards, which was obviously flirting with danger, or get pinned with nowhere to go or successfully get out of the way.

So I spent hours and hours with Ramps pinging balls through at me destined for the armpit and chest. Don't get me wrong, these sessions are not enjoyable, but I found them worthwhile. No one really fancies being battered by balls at 90 mph, but if you want to be the best you can be, you have to deal with that kind of thing. The reward is the improvement you can see as a result. Every time we finished a session, I felt more and more confident that I had a game to combat Johnson.

The Ashes experience in Australian conditions had also taught me that I needed to alter my approach to playing off the front foot. Whenever the ball was full, I kept trying to get massive strides in, and just as I had found with the short stuff, there simply was not time. In terms of my technical change here, I tried to concentrate on getting all my weight going into the ball when I struck it rather than worry about the length of the stride I was getting in. Now I get my head as close to it as I can rather than my foot. When you assess the top batsmen around the globe, very few are able to get right out to the pitch of the ball and those that do tend to be taller like Kevin Pietersen – his stride length is enormous. But as I don't have that kind of stature, and I'm therefore a different kind of player altogether, I've come to realise that it's not how far I get forward but how in control of the shot I am that matters most.

During these intense periods of practice – Ramps's competitive streak means he slings the ball down with the mentality of a fast bowler and gets grumpy if you get too many out of the middle of the bat – I also came to realise that when facing spells of extreme pace you might not be able to whack every front-foot delivery for four. It might be necessary to give up a few drives and soak up a little bit of pressure, concentrating on capitalising when they bowl a shorter length.

To be fair, I owed Ramps for this, because he was the one that initiated the original idea about preparing for Johnson well in advance. I agreed with him and so we started our work outside main net sessions. When news filtered around the team, others showed an equal willingness to get stuck in. Ramps didn't necessarily urge them to repli-cate our practice sessions to the letter, just encouraged them to do something to prepare for the increased pace and hostility.

Not everyone benefits from the same practice – it depends on your individual technique – but as a group we knew that going from the relatively mid-range pace of New Zealand, who nevertheless possess a high-class attack, to that of the consistent 90 mph stuff from Australia was going to be a bit of a shock to the system, and once you're on the international circuit it is important to instigate what you might call long-range practice. And this kind of work not only prepared me for Johnson and Mitchell Starc. With a tour of South Africa scheduled for the end of 2015, where the likes of Dale Steyn and Morne Morkel were likely to be the main threat, it was important to top up on this aspect of my batting.

If the 2013–14 whitewash Down Under left the England team looking for answers, the same was true of me as one of its components. I had travelled to Australia as an opening batsman, mentally prepared for going in first. However, things were to change very quickly. For the first warm-up game of the tour, against a Western Australia Chairman's XI in Perth, it was decided to give some game time to Michael Carberry. We opened together and he hit 78. Kept in the side for the second game, against Australia A in Hobart, he hit 153 before retiring. Suddenly, the selectors considered him to be in good enough form to warrant a place. When it came to Test selection, he had to play.

It was felt that the only place he could be accommodated was at the top of the order, and I was fine with that. I was told I would bat at six, somewhere I had batted before in Test cricket. As I felt comfortable there, I went into that first Test match feeling relaxed about the whole situation.

The first innings at the Gabba proved to be a bit of a whirlwind. I walked out to bat after the loss of a couple of quick wickets and the noise was something I'd never experienced before. Even in India I'd not encountered that level. All I could hear was blokes singing, 'Rooty is a w*****.'

The din made by 35,000 people in Brisbane sounded particularly intimidating because of the acoustics there. The cheering and jeering seems to bounce off the stands to make the most incredible racket imaginable. It was almost too much for me, if I'm being honest. It took me completely by surprise and before I knew it I had played a massive drive and been caught at third slip off the hometown hero Johnson. The atmosphere had clearly spooked me and knocked my focus. This was all new to me. I was out in Australia on an Ashes tour, something I'd not done before. As a team, we were on the back foot, Australia were all over us and a combination of all of those factors derailed me.

In the second innings I felt a lot more comfortable, probably because I was out there when Stuart Broad walked out on a hat-trick for the second time in the match and the focus was so obviously on him not me. Even more people were shouting that he was a w***** than had shouted the same obscenities at me. Although we lost heavily, I finished 26 not out and considered it to be a first building block into the series.

Then came the news that Jonathan Trott was going to be leaving the tour. It prompted a discussion between myself and Andy Flower, the England coach, in which he asked me whether I would like to bat in the vacated number three position. On balance, I considered it a good opportunity. Less than a month earlier, I believed I was going to be walking in first. There were no other stand-out candidates for the role, other than Ian Bell, and there was a reluctance to move him because in the previous series he had batted at number five so successfully – hitting three hundreds from that position during the 2013 Ashes. He looked really settled there. Kevin Pietersen had been number four for 90 per cent of his Test career, so there wasn't really any other choice than for me to do it.

In the second Test match, on a typically slow Adelaide Oval wicket, I felt in good touch and as though my game was in pretty good order, making 15 and 87. But after that the wheels fell off a little bit, both from a team point of view and a personal perspective. In the first innings of the third Test at Perth, I was given out erroneously, shortly after arriving at the crease, when the Australians appealed for a caught-behind off Shane Watson's bowling. I knew I had not hit it, and there was no Hot Spot to disprove me, nor any kind of spike on Snicko. However, despite there being no conclusive evidence that I was out, the protocol was to stick with Marais Erasmus's on-field decision. I was absolutely devastated.

Unfortunately, that episode brought out the stubborn side in me when, during the second innings, I played a drive to a full-length ball wide outside the off-stump and bashed the floor with the toe of my bat. Or at least that is what I thought I had done. Brad Haddin, behind the stumps, dived to catch the ball, Australia appealed and I was given out.

Instinct told me I had struck the pitch not the ball and so I reviewed it straight away, without consulting my partner at that time. Kevin Pietersen, the man at the non-striker's end, clearly hadn't seen me do so and advised me not to refer it when we gathered in the middle of the pitch. 'You smashed it,' he said. Embarrassingly, it was too late.

Marais Erasmus is one of the umpires I get on best with on the international circuit but because he had given me out in the first innings, I was just not having it. 'You've got it wrong again!' I thought. Only he hadn't. That fact was confirmed when I looked over at the replay screen to see a massive Hot Spot and Haddin taking a catch for the wicketkeepers' union scrapbook in front of first slip's right knee. It was an horrendous decision to review and I have never felt so stupid walking off a field in my life.

Following those two fleeting visits to the crease at the WACA, I batted two hours for two dozen runs in the first innings of the Boxing Day Test in Melbourne, having been forced right back into my shell. In the second, after conversations with the coaching staff, my intention was to change tack and express myself a bit more. When your opponents are on top it is very easy to get a bit internal and to withdraw from the challenge. The outer confidence displayed when I had been playing well earlier in the year had been eroded, and with no experience of this kind of thing before I didn't know quite how to deal with it.

I was persuaded to try to change tempo, and soon I was hitting the ball nicely again, manipulating it into gaps and rotating the strike. Then I came down the wicket to Nathan Lyon and drove all along the floor wide of mid-off and set off for a single. As the ball reached the popping crease at the far end, it struck a bobble and popped up perfectly into the fielder's left hand. Unfortunately, the fielder happened to be left-handed and arguably I should have been aware that Mitchell Johnson was stationed there. A clean gather and direct hit at the bowler's end left me run out by six inches.

I arrived in Sydney for the last Test match thinking that I needed to do some extra work and I had just finished an individual session, in fact, when the rest of the guys turned up and I was invited for what turned out to be a very difficult conversation with Alastair Cook. He told me I would be missing out on selection that week. There were no other words to describe the feeling it left me with. I was distraught.

I could not help thinking, 'Why me?' When I analysed my performances, I couldn't see how I had done anything drastically different to the other guys. Experience tells you that this is not the way you should look at that kind of situation at all, and I now look back on my initial reaction as being unacceptable and not befitting my personal standards. I have always set a high benchmark for myself and as I wasn't reaching it, why wouldn't I expect to be dropped? Being dropped certainly made me do a lot of growing up. It wasn't really important what I thought; it was what was considered to be best for the team. I think my reaction was driven more by frustration than anger – frustration that I had not done better.

Straight after the decision I reflected that I'd made 87 just two Tests previously, but even in my room at the InterContinental Hotel that evening, picking at my room-service order, I accepted that was the wrong way to look at it. I realised that things were not going to get any better moping around, feeling sorry for myself; it was important to help the England team try to win the last Test to save a bit of face. I pledged to wake up the next day and be as helpful as possible to the rest of the guys. If

I was playing, and they weren't, I would expect the same treatment from them.

It is important to go through periods like this and feel the pain of missing out. It can't have been very easy for Gary Ballance, either, a long-term mate who had to suppress his own elation somewhat to come and knock on my door to let me know he was going to make his Test debut. Here was a reason to stop feeling sorry for myself if I still needed one – I knew exactly how hard he had worked to get himself to the brink of selection.

No matter the circumstances, when you get dropped it is only natural to consider whether you'll ever get the opportunity to play Test cricket again. All I could think of was how much more I wanted to achieve. I was only young, but how was I to know what lay in store in the future? I wasn't really an established player going through a bad patch. In those kind of circumstances I might have found it easier to get back in.

During the one-day and Twenty20 series that followed, I lost and then regained my place but my priority remained to get back into that Test team. With three weeks between getting back from Australia and heading off to the Caribbean for a limited-overs tour in February and March 2014, I was determined to turn things around. So I turned to a couple of people to see what they had made of my recent batting.

First, I spoke to Kevin Sharp, my old mentor from

Yorkshire, over the phone, and then sought the advice of Michael Vaughan over a coffee in Sheffield. Nobody knows the workings of my game better than Kevin, while occasionally it can be beneficial to speak to someone who works in the media. Commentators watch every ball and can provide a different insight. Not only do people like Michael have huge amounts of experience from playing the game; their job is to assess. A coach will watch every ball but equally it is a coach's job to watch every player, and coaches don't see situations in the same way as a commentator. Sometimes you need a different opinion, with no vested interest.

It turned out that Michael's answer – to work on my strengths, bang out my best shots in practice – reiterated what Kevin had said to me. I had been spending a lot of time at practice trying to be the complete player rather than concentrating on all the strong aspects of my game. If your base elements are functioning effectively, then other areas of your game can evolve later. So I went back to drilling my most profitable shots – the cut, back-foot drive and the clip off my legs. Simplifying things in this way meant that the core of my batting had been stripped back to playing three shots rather than worrying about every one in the book. I concentrated on them, with a pledge that if the ball came into a certain area, it was going for four.

In one of the warm-up games in the Caribbean I felt at ease playing this way and it gave me the confidence to back my natural instinct, then slowly increase my range of strokes throughout an innings. Confidence grew throughout this tour for me, peaking with a hundred in the third match, in Antigua. Unfortunately, however, the blow I received to my right thumb from a rising Ravi Rampaul delivery early in that innings curtailed it for me ahead of the trio of 20-over internationals and forced me to miss the World Twenty20 in Bangladesh that followed. On the Monday morning after returning from Antigua, a scan revealed my thumb was shattered into seven pieces. It kept me sidelined for six weeks.

Thankfully, when I returned to the Test team in the first match of the 2014 summer against Sri Lanka, I could not have done so more emphatically. That unbeaten double hundred at Lord's set the tone for my next twelve months in that form of the game. Undefeated scores of 154 and 149 followed at either end of the following home series against India.

Within the England dressing room we speak a lot about big hundreds and there's no doubt that the moment had got to me after I registered my first Test century on my home ground in 2013. I felt a sense of release – and got dismissed soon afterwards. It led to a bit of a roasting from Graham Gooch – a man who likes his daddy hundreds. Could I convert three figures into something even more substantial? That appeared to be something I had answered with those scores and the 182 not out against West Indies. But the question still tormenting me was whether I could handle Australia's pace attack – and Johnson in particular. There was a lot of media talk about what a nightmare he was going to be to deal with. Behind the scenes, however, I felt prepared.

Such is the nature of the way Australia play the game, their hostility is not solely confined to what their bowlers put on the ball. Before the 2015 series I knew I would also have to prepare my mind for their verbal assaults. I was expecting them to come extremely hard in this regard and accepted I needed to deal with it better than I had in their backyard two winters previously.

When Australia are on top they can get to you. One of their strengths is that they get tight as a team, become very vocal and aren't particularly nice with what they say. It's a tactic that's worked for them over time and is important to the way they play their cricket. Once you accept that, you have to find your own method of coping with it. If they get on top, which is inevitable at some stage for a team that has been towards the top of the world Test rankings in recent times, how will you respond?

The worst way, in my estimation, is a policy of ignoring it, because that's impossible. You cannot help but hear what's being said. In Australia in 2013–14 I had turned a deaf ear but it hadn't worked, simply because when they're on top they can be so in your face and loud. When batting, it's a necessity of the job to switch off between balls, and that's when they infiltrate your consciousness with their verbal shots.

So this time around I came up with my own method of response. I decided that whenever they went for me with their one-liners, I would offer a retort under my breath. Inevitably, there would be some not nice thoughts being mimed or registering in my head, laced with one or two expletives, but I did not want to get into verbal spats, so combating it in silence would allow me to crack on and play.

Having played in two Ashes series before, I knew what to expect in terms of hype. It is incomparable to other series you play in for England. So I and other senior players tried to get across to the lads who had not played before exactly what it was like.

There is always a lot more scrutiny when you play Australia; people who would not normally watch cricket take an interest in it. And it's such a massive sporting occasion, the pinnacle of Test cricket for Englishmen, that you are already heaping excess pressure on yourself. Doing this is understandable. Part of an English cricketer's DNA is a desperation to succeed against Australia. It's no use pretending otherwise. It means a disproportionate expectation of what you want to achieve, even compared to playing the other top sides like South Africa and India. Certainly, travelling around the country, you can see that the public feel the same way too: advertising is everywhere, and that doesn't happen when you play other countries. The intensity is something you need to get your head around.

One change from my past experience was that it was obvious we were the underdogs heading into the 2015 version of cricket's greatest rivalry. And not only because of the 5–0 scoreline from our last meeting. Comparison of the two teams' build-ups told its own story – both teams had gone over to West Indies, but with contrasting results. We were held to a draw, while Australia battered them.

As far as I was concerned, this made a good start a necessity. My mind went back to 2013 and how important it had felt winning at Trent Bridge – although Australia lost by only 14 runs, it was a psychological blow to their hopes – and also how shocked we were by getting beaten up in Brisbane at the start of the 2013–14 campaign. I had experienced the two extremes and recognised how the first Test match of a series can shape what follows. Momentum can be vital as you head into such a long series.

Equally, I've always found that a good score at the start of a series can settle you down as a batsman and provide confidence in future games. In my case, the importance of this has been even more keenly felt because of an irritating pattern of mine. I have tended to follow a big score with next to nothing in the following match. For example, I felt in amazing nick at Lord's against the New Zealanders in May 2015 and then went up to Headingley and scored a single run.

* * *

There certainly seemed to be more excitement in the build-up to the 2015 series compared to two years before, when Darren Lehmann, the Australia coach, said afterwards that we played dull, boring cricket for our 3–0 win. We had been expected to be successful back then, so it perhaps hadn't captured the imagination as much as an Ashes should. It's almost more enjoyable for your public when you are not favourites.

This time, all the talk was about Australia and they were not shy about joining in themselves. It was not until much later in the summer that I was to be told of Steve Smith's comments of 29 April: 'I can't wait to get over there and play another Ashes against England in their conditions. After beating them so convincingly in Australia it's going to be nice to go into their backyard. If we continue to play the same way we've played over the last twelve to eighteen months, I don't think they'll come close to us, to be honest.' I wish I had heard those comments at the time. They would have been powerful words of motivation.

We were on the pre-series trip to Spain when Peter Siddle, asked who were favourites for the Ashes, replied, 'Is that a serious question?'

All typically Australian, I guess. That is the way they have acted for as long as I can remember. Glenn McGrath habitually claims Australia will wipe the floor with England, and I suppose he's in a safer place to say such things now he's retired. In the cases of Smith and Siddle, you really have to win if you say things like that, because the game of cricket has a tendency to bite you on the behind and make you look stupid.

In contrast, we worried much more about our game than about Australia, focusing our attention on getting absolutely ready to perform rather than having a pop at others. One of the characteristics of the England team since I have been a part of it is that when we concentrate on our strengths, rather than looking at what the opposition are going to do, it serves us much better.

In simple terms, that is what we discussed on our pre-series excursion to the Desert Springs resort near Almería in Spain. We got used to being together as a team and learned how our new coach Trevor Bayliss was going to operate and what he expected of us. It would have been very hard to rock up three or four days before the first Ashes Test, meet a new coach for the first time and try to understand what he was about, then think about the twenty-five days of cricket ahead the following day. This environment allowed us all to settle in.

My initial impression of Trevor – we met with a handshake and how-do at Birmingham Airport on Saturday, 27 June – was that he was very laid-back and quiet. Even by the end of that four-day trip, it did not feel as if we all knew him really well. Nor did it feel as if we'd engaged in a proper conversation. But as we have discovered, that's his way. He's a very observational coach, someone who sits back and studies, considers what he's seeing and then tells you his view.

On the first afternoon in Spain, we had a team bike ride down from Desert Springs to the local beach and played some bad football on a bad surface. The ball bobbled all over the place, but it was a laugh. We cycled back, passing an idyllic golf course. All I could think was 'I hope we get time to play it.'

By the time that wish came true, I could hardly grip the clubs, so sore were my hands from catching practice. We did so much catching out there that they felt swollen by the end and they were covered in bruises. Told in advance to take only training kit and spikes, those of us who occupy places in the slip cordon found ourselves having sessions twice a day. It wasn't just about the actual catching; it was about getting an understanding between those of us who were going to form the unit.

During the previous twelve months there had been numerous changes in personnel in the slips and the aim was to establish a bit of consistency again – to get to know the bloke next to you, the size of the gaps between you and how much ground each one tended to cover. A good slip cordon works in unison and so it wasn't just about how we caught as individuals but as a group. As the slip fielders play such an integral role in dictating the course of Test matches, it was an astute call by the management to highlight this as an area to sharpen up on.

We worked for hours – Alastair Cook at first, Ian Bell

at second, me at third, then Lyth; Stokes at gully. We also put Gary Ballance in various positions as a reserve in case he needed to fill in during the series. Taking your catches or not can alter the momentum of a contest, so you need to be as ready as possible to take advantage if the ball is seaming around early on. Pitches can go flat and it is important to take those chances before they do.

I had dropped a catch at Lord's against New Zealand, but the life I gave to Ross Taylor didn't prove costly. However, we'd been bad at Headingley as a collective. Hence, a daily session each morning before breakfast, followed by one in the evening before we packed up for the day. We did a lot of hard gym work too, but because we were away from home, and away from any Ashes build-up attention, we stayed relaxed.

Not that we discarded the opportunity to go through Australia's individual players and our plans for each of them. That's important ahead of any series and we did discuss them in depth at a team meeting on the Sunday. Trevor – who previously had ten of the Australia squad playing under him at New South Wales, and had coached others when deputising for Darren Lehmann for Twenty20 internationals in late 2014 – offered an insight into how he thought their attack would look to bowl and what we should consider when bowling at their batsmen. But he reiterated that primarily he wanted us to look after our own skills.

Over dinner in the evenings, we broke down into smaller

groups so that Trevor could get to know us as individuals a little better, and we also had a quiz night one evening to lighten the mood, with the four quizmasters, of which I was one, clad in fancy dress. Ben Stokes was a Brit abroad sporting fake sleeve tattoos up his legs to match his arms; Chris Taylor, the fielding coach, wore a woman's wig trimmed down and the legendary black Slazenger sweater and came as Seve Ballesteros; I scrubbed up pretty well as a matador; and Mark Saxby, the England team masseur, for reasons known only to himself, came as a female salsa dancer. Needless to say, there were a few drinks enjoyed and it was a really good night to finish off a really good trip.

It is important sometimes to spend time with the other lads outside a cricket environment. Additionally, sometimes you speak best about cricket when you are away from the ground, in another kind of atmosphere; you can find the conversation is quite different from how it would be in a dressing room. I remember Jos Buttler asking me over a beer what he should be expecting when the Tests came round. His excitement, and that of others around the group, provided me with the kind of energy that meant I wanted to start the series as soon as we got back home.

On our return, one thing that caught my eye was how, during Australia's warm-up matches and the one against Essex in particular, Nathan Lyon, their off-spinner, had been smacked by county batsmen. He was someone I had thought we had a chance of trying to dominate, so I considered this a positive sign.

Getting on top of Lyon and not letting him settle had been one of the tactics we had discussed on the Spanish sojourn. Although it didn't quite materialise as anticipated, Alastair Cook set the tone for this on the very first morning of the series in Cardiff when he used his feet to attack the spinner. Unfortunately, he kept nailing the ball straight to fielders. Nevertheless, it set the tone for everyone else.

From a bowling perspective, it was felt that the fact we use the Dukes ball over here also gave us an advantage. As an English seamer you operate with one from the first day at work playing second-team cricket. There was a period when a Tiflex ball was used in the second division of the County Championship, but otherwise the Dukes has been universally present. We were aware as a batting unit that it might take their bowlers a while to get into rhythm with it, and that arguably their best technician of swing and seam movement, Ryan Harris, had lost his fitness fight. But what about those that remained – how were they going to control the swing? Arguably they were not used to it swinging that much. Also, how were they going to control their length? When the ball is swinging you look to bowl it a bit fuller.

In our team meetings we spoke about bowling with discipline and making the Australians play with a straight bat as much as possible. We wanted them fending with it coming down straight so that our slips and wicketkeeper remained in the game. Australians are brought up on cross-bat shots.

We also talked about how, despite the fact Steve Smith was in such fantastic form coming into the series, Australia moving their best batsman up to number three provided us with the chance to expose him to the swinging ball if we could get an early breakthrough. It was an excellent opportunity to get at him when the bowlers were at their freshest, and as he had not spent a lot of time batting in that position, we wanted to exploit a potential lack of experience against lateral movement in the initial stages of an innings. We felt that anything the ball did in the air or off the surface was going to work in our favour against him. If this plan worked, it would offer the added bonus of getting Michael Clarke out in the middle before he would like. Of course, for all this to fall into place, we needed the kind of surfaces to encourage our quality new-ball duo, Jimmy Anderson and Stuart Broad.

7 AN EXPLOSIVE START

I T is no secret that I have history with David Warner. Not pleasant history, but history nevertheless. And as far as I was concerned, that history, for both our sakes, was best left in the past.

So when Warner, just before the England and Australian teams travelled to Cardiff for the start of the 2015 Ashes series, opted to revisit the issue of his punching me in Birmingham's Walkabout bar two years previously, and then came out with some cock-and-bull story to justify his actions, it made my blood boil.

In an interview with the Australian press, he suggested there had been provocation for what was universally and accurately reported in June 2013 as an 'unprovoked physical attack', for which he served a Cricket Australia-imposed suspension. To claim that he did so because he believed I was insulting Muslims like Hashim Amla by grabbing a green-and-gold party wig off someone else's head and placing it on my chin was just crass.

Unfortunately, this was not the first time I had heard such a ridiculous claim. The day after it happened, Warner had sent me a text message apologising for what he had done, and during our exchanges he used the same useless excuse for his actions that he was now repeating to journalists twenty-five months later. My reply at the time was that it was ridiculous. Asked by him to go for a coffee to talk about it face to face, I declined the invitation, thanked him for the apology and informed him that as far as I was concerned it was time to move on.

On Saturday, 4 July 2015, I was sat on my sofa when word of the Australian newspaper reports reached me. I was furious. Absolutely furious. It took me a full ten minutes to calm down to the point where I could speak to anyone about it. Within a few minutes the abuse I was getting on social media was mushrooming. Clearly, people had taken what he had said at face value. If you are presented with something like that, it is very easy to automatically believe it. So I felt I needed to say something, not in retaliation, but to get my point, and the truth, across. After consultation with my agent Neil Fairbrother, I decided to take to Twitter with a simple statement: 'Disappointing to have my character questioned – those who know me realise how ridiculous Warner's excuse for hitting me sounds but that's his choice to try and justify his actions. I'm just extremely excited about next week and getting back out there.'

By now it had sunk in that it was an obvious ploy to try to unsettle me, and by extension the England team, ahead of the series. The timing of it, four days before the start of the first Test, screamed out that they were trying to mess with my preparation. Mind games it might have been, but the last thing I wanted was for the claims to remain unchallenged. I wanted to address them so that when we all turned up for practice, it had been put to bed. I certainly didn't need stuff like that hanging around me.

In my eyes, since his attack on me in the Walkabout, I had been almost doing him a favour by never bringing the subject up. Now, in a way, it was a bit of a compliment that he chose to do so, because if he and his colleagues wanted to disturb my preparation, they obviously saw me as one of England's leading players. To think in so much depth about me, to try to throw me off my game like that, must have been because they were scared I would be able to hurt them on the field. They had tried to hit me with a negative. But I transformed it into a positive.

There had been the odd on-field word exchanged between me and Warner in the interim but no more than that, and the relationship between us, or lack of one, had been pretty irrelevant to me. After this episode, I actually turned up to the game at Cardiff feeling a bit sorry for him. The fact he felt the need to bring it up was pretty pathetic. It had the effect of taking all the sting out of any verbals Australia had stored up for me before a ball had been bowled.

My previous experience of an Ashes opening ceremony on home soil had left me with butterflies in the stomach. That match, back at Trent Bridge in 2013, was the first time I had opened the batting for England. The Red Arrows flew overhead and this huge extravaganza unfolded immediately before I walked out into the middle with my pads on. Within ten minutes or so of singing the national anthem as passionately as an Englishman possibly could – as a patriotic person, being able to belt out *God Save the Queen* always gets me going – I began the mental preparation ahead of facing my first ball. I admit it flustered me.

This time, in Cardiff, I loved the entire experience. But I gave a warning to Adam Lyth about how such a rush ahead of the first over can throw you off-kilter. I knew how important it was to get yourself ready as soon as the anthems were over. The occasion is something you will always remember, but as soon as you head back to the dressing room, you need to make sure your head is in the right place to play. Thankfully, this time, carded at number five, I was not in as much of a rush.

I was at the crease ahead of schedule, however, following the loss of three wickets inside the first hour, including that of Alastair Cook, who had won the toss and then edged Nathan Lyon, the off-spinner, behind, to be second out between Adam Lyth and Ian Bell.

A start of 43–3 was fairly dramatic, and I could not have faced a more challenging beginning to my own innings. My initial thoughts were to get through the first twenty balls, find my feet and get used to the pitch conditions and the atmosphere. But my first delivery, swung back into me by Mitchell Starc, was right on the money at 90 mph and struck me on the front pad as I jabbed down.

'Jeez,' I thought.

The Australians behind me were equally excitable and after their appeal for lbw was turned down appeared to be considering a review. However, although I accepted it was a good delivery, I was not too concerned because I knew I had got a piece of the ball on my bat on a journey I estimated was passing leg-stump. Wisely, they declined the opportunity to review.

From point, amongst a chain of expletives, David Warner shouted, 'You're not facing Trent Boult's eighty-mile-an-hour half-volleys now, mate.'

Next ball, looking to score, I went after what I thought was a half-volley. Only it wasn't one. This delivery was a bit fuller, and as the ball went past the bat I genuinely believed I had struck the ground. Until I saw the replay on the big screen, that is. It was a bit of a shock that the slow-motion pictures told me otherwise as it flew off the edge and was floored by Australia's wicketkeeper Brad Haddin, diving to his right.

As we discussed the incident in the middle of the pitch, I told my partner Gary Ballance that I would have reviewed it had Haddin held the catch and I'd been given out.

'Shock – you reviewing another one,' he said.

You see, I have a bit of a reputation in the team as a batsman who reviews everything. So much so that there was an internet meme doing the rounds during 2014 that showed the stumps spread-eagled across the turf and me in a picture alongside it making the T sign for a review.

The other lads in the England dressing room are always taking the mickey out of me for using them up. Gary's deadpan words made me chuckle.

I am no expert on wicketkeeping but I was grateful for what looked like Brad failing to get his hands in the right place. The ball went quite quickly and that might be what saved me on this occasion. When it is travelling at that kind of speed and the wicketkeeper has to move so far, he can over-compensate. In this instance, he actually got there too quickly, moving better than he perhaps anticipated. Thankfully, he could not pull back on the catch.

Normally, when you nick it, you hear the initial stages of an appeal, but there was nothing like that on this occasion. This time, there had been a bit of a lull, a hush, and as I looked around, I saw the Australians looking at each other quizzically – as if to ask, 'Did he hit that?'

The pre-series batting work I had done was mainly with Mitchell Johnson's extra pace in mind, and while there is no doubt that his fellow left-armer Starc possesses a similar level of speed, the characteristics of his bowling make him quite a different proposition. My experience of facing him in the past had been mainly in white-ball cricket and in the nets when we were team-mates at Yorkshire.

In contrast to Johnson, Starc's action is so classical that you see the ball from the moment he begins to bring his arm over the top. Because of this you can track the length of the delivery a lot quicker, which effectively provides you with an extra split second to play. For example, if he bowls short you get that little bit longer to rock onto the back foot. Generally, as he is primarily a swing bowler, he tends to bowl fuller, and although he gets prodigious amounts of aerial movement at times, the fact you get a good sight of it means you have that extra time to process where the ball is going. But then at that pace, if he gets it absolutely right, it is still extremely hard to adjust.

Even though the speed gun will tell you they are bowling the same pace, he doesn't quite feel as quick as Johnson, someone who hurries you partly because of his action. When he loads up for his delivery, you lose sight of the ball as it goes behind his back; it then reappears as he slings his arm round to propel it down at you. One of the other perils of facing Johnson is the inconsistency of his wrist position. It is not always behind the ball because of the angle at which he lets it go, and that provides natural variation in pace and bounce.

There are times when his wrist is right up behind it and he gains that extra bit of bounce, and it feels a lot quicker facing up to him, while at others his wrist is alongside the ball and the bounce can be up to a foot lower. When you are talking about someone bowling in the high 80s and above, such a difference in bounce is significant. Initially, as you shape up to play, one delivery can feel the same as the last. But although it feels like the same length, one can go whistling past your chest and the other goes whistling by at eye level, forcing you to drop your hands out of the way. This inconsistency of bounce, created by a variation in release points, is one of his strengths. The bounce Starc generates is a lot more consistent.

Looking around, it was a déjà vu moment from earlier on in the summer. Behind me was a heavy slip cordon, reminiscent of the one New Zealand had put together. Here was a chance to take the game to the Australians, hit them off their lengths and force them onto the back foot. With Starc looking for swing, in his next over I was able to drive him down the ground for four when he overpitched and then force him square for another boundary when he pulled back his length. My aim was to get to 20 as quickly as I could.

Before I reached that mini-milestone, though, Michael Clarke turned to Mitchell Johnson. Anticipating a short one to start with, I jumped to carve his first ball over point for the four that took me into the 20s. That shot settled me down completely. During the series in Australia I had not taken Johnson on at all, so here was a sign that things were going to be different. I felt prepared for everything they had to throw at me.

I knew that both their left-armers would bowl two lengths to me – they would either look to hit me full on the pads or nick me off pushing the ball across me, or go hard targeting my ribcage. My policy was to take them on.

However, I soon assessed that Josh Hazlewood would be a more dangerous bowler in these particular conditions, with his policy of trying to bowl a full length to take advantage of a bit of sideways movement. Hazlewood has something of the archetypal English seamer in his approach – trying to consistently hit the top of off-stump with a heavy ball. My main focus was therefore to get my feet moving well against him to combat any help he got out of the pitch. They were moving well by the time I faced him, as I witnessed the first three overs he sent down from the non-striker's end.

Having survived those two deliveries of wicket-taking potential from Starc – he has the knack of producing pearlers amongst four-balls – I was able to latch on to some of the latter variety to score freely. You know he has that ability to dismiss you at any time, but equally you have to be ready to score off him. I have always viewed him as a confidence bowler. When he gets on top of you it is very difficult to wrest the momentum back, but if you are positive against him you can knock him off his length, and that can set you up against him for the rest of your innings.

As with Starc, against Johnson I prospered because of my positivity that morning. One cut off him early on would have been caught had Australia placed a fielder in a normal point position – the ball travelled through the region at head height but they had opted for an extra gully and that saved me. I felt confident that I could take Johnson on over the off-side, and with no third man back I was happy to get my hands underneath the ball and hit him aerially. Because of the pace he was bowling, even if I top-edged an upper-cut the ball would fly for six.

Previously, I had felt under pressure when facing Johnson,

but now, with these attacking shot options at my disposal, I felt quite different. During this innings, for the first time in our tussles, I felt I was the one on top. This undoubtedly helped fuel my confidence against the other members of their attack. Despite the precarious situation I had walked into, I felt surprisingly calm that morning and it helped to have Gary at the other end. He is a very relaxed character, even under intense pressure, and doesn't tend to say a lot. More than anything, though, he is a genuine long-term mate and here we were playing together in an Ashes Test match.

We had lived together in Idle, Bradford, for a year as first-team players at Yorkshire after I decided that the commute from Sheffield to Leeds was too much. The house was owned by our former team-mate James Lee and we considered it a good place to base ourselves. Being twenty minutes away from Headingley, we estimated it would keep us out of the pubs and bars that were an easy stroll from the ground, and decrease temptation to go out every night off. Unfortunately, that planning did not come to fruition. We just had a lot of taxi fares to pay instead. During the 2012 season, we were both told in our appraisals that if we had any aspirations of playing for England we should no longer live together. Despite our successful records on the field, we had picked up reputations for having a great time off it and while we gathered some great memories, we also put on a bit of timber around our waistlines. That might have been something to do with the mountain of takeaways we tackled. A matter of weeks later, I got a call-up to go on the Test tour of India; a year later Gary was playing in Sydney. By then, we were ex-housemates.

It was during that period that I first met Carrie. She is now a medical rep but back then in her student days, she worked in Arc, our favourite Headingley haunt, and would have to contend with us appearing on random quiet nights ordering ridiculous rounds. She used to hate us. We would be loud and annoying, never more so than on our season-ending drinks in 2011. It was going to be the last time we saw each other for quite some time, heading into the winter, and the whole group was determined to have a good time. Not that we had much to celebrate, as Carrie bluntly pointed out to Gary as he arrived at the bar to get a round in. 'What are you all drinking for?' she asked. 'Haven't you just been relegated?' In those days my conversations with her were few and far between. Then, quite bizarrely, I bumped into her on a night out in Nottingham during the summer of 2014. We recognised each other, got talking, went on a few dates, and the rest as they say . . .

As I had told Carrie on our Stanage Edge jaunt, one of the things that concerned me was that my previous Test average against Australia was just 33. I wanted to prove to myself that I could score runs against their celebrated bowling attack. I had certainly struggled against them abroad, but it felt more achievable to change my returns against them here in more familiar conditions. I'd found myself questioning whether I was good enough to do it and whether I was able to cut it against attacks with that extra bit of pace. I also knew that to turn this around I needed to make a big statement, and that meant a big score early on in the series.

There had been times in Australia when Johnson bowled some really quick spells at me, particularly in Melbourne, where he hit me quite hard on the helmet and then on the shoulder in quick succession. The second blow was right on top of the bone and left me in agony. I didn't want to retire hurt, as I have always had this thing about not showing signs of weakness. Luckily, because it was only ten minutes away, I managed to scrape through to lunch before being able to get some more intense treatment. It was a relief to get off the field.

Here in Cardiff, I felt I was heaping some of that pain back on him every time I got a boundary off him. I used those cuts and pulls to drive myself forward and exorcise some of the frustration I had felt on that previous tour. I didn't necessarily think about it in the middle, but certainly between sessions. So that spell, during which Gary and I played with a bit of skill, began to put Australia under pressure. With him being the front man of their attack, our approach towards him helped swing momentum back towards us. If you see your main bowler receiving some harsh treatment, it affects the confidence of a side, and that is what we were trying to play on.

A right-hand/left-hand combination tends to put bowlers

off their line and length and the pair of us have complemented each other well in the past. Back in our academy days, we were the opening partnership, so we were used to facing the new ball in tandem. Only the intensity now was a bit different. Gary was under a lot of pressure, as there had been talk about his technique and suitability for England's number three position following the New Zealand series, and Australia bowled very well at him. So to bat like that in the first innings of the series showed how much guts and determination he has. These are the qualities that sum Gary up for me. He has that combination of Yorkshire grit and Zimbabwean obstinacy about him. He might not possess a massively dominant personality, and is not particularly outgoing, but you will find he is far from a pushover. He never backs down from a challenge and is exactly the kind of guy you want in the situation we were confronted with in Cardiff.

Our fourth-wicket partnership of 153 was crucial in setting up a good score. Gary's contribution to that 39-over alliance, and the entire innings, was undervalued. I did all the pretty, fancy work and was the aggressor of the two of us, but he did all the hard graft. Facing two left-armers, who were swinging the ball away from him, made it a real challenge and they were well in the groove because they'd also bowled at Alastair Cook and Adam Lyth, our two left-handers at the top of the order.

Arguably, I got more balls to score off as the pair of them found it hard to make the adjustments. Gary was also a victim of his own success to a degree when he forced

Johnson to change his mode of attack. Life became very uncomfortable for a while after a switch to round the wicket and short balls targeting the body in a bid to get him fending to short leg or leg gully. It would have been easy to flap but, typically, Gary took his medicine via a couple of blows to the gloves and arm.

It was not until after tea that Gary and I were separated, and by that time we were in a dominant position as a team. The nothing-to-lose mentality I had carried with me to the middle – of course I would have been left with nothing had Haddin clung on second ball – got me to 50 from 56 deliveries. The pace of my innings only slowed marginally thereafter, because when Gary got out, I had Ben Stokes for company. I have always found that with Ben around you don't have to be overly aggressive and can still find yourself scoring at a fair old lick.

He top-edged Johnson for six from his second scoring stroke and then got to 20 with another six down the ground off Nathan Lyon. With someone like him at the other end, you never feel under pressure from the scoreboard not moving. You have to accept that the opposition are allowed to bowl well at times and put you under pressure, and these times tend to follow the taking of a wicket. Part of a batsman's skill is to recognise these periods as being the ones to get through. People like Ben will be more expansive, and take risks, but I recognised my job was to stay in.

Ben and I had only been together for nine deliveries

when I got to my hundred – a moment that brought a great amount of relief as well as pride. One of my pre-series goals had been ticked off at the first time of asking, as I opened the face of the bat and struck a square drive off Josh Hazlewood to the boundary. I ran through to the other end where Ben was, removed my helmet and embraced him. We have been in each other's arms a few times before. It is remarkable how often he and I are at the crease together when one of us reaches a milestone.

It was while composing myself after acknowledging the applause from the crowd and my team-mates on the balcony that I recognised the need to push on to 150, and even 200 if I could. That would really stamp my mark on the series, but more importantly I saw the opportunity to propel us towards a team score of 450. With that many runs on the board, I knew it would remove the possibility of us losing the Test match. To think of not losing might sound negative and not befitting the ethos I have spoken about, but I saw this as a necessity. Of course the number-one target was to win, but to begin with a draw in the first Test would put us in a really good place for the matches that followed. A good start was crucial and so getting into that frame of mind helped remove any sense that my job was complete.

Unfortunately, I only got part of the way there, ending up with 134. I had been quite disciplined outside off-stump throughout the innings, so it was disappointing to nick Mitchell Starc's first ball of a new spell, a delivery that wasn't a half-volley. I just got a little bit complacent and poor shot-selection cost me. That suggested a bit of tiredness in the mind; with it being such a big occasion, you expect mental fatigue to take effect at a quicker rate than in other matches. It was also quite late on that first day.

Ben followed soon afterwards, immediately after reaching his half-century, but the lower order all made solid contributions to build on the platform Gary and I had laid. Numbers seven to eleven took the game to Australia, with Moeen Ali's contribution being simply awesome. He came out to bat with question marks against his name regarding the short ball. But you could see how effectively he had worked on this when – after surviving a couple of uncertain moments – he gauged the pace of the wicket and started taking their bowlers on. Moeen times the ball so beautifully, and possesses such a lovely swing of the bat, that he is a joy to watch – the kind of carefree player you like if he's on your team and hate if he's on the opposition.

It should not be underestimated how difficult it is for a front-line batsman like him to come in at number eight. But from a team perspective, if everything is going your way, having someone like him walk in with a licence to entertain is so exciting. You couldn't ask for a better person to come in a couple of blows shy of the 300-mark. He can bat for long spells, scores quickly and takes the game further away from the opposition in a short period of time. Coming in at that position, he is often confronted with a second new ball, something he is used to from his many years as a top-order batsman. His contributions were to prove vital in this game – half-century stands with Jos Buttler and Stuart Broad getting us up to a pleasing total of 430.

During the first morning, the pitch was a little bit tacky and on the slow side; there was some movement off the surface, rain hung in the air and conditions were bowler-friendly. But we battled through that period and vindicated the decision to bat first. Moeen now capitalised on it. Because he is so disruptive, it works in his favour when he is with the tail because opponents let him take singles whenever he wants so they can have a bowl at the others. I know from experience that when the opposition allow you to get off strike and set the fields back, it takes pressure off you. Things get easier when the feeling that the bowler is trying to get you out is removed. When all they are trying to do is get you to the non-striker's end, they generally serve up more balls for you to score off. Not for the first time, Moeen took advantage of this, combining farming the strike with the crispest of boundary-hitting in a wonderful innings of 77.

The fluency with which Moeen played demonstrated that there were no obvious demons in the pitch, so it was not too disheartening when Australia got off to a good start in response. David Warner's edge to slip off James Anderson was the only wicket we claimed with the new ball and it was clear that dismissing the Australian batsmen in conventional ways was going to be hard work.

Having taken the diving catch to dispatch Warner, Alastair Cook discovered in the most painful way that not all nicks were going to carry when one dropped short, bounced up and hit him where it hurts. When that happens to you, it is the worst thing imaginable; it feels absolutely excruciating, to the point you think you might be sick. But when you see it happen to someone else it's completely different and you cannot help but smile. What he didn't know, as I stood over him while he squirmed on the floor, was that I was struggling to suppress my giggling. However, when he returned to the field after treatment to resume captaincy responsibilities from me, he gave me a huge serve.

Both at the afternoon drinks break and at tea, Alastair led discussions amongst the group, recognising that the pitch was slow and that the ball was not moving laterally. We knew that we would have to be a lot smarter with our plans, with bowlers mixing up their paces, and bowling dead straight, with catchers positioned in front of the wicket rather than behind it. The ball hadn't carried through as far as the slips on a couple of occasions and so we repeated a tactic of me being positioned at 'suicidal slip' – a couple of yards ahead of where a conventional third slip would stand – something we had tried in the West Indies to ensure that if a bowler located the outside edge, he got his rewards.

In fact, our experiences in the Caribbean three months earlier stood us in really good stead for this situation. We reverted to the disciplines we used there, concentrating on

Celebrating my hundred in the first Ashes Test – it's amazing how often Ben Stokes and I are together in the middle when one of us reaches a landmark – Cardiff, July 2015.

This Mitchell Marsh bouncer at Lord's triggered concerns that I had suffered concussion.

MCC members queuing in anticipation of the Lord's Ashes Test, July 2015.

Jimmy Anderson's first innings spell swung the momentum back in England's favour on the first day at Edgbaston, July 2015.

Steven Finn deserved his man-of-the-match award at Edgbaston – there are few nicer guys in the game.

Stuart Broad produced a phenomenal new-ball performance at Trent Bridge. Only one man, Jim Laker, has claimed better Ashes bowling figures than the ones above Broad's head.

Stuart Broad rose to the challenge of covering the loss of Jimmy Anderson, Trent Bridge, August 2015.

Ben Stokes takes a blinder to dismiss Adam Voges on an extraordinary first morning of the Trent Bridge Ashes Test, August 2015.

England's Ashes-winning team post match, Trent Bridge, August 2015.

Australia captain Michael Clarke – a player whose career record was deserving of the guard of honour we provided at the Oval.

After struggling to counter his threat in the 2013–14 series, I felt I won my 2015 duel with Mitchel Johnson.

Relaxing on the outfield at the Oval with Carrie, having fulfilled my pre-series goal of improving my record against Australia.

he end of series drinks between the England
nd Australia teams was a good time to put any
ad blood with David Warner in the past.

Toasting Ashes success with my dad Matt –
by downing several pints from the glass urn!

view from the other side. It is a privilege to be able to witness the moment of celebration
om this perspective.

It can be sweltering in the UAE, so a wet towel down the back of the neck comes in handy.

The Test series against Pakistan was frustrating: I g[...] in on several occasions without making the most o[...] it. Here, I have gifted Rahat Ali my wicket.

The repetitive nature of my dismissals, chasing the ball outside off-stump, infuriated me.

During the away tour against Pakistan we showed we were coming of age as a white-ball team.

Twenty20 whitewash against Pakistan – winners are grinners.

It was nice to score a hundred again after a while without one. The bonus of doing so at Pietermaritzburg is that each international player to do so gets a tree planted in their honour.

Some of the cleanest hitting I have ever witnessed was by Ben Stokes at Newlands – if you blinked you missed it, as I was to discover.

denying width, drying up the runs to two an over and encouraging the Australian batsmen to force the issue. If they wanted to score runs, they would have to hit it off the stumps through a tight field.

There was some pretty smart bowling from our guys during the second half of the second day. Moeen knew the Australians would come after him; they had not been shy in letting it be known that they did not see him as a specialist spinner. But he held his nerve under pressure and took two crucial wickets. Michael Clarke and Steve Smith were both looking very dangerous but got suckered into trying to hit him down the ground; Smith picked out Cook at short midwicket and Clarke was well taken caught and bowled.

A combination of astute field placement and patience in our approach was crucial to our success. It is rare you see an Australian side with four middle-order players getting into the 30s but none going on. As so often happens, taking regular wickets had put our opponents under pressure.

At the close of play, there was further talk between Cooky and the support staff about the best form of attack from a bowling perspective. Sometimes the best ideas from a tactical point of new can come from the guys off the field and so liaising with them for a different opinion can be extremely beneficial.

Having stayed in the game by taking wickets, though, we reinforced our dominant position through Jimmy Anderson's genius the next morning. He took the second new ball and sent down an over to Brad Haddin which was simply phenomenal. Some new balls swing more than others and the one picked out of the batch to use on that morning proved to be a beauty. When you give one such to a bowler with the skill of Anderson, it can prove a lethal cocktail, and the way he kept beating Haddin both ways was high class. Australia's wicketkeeper did not make it through his second over.

Ahead of the series we all knew how dangerous Haddin could be. We had learned it to our cost in Australia eighteen months earlier when he scored a bucketload of runs against us, constantly turning around situations to Australia's advantage from positions like 134–6. He proved a nightmare opponent in that 2013–14 series and was arguably the reason they won each of those first three Test matches. Others took the headlines and he didn't get the plaudits he truly deserved for wrestling them back into positions of power. We started the 2015 summer in the knowledge that he would be one of the biggest wickets for us. His was the middle one of five inside 14 overs that third morning.

With a lead of 122 runs on first innings, we were obviously in the ascendancy as we went out to bat again, but when Australia took two wickets in quick succession, the crowd appeared to sense they had a chance in the match again. It was a really good contest in the period immediately afterwards and the advantage had only swelled to 195 by the time I joined Ian Bell in the middle.

Like a number of our players, there had been discussion regarding Ian's form in the media in the build-up to the series, and he would have been the first to admit that recently he had not scored the runs you would expect for a player of his record and talent. But here was an example of a senior player standing up to make a valuable contribution for the team right on cue. When you've had a couple of rough Tests, the last opposition you want to be facing is Australia, and it was very important that he made the 60 runs he did, scoring them very fluently in the process. Our share of 97 in 20 overs represented another healthy scoring rate and with bad weather forecast it left plenty of time at the back end of the match for us to bowl them out.

One of the pleasing things about the match from our point of view was that we were able to maintain our dominance from that first afternoon onwards. In contrast, seeing the Australians' withdrawn body language was a good sign. It reiterated that we were on top of them.

Not a team to lie down, however, they continued to search for ways to upset us. We all have our own method of ensuring we are switched on while we are at the crease, some more idiosyncratic than others, and Ben Stokes's method since entering Test cricket has been to sweep the crease with his bat at the end of every over. Aware of this, some of the Australians tried to disrupt this concentration trigger by making beelines to stand in the way and prevent it happening. Typically, David Warner was involved, as was

Nathan Lyon, someone I know well from our days as team-mates in Adelaide grade cricket. Nathan is not a malicious kind of bloke and would only have got involved in the gamesmanship, bending down to laboriously tie his shoe-laces for example, because he would have considered it amusing.

What a compliment for someone like Ben. He had not played a huge amount of Test cricket, but after the start of the summer he'd had and his success against them in the past, it had obviously registered with the Australia team that he was a player they needed to disrupt. They must have rated him to try to get into his head like that.

Our performance over the first three days challenged the received wisdom. Australia were supposed to come here and win, and you could sense a mood throughout – even as the fourth-innings target swelled – that everyone half-expected them to come back. But I am sure that as a team they did not share that confidence. We had not allowed them to live up to the hype, and in Ashes cricket you have to remember that any insecurities you have suffered when under pressure also go through the minds of the opposition. They were obviously a great side, deservedly starting as huge series favourites, but underneath they were eleven human beings.

The crowd were doing their best to expose this mortality too. Buoyed by the sense of adventure shown by Moeen Ali and Mark Wood on that third evening, the atmosphere was electric inside the ground. With your average bloke in the stands topped to the brim with Dutch courage, those two chose the perfect time to indulge in one of those happy-go-lucky partnerships. The crowd became very vocal and let the Australians know in no uncertain terms who they were supporting.

Safe to say, Mitchell Johnson had long known where he stood with those barracking from the stands. Wicketless in the first innings at a cost of over 100 runs, he claimed a couple in the second but his life was made hell at fine leg. I must admit that he took it really well, because despite his chilled-out responses, saying it is good fun is one thing, but meaning it after being subjected to constant abuse all day is another.

The fact that rain was forecast on the Sunday was something we discussed on that Friday evening. But Trevor Bayliss just kept reiterating that all that mattered, all that ever matters in Test cricket, was the next hour of the match. He insisted that we should not look too far ahead, not get too carried away if things went well and not get too down on ourselves if it took a while to get a breakthrough.

When Australia began their pursuit on the fourth morning, requiring 412 for victory, I was grateful that my flooring of a difficult early chance did not prove costly as we took the second one offered by Chris Rogers to end his sequence of seven straight half-centuries in Test innings.

We knew how dangerous David Warner could be, particularly in the second innings. Prior to this match he averaged in excess of 50 and had scored at a strike rate above 70 in the second half of Test matches across his career. Typically, when Moeen came on Warner played very aggressively and pumped him over long-on for a six as 22 runs came off his first two overs. But having got a couple to turn, Moeen was always going to come back and play a part, and so it was a smart move from Cook to bring him back immediately before lunch. This time he got one to skid on off the surface to win an lbw. That was a massive wicket in the context. We headed into the interval with increased confidence and the promise of a new batsman to bowl at when the afternoon session began.

As it transpired, Warner's departure at 97–2 was the first of five wickets in a very short spell. Stuart Broad got Steve Smith soon after lunch. Then Michael Clarke, who had experienced problems against Broad's shorter deliveries in the past, fell into a shrewd trap. With the field set for short bowling, Broad went full and wide, which lured the Australian captain into a false drive. Because his weight was on the back foot, the ball skewed off the bat to point – that is what can happen on slow pitches when you are slightly off with your timing. It had been discussed that, if at all possible, Broad should be bowling at the start of Clarke's innings. Bringing someone into the attack who has had previous success against you as a batsman, as Broad had with the short ball against Clarke Down Under, has the potential to do psychological damage. Especially if you know it's a definite plan. I knew in this series, for example, that every time I came in they would bring Mitchell Johnson on. I accepted that was going to happen before the first toss of that coin at Sophia Gardens. But it can play on your mind when opponents make such moves. Why are they doing this? Even posing that question hints at potential weakness in your game.

Shane Watson had a problem of a different sort. When you know someone has an issue with a certain mode of dismissal, you have to be really ruthless in a bid to expose it, and our pace bowlers did well to set him up perfectly for the twenty-eighth and twenty-ninth lbw dismissals of his Test career. They bowled in that corridor outside off-stump, dragged him across his crease and then attacked the stumps. If I am honest, he was quite unlucky, because both decisions came down to umpire's call and therefore could easily have gone the other way. But when things aren't going for you, decisions tend to follow suit. Once you are seen to have a leg-before problem, I guess that has to play on the umpire's mind and you might not get the benefit of the doubt. That will have tormented Watson's mind, I am sure. Just flip the situation. If we had appealed for the same deliveries, been answered with a not out and then reviewed, Watson would have survived twice on umpire's call.

When he trudged off for a second time in the game, dismissed by Mark Wood to end a wicketless 12-over spell, the blow we had dealt seemed significant. You are always keen to expose batsmen who are out of form or battling a technical deficiency early in a series, and when you have just taken a wicket and they stride to the crease, it almost gives you more confidence as a side. The fact that we were all over a few of their senior players in that first Test was telling, I felt. The reverse had happened to us in Australia in 2013–14. A few experienced guys were getting out early and once that happens at the start of a long series it feels like a slog to fight your way back.

From there, with so much time remaining, we knew only one result was possible. So although Mitchell Johnson played aggressively, there was no need for panic. Cook was quite astute in making sure he regularly changed things up with regards to the bowling and that meant Mitchell wasn't allowed to settle for large periods of time against one man or one pace.

As Moeen had bowled quite a lot at him, my off-spin was viewed as an alternative. I think I can complement him in this way. Although we are both off-break bowlers, we bowl from a slightly different angle – my arm is lower in delivery – and on different lines. Of my dozen wickets in Test cricket, the majority have been left-handers and predominantly second-innings dismissals. I have recognised this as a strength and something I can offer the team later in matches. Part-timers like me always enjoy getting among the wickets, and I hope that for Moeen seeing me come on at the other end occasionally makes him feel less under pressure as the go-to spin option.

Despite Johnson taking me on, whacking me all over the place as he took 17 runs off my first over, Cooky reckoned that, with the purchase on offer, it was going to be very hard for him to keep playing in that fashion without risking hitting the ball straight up in the air or nicking one. The ball was turning, outside off-stump especially, and that was great from my perspective – because I have got such a low arm in delivery it almost feels like the ball is going to run into the stumps from a wide angle from round the wicket, allowing me to attack the imaginary fourth stump. If the ball does spin, I can beat the outside edge, and if it doesn't it can hustle on to hit the stumps. You always feel in the game if you can find the right line early on when the batsman looks like he wants to get bat on ball.

Our catching had generally been sound throughout the Test, and the best of the lot came from Cook at a critical time during the second innings. We were massively on top but it was clear that the Australians wanted to hit Moeen out of the series. Additionally, it appeared that Brad Haddin was looking to reawaken past glories against us. For our part, we know Moeen always has a chance of taking a wicket if someone attacks him, as he had proved with the classic flat-pitch dismissals of Michael Clarke and Steve Smith in the first innings. This time, Haddin tried to smear him through the on-side, only for a spectacular parry and rebound catch from Cook at short midwicket. Similarly quick reactions from Cook at gully helped re-direct Mitchell Starc's cut for Adam Lyth to scoop up at slip, providing me with a first wicket. My second was not long in the waiting, either, as Johnson's charge resulted in a slice and another slip catch for Lyth.

In the next over it was a special moment for me to be involved in the wicket that sealed a 169-run victory and put us 1–0 up in the series. When the ball went up from Josh Hazlewood's blow towards long-off, I thought it was sailing over my head. But the wind grabbed it and held it up nicely. As pandemonium ensued in the stands, I trudged off the field contemplating how long a Test match it had felt, despite the fact we'd only been playing four days and there were four more matches to go.

To be handed the Man of the Match award half an hour later settled me in for the duration. You want to be off and running at the start of any series and once you have a score on the board you relax. Until you get one, you do tend to remain concerned about your own form. I already had 194 runs to my name and had performed in line with my expectations.

From a team perspective, our performance might have gone above and beyond that. Trevor Bayliss chaired an informal review over a beer or two in the changing room, during which he praised our all-round effort, fight and character. We knew as a group we had played some smart cricket, assessing the conditions and adapting accordingly.

There was praise from another experienced head too. Sir Ian Botham came into the dressing room that evening and enjoyed a few glasses of wine with us. It was great to connect with him and other ex-players over the course of the five matches, just to hear some of the old stories from when they played against Australia. It gave us a sense of what the Ashes is all about from an historical perspective. Mark Wood was absolutely in awe as he sat chatting to such a legend for half an hour.

Not only is it wonderful to sit toasting an Ashes Test win and reminiscing about great victories of the past, but having former England captains come and mingle among us also helps to break down a few barriers. With a lot of them working in the media, it can reduce tension between dressing room and commentary box. When things aren't going so well, it can sometimes feel like a media-versus-players situation, so these sessions were invaluable in reminding those who now pick up microphones that they used to be pulling pads on in our dressing room. I'm sure they also remember what it is like feeling under attack both on a personal level and as a team when results don't go your way.

On the other side of the equation, it brought home to us that those reporting on the game have a responsibility to be honest and give a fair account of things. This summer we also had visits from Nasser Hussain, Michael Atherton and Bob Willis and we came to realise they are good people doing a job to the best of their ability. Even if they have made comments you might disagree with or said something critical about your technique, they have a professional duty to share their opinion. It's not meant to be a malicious attack. In Test cricket there's a lot of time to fill, and sometimes they have to pick peripheral things apart, so you mustn't let it affect you too much.

England v Australia
(1st Test)

Played at the SWALEC Stadium, Cardiff, on 8–11 July 2015

Umpires: HDPK Dharmasena & M Erasmus (TV: CB Gaffaney)
Referee: RS Madugalle
Toss: England

ENGLAND

A Lyth	c Warner b Hazlewood	6	c Clarke b Lyon	37
AN Cook*	c Haddin b Lyon	20	c Lyon b Starc	12
GS Ballance	lbw b Hazlewood	61	c Haddin b Hazlewood	0
IR Bell	lbw b Starc	1	b Johnson	60
JE Root	c Watson b Starc	134	b Hazlewood	60
BA Stokes	b Starc	52	b Starc	42
JC Buttler†	c Johnson b Hazlewood	27	c Haddin b Lyon	7
MM Ali	c Watson b Starc	77	c Haddin b Johnson	15
SCJ Broad	c Haddin b Lyon	18	c Hazlewood b Lyon	4
MA Wood	not out	7	not out	32
JM Anderson	b Starc	1	b Lyon	1
Extras	(b 17, lb 3, w 5, nb 1)	26	(b 7, lb 6, w 6)	19
Total	(102.1 overs)	**430**	(70.1 overs)	**289**

AUSTRALIA

CJL Rogers	c Buttler b Wood	95	c Bell b Broad	10
DA Warner	c Cook b Anderson	17	lbw b Ali	52
SPD Smith	c Cook b Ali	33	c Bell b Broad	33
MJ Clarke*	c and b Ali	38	c Stokes b Broad	4
AC Voges	c Anderson b Stokes	31	c Buttler b Wood	1
SR Watson	lbw b Broad	30	lbw b Wood	19
NM Lyon	lbw b Wood	6 (11)	not out	0
BJ Haddin†	c Buttler b Anderson	22 (7)	c Cook b Ali	7
MG Johnson	c Ballance b Broad	14 (8)	c Lyth b Root	77
MA Starc	c Root b Anderson	0 (9)	c Lyth b Root	17
JR Hazlewood	not out	2 (10)	c Root b Ali	14
Extras	(b 6, lb 11, w 3)	20	(b 4, lb 3, nb 1)	8
Total	(84.5 overs)	**308**	(70.3 overs)	**242**

AUSTRALIA	O	M	R	W	O	M	R	W
Starc	24.1	4	114	5	(3) 16	4	60	2
Hazlewood	23	8	83	3	13	2	49	2
Johnson	25	3	111	0	(1) 16	2	69	2
Lyon	20	4	69	2	20.1	4	75	4
Watson	8	0	24	0	5	0	23	0
Warner	2	0	9	0				

ENGLAND	O	M	R	W	O	M	R	W
Anderson	18.5	6	43	3	12	3	33	0
Broad	17	4	60	2	14	3	39	3
Wood	20	5	66	2	(5) 14	4	53	2
Ali	15	1	71	2	(3) 16.3	4	59	3
Stokes	14	5	51	1	(4) 8	2	23	0
Root					6	1	28	2

Fall of wickets:

	Eng	Aus	Eng	Aus
1st	7	52	17	19
2nd	42	129	22	97
3rd	43	180	73	101
4th	196	207	170	106
5th	280	258	207	106
6th	293	265	236	122
7th	343	265	240	151
8th	395	304	245	223
9th	419	306	288	242
10th	430	308	289	242

Close of play: Day 1: Eng (1) 343-7 (Ali 26*, Broad 0*, 88 overs)
Day 2: Aus (1) 264-5 (Watson 29*, Lyon 6*, 70 overs)
Day 3: Eng (2) 289

Man of the Match: JE Root
Result: **England won by 169 runs**

8 A DIFFERENT TUNE

ONE of the bonuses of finishing the first Test ahead of schedule was getting to see Ed Sheeran perform at Wembley Stadium on what should have been the fifth evening in Cardiff. After a Sunday roast with Carrie's family just outside her home city of Bristol, we headed down to London to see a bloke with a guitar and a loop pedal holding 80,000 people in the palm of his hand.

Michael Vaughan had got hold of some tickets and offered us the chance to watch this genius performer. To have a packed house at Wembley either on the edge of their seats or on their feet up singing the words must be an amazing feeling. I've always loved music and although heavier stuff like Foo Fighters and Muse are more my thing, I fully appreciate the appeal of someone like Ed who strips everything back.

I've never had lessons, but I play a bit of guitar and ukulele myself. It all stemmed from the tour of New Zealand in 2012–13 when I was keen to come up with something to occupy my time. Most of the other players had wives and girlfriends with them on that trip and being single at the time meant I was going to be spending plenty of after-noons and evenings on my lonesome.

One day when I was out shopping, I passed a music shop and this ukulele in the window display caught my eye. I had tried to learn a bit of guitar as a kid but not got very far, and as it had remained on my bucket list of things to do away from the cricket field, this little instrument seemed a suitable alternative. It fits in my suitcase and Phil Neale, the England operations manager, doesn't have to worry about finding extra space in the golf-bag-dominated excess baggage on tours as he would if I was lugging a guitar round. (On at least one tour he also had to contend with Matt Prior contributing a bike to our load.)

So I took the ukulele away with me that day and have carried it round ever since. Playing a few tunes is good fun and there is a sense of accomplishment when you've mastered one. Not that I can even read music. I just go on YouTube, watch some instructor tutorials and then try to copy what they do. I would like to say that Arctic Monkeys' 'Mardy Bum' and 'Don't Look Back in Anger' by Oasis never sounded so good. But my mum always taught me not to tell lies, so I'll have to keep practising.

Social events like that Ed Sheeran gig or playing golf against Adam Lyth and Stuart Broad at The Grove, Hertfordshire, the following day play an important part during a series with such a relentless schedule as the Ashes. Being able to switch off and keep your mind fresh is crucial when there are five Test matches in just forty-two days.

Without that kind of relaxing distraction, you risk turning into a cricket robot.

Days away from the international environment help you feel fresh when you next turn up to training. You never want to feel that a net session is a chore or experience those 'here we go again' moments. I play cricket because I love everything about the game and that includes the practice, so it would be very disappointing if I ever got to a point where I was fed up with doing it. To avoid that, it is important to get a balance between doing the stuff required to be ready to play and getting away from things completely. When you maintain that freshness, it feels as if you can train with a real intensity and purpose.

There had been little to concern us in South Wales; everything had gone smoothly from the moment we crossed the Severn Bridge. But the same could not be said when we gathered in London NW8 on the evening of 13 July. Moeen Ali turned up suffering from a side strain. Obviously, given that he was our first-choice spinner and had scored lots of runs in Cardiff from number eight, this was a concern.

In Adil Rashid, we had someone in reserve who was undoubtedly a very exciting prospect, someone who could potentially win you a Test match, bowling leg-spin and batting in his attacking manner down the order; he is an extremely exciting cricketer. But to make your debut in a Lord's Test match, in an Ashes series, would carry a huge amount of pressure, and the way Moeen had played that first Test match made it very important to us, from a continuity point of view as much as anything, that he should be fit and ready.

Don't get me wrong: it wouldn't have been the worst thing in the world if Adil's name had been on our team sheet that Thursday morning, because by this point he had played quite a bit of one-day international cricket and he offers something different, being a leg-spinner. He may not possess the control Moeen provides in terms of run rate, and may prove to be generally more expensive, but in the second innings leg-spinners can be very dangerous operators. If the pitch is responsive, having a bowler able to turn the ball both ways is invaluable.

Had Moeen not pulled through after training on the Wednesday, Adil would have been good to go. One of the positive things about having our camp in Spain was that guys around the squad like Adil, Liam Plunkett and even Mark Footitt felt part of the series from the off. When you feel like a member of an expanded squad, as they hopefully did, and you are drafted into the starting XI, it is an easier transition to make than it would be had you been called in out of the cold. In previous years, guys have been taken straight from county cricket.

This trio of players were already established within our Ashes series environment. If they were to be called up, they were ready to go and knew what everyone else in the squad was about. They knew of our pre-series plans, how we wanted to play and what was expected of them if they were required. With that kind of preparation, it is not as daunting a proposition if you are asked to play. Contrast this to when I first turned up at the airport for my maiden trip away with England, the tour of India, in the autumn of 2012. I looked around at all the guys I'd been watching on the television. Here in front of me were Kevin Pietersen, Graeme Swann and Alastair Cook. It was quite intimidating, which was not their making at all. But I had idolised them for years and suddenly there I was on an equal footing to work alongside them.

Trips before a series can help ease you into international cricket. You find that no one bites, that you are as welcome as anyone else and that the players already with places in the England dressing room are all just normal blokes. Having guys travelling around the country with us – Adil was named in all five squads – was taken on positively by those concerned too. Although it may have meant a few extra motorway miles and little time to rest at home, playing County Championship matches in between, they knew they were within touching distance of playing Test cricket. Being in and around net sessions provides the chance to impress influential people and put forward your case for inclusion.

As our selection was resolving itself, after Moeen came through net practice unscathed, Australia's was developing. You never want to see anyone miss out in the circumstances Brad Haddin had to. With his young daughter ill in hospital, he did not feel it right to play. All our thoughts were immediately with him and his family. Being away on tour, it would have been a tough time for them all.

Brad's a really good fella. At the end of the various Ashes series I've been involved in, he has always been the first member of the Australian team to approach with a handshake, crack open a beer and say 'well played'. He's a model professional, someone who would not give up the Baggy Green lightly. But he made the only decision he saw fit. Family came first.

Even later in the series, when he made himself available once more and was overlooked, all the noises from the Australian camp were telling you that he was only too willing to help other guys in their practice drills and was usually the last one to leave the pitch after every session finished. As I understand it, he couldn't give enough time to Peter Nevill, the wicketkeeper who took his place behind the stumps.

Purely from a cricket perspective, disregarding emotional reflections, it was a massive positive for us in the England dressing room to know that someone of Brad's stature was going to miss out that week at Lord's, because he had hurt us so many times previously. In recent matches he had regularly been the difference between the two sides. As for his replacement, you are always looking to exploit possible areas of weakness in the opposition and although we considered Nevill a good player, this was his Test debut and he was new to English conditions. Throw in the fact that he had to get used to the Lord's slope, that it is not always the best seeing ground, and that he was being asked to replicate Haddin's productivity at number seven in the batting order, we felt he would be under pressure.

Further confidence in our camp came with the news that despite the disruption with regard to the wicketkeeper's berth, Australia felt it necessary to make a second change, with Shane Watson being replaced by his fellow all-rounder, Mitchell Marsh. This, on reflection, was an admission that they had not played their strongest side first time around in Cardiff. It's never easy for a player to come into a series and make an immediate impact, so selectors tend to try to get the right XI from the off. No matter how you dress it up, a player coming into a series that has already started always feels as if he's playing catch-up.

In the build-up to the match, I spoke to Mick Hunt, the Lord's groundsman, and he was concerned about his pitch preparation. He had not had the weather he'd wanted in the preceding week and that, he told me, had affected how he was able to prepare the surface. There had been a lot of rain and he had not been able to work on the square anywhere near as much as he wanted.

This got me thinking about how we might make preparations easier for ground staff in this day and age. For example, during pre-season, it has become common for marquees to be put up over cricket squares to allow outdoor practice to take place whatever the weather. Is there any reason similar temporary structures could not be erected to allow work on the pitch to proceed as scheduled, regardless of the elements? If you think there's going to be bad weather in the region, you hoist one across the critical area and carry on as was. Groundsmen would probably tell you that direct sunlight is also a necessity, but presumably you could have a retractable roof. That would certainly have helped Mick that particular week, having got to the eve of the Test without being able to do all the work he'd intended to. The pitch felt a bit underdone when we played on it, to be honest, and when you considered the outstanding pitch that had been prepared by the same team for the New Zealand match, the contrast was staggering. For that encounter, Mick had created the perfect cricket wicket: with pace, bounce and carry, it offered a bit for everyone. This provided a stark contrast.

In the circumstances, it was a great toss for Australia captain Michael Clarke to win and we would have batted first as well that Thursday morning. The thing with the Australians is that when they have lost a match, you expect them to come at you even harder in the next. It's in their genes. Australian teams have always done it. The 2015 version were desperate to get back into the series, we knew that, and there was certainly no sign of complacency on our part as we prepared to walk through the Long Room, and its rousing applause, and onto the field that morning. If anything, having spent all pre-series talking about our own games, for the first time we became a bit more concerned about how they were going to approach it. That shift in focus certainly wasn't for the better.

Credit to Australia, though, as they had to make use of

the conditions, and whenever you play a Test on British soil you always feel the bowlers will be able to create opportunities on the first morning. In the first over, in fact, there was a half-chance as the ball flashed over the heads of me and Ian Bell, positioned at third and second slip respectively. It would have been a really good catch had either of us reacted more decisively, but we had taken those chances in the match at Cardiff. Games can hinge on accepting the slightest sniff like that.

Grabbing it would have got Steve Smith in early against the new ball rather than it being 15 overs old when he did come in. That's a big difference. Chris Rogers has a fantastic Ashes record and with that streaky boundary he was away. To show the fine margins that exist at the top level, Jimmy produced the same ball later in the over, looking to lure Rogers into another false drive at a wide one. This time, however, he played it much better, timing it perfectly for a more authoritative boundary, and suddenly they had eight runs on the board.

Instead of being one down, they were off to a flyer. We had been faultless at Cardiff with our catching – bar one, no names mentioned, just the initials, JER – yet here our reactions were not as sharp. It was not until the 50th over of the innings, immediately after Smith had reached his half-century, that another was created and Ian Bell floored it low at second slip. Australia were 167–1 at that stage. They went on to double that score by the close, and with our opponents 337–1 we ended the day well and truly on the back foot.

We did not bowl particularly badly on that first day. It was a good wicket, we missed a couple of chances and they batted really well. One of the improved features of their play was that in comparison to their alpha-male attitudes towards him in Cardiff, they were playing Moeen Ali a lot better. There, their over-aggression towards him – in trying to hit him out of the attack at all costs – had proved fatal. On this occasion, their second-wicket pair of Rogers and Smith took bravado out of the equation and looked to knock him around. They removed any unnecessary risks and instead of looking to hit fours off him, they just concentrated on their percentage options, milking him for singles when they were available and taking advantage of their best individual boundary options whenever they were given the opportunity.

In short, they benefited from playing much smarter cricket. They had clear game plans. Rogers was looking to late-cut and generally play through point as much as he could off either front or back foot. In contrast, Smith used his feet and looked to hit him primarily through midwicket, or, when his footwork was precise enough, through the gaps in the off-side, by getting his hands to the left side of the ball.

They both played to their strengths rather than trying to force things they might not normally do. Arguably, going outside their normal games had seen several Australian batsmen perish in Cardiff. At times the pitch there had felt two-paced and while we looked to exploit that by placing men in front of the bat in catching positions, in contrast the bounce of the Lord's pitch was quite true, and so mishits were at a premium. In fact, given the conditions, we had to turn our attention to restricting them as much as trying to get them out.

Steve Smith had a few things to say about our tactics in the post-play press conference that evening. 'Look, I was a little bit surprised that Trevor Bayliss would allow Alastair Cook to have a deep point for as long as he did, to be honest. I think it was a good pitch to bat on but they got defensive quite quickly. I know that's one thing we're certainly not going to do. We didn't play as well as we could in Cardiff and we copped a lot for that and rightfully so . . . it's pretty crucial to make this first innings count.'

As a captain, when confronted with a flat pitch and a fast outfield, you have to get the balance right between trying to take wickets and controlling the run rate. There were undoubtedly a few mind games in what Smith was saying, acutely aware that in the recent past some members of the media had attacked Cook's captaincy. This kind of talk suggested he was trying to throw him off his game again.

Not that it worked. Alastair showed throughout the summer that he was willing to set aggressive fields whenever he could. At other times, he had to set more defensive ones because of the situation of the game. This was one of those occasions. The pitch gave us so little to work with on that first day and at least one ex-Test captain, and an Australian one at that, Ricky Ponting, recognised how tough a job it had been, claiming the balance between bat and ball had been altered too much in favour of the bat.

Reports later circulated that this England team's preference was for slow pitches to nullify the threat of Mitchell Johnson. Andrew Strauss later denied there had been a formal request to the groundsmen encouraging the preparation of such pitches and, to be honest, if we wanted anything it was not a lack of pace but a prevalence of seam movement.

Having played international cricket for three years now, my take is that the hosts get to choose where you play and what you play on. I definitely don't have a problem with pitches being prepared in the home side's favour. Consider what happens elsewhere around the globe. If you go to India – as I did on my first trip abroad with England in 2012 – you are thrown onto turning decks and can face anything up to four spinners.

Part of playing away from home in international cricket is tackling the question of whether you can adapt. Test cricket throws up all kinds of different conditions and the challenge is to be successful in all of them. Everywhere you go, you conquer or are conquered. When you go to Australia, you are faced with quick, bouncy pitches and the ball carries through above stump height. You have to adapt your game to deal with that, and the same is required of other teams when they come over here. Why wouldn't we have pitches that suit our bowlers? Our guys have grown up used to batting with the ball moving around off the seam and in the air, so why not play to those strengths?

When you are playing against world-class opposition, you expect that their bowlers will get similar rewards if they are able to bowl in those same areas. It's not as if the ball will not seam around for them in the same way – if they are skilful enough. In sport, home advantage plays its part in many different ways. In football, it might be the crowd or the dimensions of a particular pitch. It has always been the case that you find variations in all aspects of a pitch or venue wherever you go. As a player, you expect to have to show your versatility when you play away.

Previously in England there had been accusations of counties trying to make sure they got five days of cricket by producing unresponsive surfaces – the financial bonus of doing so being fairly obvious. If they only had a three-day Test match on their hands, it is nowhere near as profitable and can even result in a loss. But from a playing perspective, you just want to be given the pitches that offer you the best chance to be successful. The last thing you want to do is cede home advantage; it is the equivalent of taking on the opposition at a neutral venue.

In this instance, Australia played the conditions perfectly and part of Test cricket is knowing that if you get them in your favour you have to make the scores to justify it. Australia, with Chris Rogers effectively batting on his home ground due to his long-term association with Middlesex, had answers for everything that we threw at them on that opening day.

Another issue to contend with – though not an excuse – concerned our bowling attack. The relatively quick turn-around between back-to-back Tests can be quite tough on the body, and having bowled last in the first one, here we were bowling first in the second after just a four-day gap. On a surface as flat as this proved to be, that represented a considerable amount of hard graft for the seamers, and the fact that Australia kept us out in the field for an extended period of time would also have been viewed by them as a tactical box-tick. Fatigue undermines many a batting reply. Tired bodies and minds lead to tired shots.

Although Rogers missed out on his double hundred, his dismissal for 173 on the second morning – a first of four rewards for Stuart Broad's endeavours ending a 284-run stand for the second wicket and Australia's highest-ever partnership at Lord's – Smith was able to celebrate that personal landmark. By the end of the Australian innings, which was signalled by a declaration, I had been brought on to give the front-line attack some respite. I hope I don't get too many more batsmen out for 215. Playing at Lord's is a really unique experience. Walking up the stairs to the dressing room you pass portraits of England heroes like Len Hutton, Graham Gooch, Michael Atherton and Michael Vaughan. It's like you're walking back through history. You feel part of something special when you open the door and enter. Every time you glance up at the honours board it reminds you of what you are trying to live up to.

The pavilion feels like a timeless building. The changing rooms have not changed over the years, yet they do not feel dated. They are far from old or shabby. You can smell the tradition when you stroll down the stairs on the way out to bat. Halfway down and the hum of the crowd in Long Room gets the hairs on the back of my neck to stand up. This journey as an England batsman has always been extra-special for me because my dad, as an MCC member, is amongst the throng. We always high-five on my way in and out. Unfortunately, on this occasion, these acknowledgements were too close together for my liking.

By the time Australia pulled out a few minutes after tea, with 566 on the board, there had been quite a change in the weather. Their bowlers, fresh after sitting up on the balcony for a day and a half, would have been licking their lips. Suddenly the sky grew overcast and the floodlights were required to aid visibility. That can make a big difference to how the red ball behaves; it definitely helps it swing around a bit more.

The Australian bowlers profited from getting the ball as full as possible, we didn't play that well and, without making excuses, conditions were well and truly against us. Being brutally honest, we didn't help ourselves by playing some poor shots. It is very hard to get back into a contest when you start the way we did, and I was as culpable as anyone.

The situation I was confronted with was one I had seen before. Entering the contest at 29–3, I was trying to find a happy medium between putting the pressure back on them, as I had done at Cardiff, and not allowing them to get further on top. Unfortunately, this time I got it a bit wrong and that is the danger of playing in a positive fashion from the start. When your shot-selection is slightly off, as it was on this occasion, it can look reckless or stupid. Whatever the situation of the game, it is always nice to get off the mark as soon as possible and, having done this with a single off my first ball from Josh Hazlewood, I found myself at the other end for Mitchell Johnson's second over. I attempted a forceful back-foot punch through the off-side but only succeeded in feathering the ball through to Peter Nevill, the wicketkeeper. Arguably, I should have taken a bit more time to get used to the pace of the wicket.

Even though Alastair Cook and Ben Stokes prevented further damage, when you come off the field four wickets down inside a session, as we did that night, you start wondering how on earth you are going to get anything out of the match. The most obvious thing to stress amongst yourselves is that the next day starts afresh. It's a new challenge. The previous summer, we had been in that kind of position against India and shown the skill and fight to get out of trouble.

On the third day, the pair of them played really well to defy Australia for a quarter of an hour shy of the full morning session. Australia began with confidence, I am sure, but the momentum of their previous day's exploits had been halted by our fifth-wicket partnership and they showed the rest of our lads exactly how to play on that kind of surface. Had they reached lunch, the second session would have taken on a completely different feel, but as it was, it didn't quite materialise.

Credit to Australia, and Michael Clarke in particular, for

recognising that bowling straight made it hard to score on that surface, and so although both Stokes and Cook could consider themselves unlucky with their dismissals, they were also victims of a smart form of attack. With the faster men unable to blast through, the seamers of lesser pace prospered. When you have that difference in pace amongst your bowlers, the 80 mph guys feel like a totally different challenge. Even though they are still brisk enough, when you have just faced the Mitchells, Starc and Johnson, it feels as if there is no pace to work with, and it can be tricky to maintain scoring shots when they bowl wicket to wicket.

This contributed to identikit dismissals for our unbeaten overnight left-handers, with two drag-ons to Mitchell Marsh. It was a real shame for Cooky to get so close to that elusive hundred and then depart in that way, with the second new ball imminent. He maintained very good shot-selection throughout and his innings had the class of a hundred about it. You can't get much closer. To the extent that when he clipped his first ball in the second innings off his pads for four, he chuntered, 'Why couldn't I do that in the first innings?'

He batted for five and three-quarter hours for his first-innings 96 and that's a long time to be out there keeping your concentration, especially when faced with such a tricky situation. He got through what were high-quality spells of bowling, in favourable conditions, and emphasised just how important he is to our side. With his solidity at the top of the order, if we can just get more out of those first few part-nerships, we will show ourselves to be an even more dangerous team. With the right foundations, I am sure you will see the more expansive players take greater advantage, batting around him or building on the foundations of the innings.

Despite securing a 254-run lead, with so much time remaining in the game it was no surprise when Michael Clarke snubbed the chance of enforcing the follow-on. Australia were intent on getting as many runs as they could and in typical style tried to do it as quickly as they could as well. With licence to play in an aggressive manner, their aim was to push towards an unassailable advantage as quickly as possible. In England, when wet weather has a habit of lurking around the corner, you sometimes need to factor in extra time. Under Clarke, Australia's tactic was always to manoeuvre into positions where they had the chance to bowl opponents out inside a day and a half.

Our only hope of getting back into the game was to have a crazy hour with the new ball. Once again, we were given a glimmer of hope early on when David Warner slashed a delivery from Jimmy through the hands of Adam Lyth at gully, but just as in the first innings, we were unable to seize on a loose Australian stroke. As a bowler there can be nothing more devastating than when, having created a chance on a flat wicket, you see the ball go through someone's hands and hit the turf. It must be a real challenge to stay positive after something like that and Jimmy was to endure a rare wicketless Test.

By the start of the fourth morning, Australia's opening

pair had swelled their advantage by a further 106 runs. But it soon became apparent that all was not well with Chris Rogers. Standing at the non-striker's end at the end of the second over, he lost his bearings and signalled to the dressing room that he needed treatment. At first I thought he must have a fly in his eye or had swallowed a bee, something like that. Then David Warner encouraged him to sit down. You don't normally see someone go down like that, and I don't think anyone expected him to leave the field. Only later did we find out it was potentially a result of the blow he had taken on the second morning of the match when a delivery from Jimmy Anderson had struck him above the ear. In 2015 he had had a succession of concussion problems – forcing him to miss the Tests against West Indies before the tour – although the Australians later revealed that he had been cleared of this following tests and that the trauma to the ear had caused an imbalance problem.

Following the tragic accident that cost Phil Hughes his life, there is always concern when people get hit while batting these days, but thankfully he was fine. We are all so much more aware of the dangers. This is a game that we play for fun and while we want to be competitive – we are all hugely passionate about playing for our country – you have to look after yourself and each other. Health is what matters.

It was so sad to lose someone from the cricket family, especially a bright young talent like Phil. But one thing that has been important since that tragic match between New South Wales and South Australia in November 2014 has been the retention of the bouncer in our game. It's a vital delivery in cricket. For a fast bowler it is an essential tool of the trade, used to force the batsman onto the back foot, so that the bowler can attack the stumps with their opponent less sure about getting forward. The crucial thing is that the protective equipment players wear should be the best it possibly can be. Safety is paramount. That's why the helmet manufacturers are putting so much effort into producing models to meet new standards.

Some manufacturers have been to county and Test grounds since, talking to players about safety, showing us their new equipment following hours of laboratory testing and emphasising exactly how sturdy it is. There is no doubt you want to be wearing the most robust kit available and so when I was given the opportunity to sport the newly designed protective clips that cover the back of the neck, I took up the offer. I wore one of the prototypes throughout the series in the Caribbean and did so all the way up until the second Test at Lord's.

As it happened, I was actually grateful for the new technology used on the front of helmets when, after walking in to bat at 42–3, the fifth ball I faced, from Mitchell Marsh, took a tiny top edge from an attempted pull shot and clunked the ball into my protective headwear. At first, I believed it had struck me directly on the England badge. However, it turned out its impact was right in the gap between the helmet's peak and grille. Previously that might have resulted in the ball spinning through the gap, but advances made in manufacture since Stuart Broad was struck in the face by a Varun Aaron bouncer in the Test match against India at Old Trafford in 2014 now prevent this from happening. Where once there was one metal strip running below the eyeline, there are now two, with the secondary protection, set back by about half an inch, negating any momentum towards the face. Importantly, you can no longer squeeze a cricket ball through the gap.

A helmet needs to be discarded once struck and players are now reminded of this by instructions printed inside. Naturally, after I received that clunk I was forced into a switch to another one, unfortunately forgetting that the protective clips remained on my original. Only later did it occur to me and by the time the damaged one was brought up to the dressing room after the day's play, someone had removed them. Hence, I did not have them as extra protection in the final three matches – as the only ones available were pre-sale prototypes like mine.

At the time, this was the least of my worries as the medical team feared I had incurred mild concussion. These days medics err on the side of caution when it comes to the subject and so I had to get through several checks with Craig de Weymarn and Mark Wotherspoon, the England physio and team doctor respectively, before being cleared.

Whatever the results, I was determined that news of this should not get outside the walls of our dressing room. As a Yorkshireman, I was brought up to never show weakness to the opposition and I didn't want the Australians think they had unsettled me in even the most minor of ways. Any indication that I had troubles against the short ball and they would have made it a greater focus of their attention. And the truth was I felt much better prepared for it anyway.

We were simply blown away in that second innings, my dismissal, the penultimate one, bowled by a Josh Hazlewood delivery that kept a bit low, coming at 5 p.m. that Sunday evening. We only just scraped to three figures and the way we applied ourselves suggested we lost our heads a little. Alastair Cook said at the post-match presentation that he felt the 405-run defeat was a 'real kick in the teeth', and we couldn't disagree with that assessment.

Having the contrast between the performances and emotions from Cardiff and Lord's was tough to take. After all that hard work it was almost as if we were back where we started. Afterwards, we sat down in the dressing room and expressed how we felt about the display. Trevor told us that it simply was not good enough from an England side. It was only his second game in charge but he nailed it really. We all knew it, but we needed to hear it.

'Australia were ahead from pretty much ball one and never let us back in,' Cook said on the podium during his TV interview. 'It shows how important the first couple of days are of the next Test match. The side that gets on top tends to dominate.'

England v Australia
(2nd Test)

Played at Lord's Cricket Ground, London, on 16–19 July 2015

Umpires: HDPK Dharmasena & M Erasmus (TV: CB Gaffaney)
Referee: RS Madugalle
Toss: Australia

AUSTRALIA

CJL Rogers	b Broad	173	retired hurt		49
DA Warner	c Anderson b Ali	38	c Cook b Ali		83
SPD Smith	lbw b Root	215	b Ali		58
MJ Clarke*	c Ballance b Wood	7	not out		32
AC Voges	c Buttler b Broad	25			
MR Marsh	b Broad	12	(5) not out		27
PM Nevill†	c Ali b Root	45			
MG Johnson	c Anderson b Broad	15			
MA Starc	not out	12			
JR Hazlewood					
NM Lyon					
Extras	(b 8, lb 14, w 1, nb 1)	24	(lb 5)		5
Total	(for 8 wkts dec) (149 overs)	**566**	(for 2 wkts dec) (49 overs)		**254**

ENGLAND

A Lyth	c Nevill b Starc	0	c Nevill b Starc	7
AN Cook*	b Marsh	96	c Nevill b Johnson	11
GS Ballance	b Johnson	23	c Nevill b Marsh	14
IR Bell	b Hazlewood	1	c sub (SE Marsh) b Lyon	11
JE Root	c Nevill b Johnson	1	b Hazlewood	17
BA Stokes	b Marsh	87	run out (Johnson)	0
JC Buttler†	c Nevill b Lyon	13	c Nevill b Johnson	11
MM Ali	lbw b Hazlewood	39	c sub (SE Marsh) b Johnson	0
SCJ Broad	c sub (SE Marsh) b Johnson	21	c Voges b Lyon	25
MA Wood	b Hazlewood	4	not out	2
JM Anderson	not out	6	b Hazlewood	0
Extras	(b 12, lb 8, nb 1)	21	(b 4, lb 1)	5
Total	(90.1 overs)	**312**	(37 overs)	**103**

ENGLAND	O	M	R	W		O	M	R	W
Anderson	26	4	99	0		7	0	38	0
Broad	27	5	83	4		8	2	42	0
Wood	28	7	92	1	(4)	10	3	39	0
Ali	36	4	138	1	(3)	16	0	78	2
Stokes	19	2	77	0		3	0	20	0
Root	12	0	55	2		5	0	32	0
Lyth	1	1	0	0					

AUSTRALIA	O	M	R	W		O	M	R	W
Starc	22	1	86	4		7	3	16	1
Hazlewood	22	2	68	3		8	2	20	2
Johnson	20.1	8	53	3		10	3	27	3
Lyon	16	1	53	1	(5)	9	3	27	2
Marsh	8	3	23	2	(4)	3	2	8	1
Smith	2	0	9	0					

Fall of wickets:

	Aus	Eng	Aus	Eng
1st	78	0	165	12
2nd	362	28	210	23
3rd	383	29	–	42
4th	426	30	–	48
5th	442	175	–	52
6th	533	210	–	64
7th	536	266	–	64
8th	566	294	–	101
9th	–	306	–	101
10th	–	312	–	103

Close of play:
Day 1: Aus (1) 337–1 (Rogers 158*, Smith 129*, 90 overs)
Day 2: Eng (1) 85–4 (Cook 21*, Stokes 38*, 29 overs)
Day 3: Aus (2) 108–0 (Rogers 44*, Warner 60*, 26 overs)

Note:
CJL Rogers retired hurt with his score on 49 and the total on 114–0 in Australia's 2nd innings.

Man of the Match: SPD Smith
Result: **Australia won by 405 runs**

*　*　*

As a group, we went our separate ways, reflecting on how we could improve, and on this occasion the way the fixtures were laid out – there were ten days before the next game in Birmingham – allowed us time to get into a better frame of mind. Had we played so badly in the first of back-to-back matches, it might have been a different story.

Jos Buttler and I had already discussed the break in the dressing room at Lord's and decided to do our own private sessions in expectation of increased hostility from the Australian attack. Jos and I love working together and whenever I have a one-day issue that needs addressing I turn to him. On the flip side, when he wants to work on his Test batting he tends to come to me. On this occasion, I asked him to pop across the Pennines for a little session at Abbeydale Park on the evening of Thursday, 23 July.

We took the end net at Sheffield Collegiate's club training night – an AstroTurf strip. We grabbed a bin full of water and completely soaked the surface to ensure the ball would skid through off it. We were both expecting to get a barrage from the Australian fast bowlers in the next game and so we mixed things up with full and short balls.

The session lasted about three hours: facing a high volume of deliveries on a quick surface was just what we needed. Coaches often promote practising at higher intensity than you experience in a game situation and we certainly met that criterion on this occasion. For me, it's all about feeling ready when I go out to bat, and that means occasionally going through sessions that are not enjoyable. It's no fun facing 90 mph bouncers for an hour and a half. But the more you do it, the easier it feels and the better you get at it. We each took a few blows early on, but by the end it felt worth it.

Just as it had been in the Caribbean with Mark Ramprakash three months earlier, this preparation was with Johnson in mind and, as then, seeing development in practice provided confidence that I was ready for whatever he had in store for me at Edgbaston. Jos and I used the ball-thrower with a flick of the wrist to the left side of the ball to try to replicate the Johnson angle and others queued up to ping pain our way too. Collegiate coach Josh Varley threw at us for a while, as did the club professional Simon Guy, but the most helpful of all proved to be my former schoolmate Ben Fielding, who despite being a left-arm spinner by trade was nevertheless able to recreate the Johnson release position the best out of anyone.

Although I felt topped up on a personal level, concerns about the team starts triggered a change in the batting when the squad for the third Test was announced less than forty-eight hours after defeat at Lord's. In the four innings of the opening two matches, the third England wicket had fallen on scores of 43, 73, 29 and 42. Not to mention the first-morning collapse to 30–4 against New Zealand in the first Test of the summer.

'It's a few games now we've been three down for 40-odd

and it's hard to always expect the middle order to get us out of trouble,' Cook said. 'So that's obviously an area of concern.'

Enough of a concern for it to cost Gary Ballance his place, and for another of our Yorkshire colleagues, Jonny Bairstow, to be called up. I felt deeply sorry for Gaz. A Test match earlier, we had celebrated going 1–0 up over Australia thanks to a really gutsy 61 he contributed in challenging circumstances. Sometimes Test cricket forces difficult decisions and I cannot imagine it was very easy for those who made this one. He was the reigning ICC emerging player of the year, lest we forget, and I believe he will show the class typical of the best players by bouncing back from hardship with strong performances. I am confident we will be sharing an England dressing room again in the not-too-distant future.

9 ROARED BACK IN FRONT

THE atmosphere at Edgbaston was like no other. The crescendo began with Stuart Broad's direct-hit run-out attempt from the second ball of the match and lasted for the next fifty hours. Normally even the liveliest of crowds need warming up, the vocal contingent requiring a few pints to slip down before they start getting rowdy. No need for Dutch courage in Birmingham. It was as if they had auditioned the loudest Brummies and shoved them into the Eric Hollies Stand on national service.

The moment Broady swooped to gather a shovel to mid-on by Chris Rogers and threw down the stumps to leave David Warner groping for the line with a full-length dive, the whole ground went wild. Warner clambered from the turf to learn his fate from the replay screens, but although that was survival by a split second, it mattered little to those who had come to support us. It's quite a cliché, but if ever there was a time it felt like we had twelve men on the field, this was it. From that moment you could genuinely feel the pressure the Edgbaston crowd were heaping on the Australians. It must have been quite an intimidating environment to bat in.

Jimmy had already jagged the first ball of the game past Rogers's outside edge and another delivery squirted off Warner's bat wide of gully before the first over was out. After what was a tough match for them at Lord's, our two opening bowlers, Anderson and Broad, began brilliantly here, which kept the cauldron of noise bubbling. The atmosphere was really spicy.

As an England player, you love it when the crowd supports you so fervently; it makes you feel so good about what you're trying to do. And when the reaction is like that from the 25,000 people in the ground, as strange as it sounds, you actually feel the love from everyone watching at home too.

We have a great fan base and every ground has its own unique feel. There are pockets everywhere that tend to get a bit raucous. Headingley's infamous Western Terrace can be unforgiving to opposition players when the volume goes up, and the same can be said of the huge temporary stand at Old Trafford. Trent Bridge seems to have the perfect acoustics when England get on top. It feels a bit like a football crowd at Edgbaston, with their songs, and that's great because you are left in no doubt that they are right behind you. Equally, they get into the opposition and make them uncomfortable. When you play in a home environment, one of the conditions to be used to your advantage is the hostility from the stands – particularly during the Ashes, when they are not shy of getting stuck into the opposition.

In preparation, we had spoken about the need to refocus on what we do well, not on the Australian team. That had worked for us in Cardiff, yet at Lord's we had gone away from that policy. In our huddle that morning, Alastair Cook told us that all he was interested in was how we were going to approach our cricket for that opening session. There was no point worrying about Australia. What were *we* going to do to exploit their batsmen? How were *we* going to get on top of them? It was about what *we* could do. To hear that was really good for a team with a point to prove, because it helped us concentrate on working on our individual strengths.

Every member of this England side understands how much a defeat like Lord's hurts each and every cricket fan in the country. We all love playing for England and count ourselves fortunate that we get the opportunity to do what a lot of those watching dream of doing. We don't take it lightly when we perform badly, and the key thing on this occasion was to learn from our mistakes, draw a line under the second Test defeat and move on. True, they had humiliated us at the home of cricket, but then we'd wiped the floor with them in Cardiff. We knew we weren't metaphorically a million miles – or statistically 405 runs – behind them. Taking emotion out of things and performing at our best was going to serve us well.

On the face of it, things started badly when Michael Clarke opted to bat first. But, just as it did ten years earlier at the same ground, this proved a good toss to lose. Ricky Ponting's decision to insert England in 2005 will always gain more attention because it proved such a critical factor in England's resurgence in that series, their scoring rate of 5.13 runs per over making their 407 all out an innings ahead of its time. However, conditions this time made it a far-from-easy decision: the rain and general cloud circling the Midlands suggested bowling might be a gamble worth taking, but the trend of the series so far had been bat first, win game.

I am sure Clarke would have considered the fact that they'd played so well at Lord's when batting first in making his choice. A repeat display would have kept us on the back foot. The Australian way has always been to bat first and control the game, and that policy had allowed them to take a grip of the second Test via a dominant first-day display. But we were determined to disrupt this chain of success and I don't think we were downhearted to be walking out onto the field first that morning.

Prolonged wet weather in the build-up had led to Edgbaston's head groundsman, Gary Barwell, using lights once employed for cultivating cannabis to dry certain areas of the playing surface. The heat of these lamps, confiscated by West Midlands Police from those using them in criminal activity and loaned to the club, was designed to make the pitch harder and therefore faster while encouraging grass growth. After two matches with minimal if any sideways movement, a bit of grass to promote it was nice to see. When Trevor Bayliss had said, 'I'd like to see a typical

English seaming wicket,' in the aftermath of the Lord's Test, he spoke for all of us. This green-tinged surface was exactly the kind we wanted to play on, one that even on the best days atmospherically – constant sunshine, for example – would still offer encouragement to our bowlers.

On this occasion, they made best use of what was overhead as well as what was underfoot. The challenge for our bowlers, set by Cook and Bayliss, was to keep that lateral movement as a permanent problem for Australia's batsmen by being extremely disciplined with the line they bowled in that first innings. Denying width would reduce the chances for cross-bat shots, a strength of a good number of their players. Cut and pull shots are what Australian batsmen are reared on because of the extra bounce their own conditions provide.

Also, at Lord's we'd been guilty of moving to each batsman's individual plans too early when confronted by a slow true pitch rather than persisting with our recipe for success of the recent past – encouraging our bowling attack to bowl their best balls at the top of off-stump consistently for a sustained period. We simply switched to our secondary form of attack too early.

What we got at Edgbaston was exactly the kind of dedicated and positive response we have come to expect from two senior bowlers with a combined Test wicket haul in excess of 700. The pair of them stayed true to the principles chiefly responsible for that success and it set the tone perfectly.

Jimmy is permanently grumpy – stereotypical for a fast bowler, I guess – but even he had a smile or two in that rain-shortened first session, coming back so strongly from his barren spell a fortnight earlier. Here, he was swinging the ball both ways and beating both edges of the Australians' bats with his wobble-seam deliveries. With wobble-seam you are never quite sure which way the ball is going to jag – it either hits the side of the seam or it doesn't – so you have to be meticulously accurate for it to be effective. If you get too straight and the ball darts the wrong way, you can be clipped off the pads for four. But the way he held his line and length was exceptional. To maintain such a wicket threat while proving so economical is a godsend for a captain, because he feels in great control of the game situation and it makes it easy to set aggressive fields at both ends. In those conditions, asking batsmen whether to stick or twist can be very rewarding. They have to decide whether to try to hang around, avoiding one with their name on it, or live dangerously by looking to exploit the gaps in the knowledge that one mistake will be costly.

You cannot keep top new-ball operators like Jimmy quiet for long, and when he got his eighth ball of the morning to nip back off the seam to defy David Warner's prod, and a subsequent review against the lbw decision, it was the perfect start. It also proved a master stroke by Alastair Cook to introduce Steven Finn into the attack as early as the eighth over of the morning.

Mark Wood had done everything he could to prove his

fitness after an ankle injury flared at Lord's, including having a cortisone injection to manage the pain, and was absolutely gutted to miss out. In contrast, Finn was elated to be back, having been out of Test cricket since the previous tour here by Australia. More than two years had passed between caps twenty-three and twenty-four. But you would not have guessed his last appearance for England in a Test was the opening Ashes contest at Trent Bridge in 2013 had you watched the quality first spell of bowling he pieced together on his return.

Dismissing Steve Smith with just his sixth ball back was a really telling blow for the team and even more significant was the mode of dismissal – feeling for the ball outside off-stump. It's always nice to see someone overcoming their problems and Steve had endured his fair share, with things like running up and hitting the stump with his knee as he got into his delivery stride.

He was given the opportunity to go back to Middlesex and work hard on recovering the form that got him picked in the first place. That's exactly what he did and he remains a good example to others who might lose their international place in future. You can either think 'poor me' or do something positive about the situation, and it took prolonged dedication from him to put things right via some really good performances at county level to get reconsidered for England again.

His inclusion maintained that extra yard of pace in our attack. Mark Wood regularly clocked 90 mph in his first few

Test matches and Steve was around that mark throughout the match at Edgbaston. It's helpful if you have that extra yard of pace somewhere in your attack, and from where I was standing at slip that morning he looked very sharp. He kept his speed consistent for that entire first spell and when there is a bit of swing in the air, and some seam movement, at close to 90 mph it makes it very hard for batsmen trying to start their innings. His dismissal of Michael Clarke with a full ball that went straight through the Australian captain's defence crowned a fine opening session for us.

Playing international sport is a real privilege but it can also provide moments of despair and no one wants to see a team-mate lose confidence the way Steve did on the 2013–14 Ashes tour. When times are hard, it is important to pull together, and it's always easier to do that when you've got a happy team. Throughout the 2015 summer, we had some great fun and that has to be maintained even when you are losing and struggling. Results dictate how much pressure there is on you to perform, but one thing that shouldn't change is the way you act around each other.

Humour plays an integral part in making our environment successful and has been crucial in helping us to stay relaxed. It is when you are relaxed that you perform at your best, I am convinced of that. And despite the result in our previous match, and some doom-and-gloom predictions that we had blown our chances of a series win, the dressing-room mood did not alter.

Away from game time, the dressing room can become a bit like a sixth-form common room. I am sure through the ages there have been lots of activities to keep players occupied, but all were probably more civilised than my distraction of choice for Lord's. I packed a load of Nerf guns in my kitbag and at lunch and tea it was all-out war. Of course, you have to get the balance right between work and play, because when a session starts it is full-on and none of us wants to be accused of not taking the game seriously once the players walk onto the pitch. Developing an enjoyment of each other's company away from the game can help you work better as a team when you switch onto the business aspect of being there.

In the toilets, for example, we have a wall of shame. One player tends to be targeted each game. Reg Dickason, our security officer, used to be the permanent butt of team jokes but more recently it's been shared around the team at the whim of Mark Saxby, our masseur. He seems to choose the victim to be targeted throughout a Test match. Everyone has had their fair share of it, so there is no chance of anyone claiming victimisation. But for that week, there will be cuttings and doctored pictures from the newspapers of the said player stuck in the smallest room. It is important to have a laugh, and more important to have a laugh at yourself. You do make friends for life in a cricket dressing room and that is something we have tried to promote.

Sometimes our larking gets caught on camera, as was the case at Edgbaston when, on one of the practice days,

I retaliated against Stuart Broad, who had been marking me throughout our football warm-up like Sol Campbell in his pomp. Everywhere I went, he went. It would be fair to say he was marking 'touch-tight'. Towards the end of the game, I'd had enough of it, so when he turned round I saw my opportunity to get one back on him and tugged down his shorts. In the immediate aftermath, he tried all sorts of things to get me back, but his tactics were not as effective as his marking and I remained unscathed.

More fun than all that, of course, are those amazing periods on the field when everything goes right, like it did when a delayed afternoon session finally got under way on the first day at Edgbaston. Jimmy's spell of four wickets for seven runs in nineteen deliveries was enough to put smiles on the faces of everyone again. No one anticipated the pitch and conditions being as conducive as they were to seam bowling. From a position of 72–3 at lunch, Australia were plunged to 94–7 thanks to Jimmy's eighteenth five-wicket haul in Test cricket. Playing on Australian uncertainty on and around off-stump delivered stunning results. Adam Voges tried to leave one and edged behind, Mitchell Marsh was lured into a drive, Peter Nevill was bowled by one that angled back and a switch to round the wicket accounted for Mitchell Johnson.

In those conditions – as predicted by us earlier that morning – the key to success was keeping things simple. Stuart Broad made the batsmen, and especially Chris

Rogers, play and miss a hell of a lot. That, combined with a few squirts off the edge, can frustrate you as a bowler – you might look to go fuller and pay for it. With anyone who plays and misses regularly, as Rogers had a tendency to do, the trap to fall into as a bowler is to search for something different. Good players like him then punish you with boundaries. The best thing to do is to allow a player like that to keep playing at the same length, because eventually he will nick one. Doing that not only makes the guy who's facing feel under pressure. It has an effect on those watching from the opposition dressing-room balcony. If a batsman's playing and missing, the scoreboard's not moving and that reminds those next in to bat that it's going to be tough.

As Broad discovered, hitting a similar spot from round the wicket was even more dangerous to the left-handers, and Rogers in particular. It took just three balls, following an afternoon rain shower, to end his dogged half-century when one that nipped back trapped him leg before. With one more wicket apiece, Broad and Anderson wrapped things up swiftly to make it seven inside the session. After their struggles at Lord's, what a difference a couple of weeks made.

We began our reply to Australia's 136 at the start of the evening session of the first day. With the changes to our batting order after Gary Ballance was omitted, there was a lot of pressure on Ian Bell to do well at his new position of number three, particularly as he had not made a score in the first two matches. In relatively early, after Adam Lyth edged one behind trying to be positive against Josh Hazlewood, the fact that Ian was on his home ground would no doubt have settled him a little, but he also knew that it was a critical stage of the match – we simply had to build on our early advantage.

He contributed what turned out to be 53 vital runs for us. The conditions had not changed a great deal, and it was therefore not easy to go out and bat. But from the outset he was very positive, looking to get on top of the bowlers by taking drives on through the covers and flicking to leg when they got too straight at him. The fact that he was scoring so freely made it hard for their bowlers to build any sort of pressure following that early wicket and he vindicated the decision by the England selectors to place more responsibility on a senior player.

Question marks had lingered in the media as to whether it should have been him or Gary that was left out after those first two Test matches and he provided an authoritative answer as to why he should have stayed in the side by playing handsomely at a venue he knew so well. You could see how devastated he looked when he eventually got out, hitting one in the air off Lyon. Stood at the non-striker's end, I knew exactly what he was trying to do. As a team, we always felt that undermining Lyon, who performed the holding role for the Australians, was a critical operation. On the other hand, it was the second frustrating dismissal that evening and came just five minutes before more rain curtailed the day's play. Earlier, Alastair Cook had pulled one straight into the body of Adam Voges at short leg and had somehow been caught as the ball got wrapped up in Voges's stomach. Nevertheless, their runs had put us into a position of real strength and one from which we could press home our advantage the following day.

Alongside me on the way to the crease that second morning, with our side just three runs in arrears, was my Yorkshire team-mate Jonny Bairstow. You would have struggled to have found a more confident cricketer in the land at that point in the summer. Jonny had been playing supremely, averaging over 100, with five centuries, including a double, in County Championship cricket. That was a phenomenal effort for someone who had missed the start of the season due to the England tour of the Caribbean. He was in the form of his life and I was so excited to see him try to emulate that on the international stage.

Unfortunately, he was the victim of one of two absolutely belting deliveries sent down by Mitchell Johnson in the second over of the second morning. Jonny had put us into the lead with a confident square drive for four off a Josh Hazlewood delivery that could not have been more of a contrast to the one that had him trudging off moments later. While the first had been full and wide, this one was short and directed with precision, the ball rearing towards his throat and taking the top glove on its way through to the wicketkeeper. It is very hard to combat that extra bounce, at that kind of rapid pace, so early in your innings. Two balls later, a replica accounted for Ben Stokes. It was quite a way for Johnson to go to 300 and then 301 Test wickets, and the fact that he can summon unplayable balls like that from nowhere makes him the most dangerous out-and-out pace bowler in the world.

It all meant that Jos Buttler and I were reunited seven days after scheming up our imaginary Mitch at Collegiate. The first thing we spoke about when he walked out to meet me was that very fact: we had done all the work to prepare for this kind of hostile attack. Johnson may have been bowling at the speed of light but that was what we had tried to replicate on the Astro pitch in Sheffield. We were up to speed and now could rely on playing on our instincts.

We just needed to stem the tide for a while, and although our partnership only lasted three-quarters of an hour, that was enough to allow us to kick on again. We made Johnson go wicketless for the rest of his spell and hopefully took a bit out of him for when the guys came in lower down the order. Pleasingly, during that entire innings of 63 I felt in control of what I was trying to do against him and extremely comfortable taking him on if the opportunity arose, as it did when I hauled him high over fine leg for six on the first day. As a batsman, it is a nice place to be in when you feel you have attacking options and time to execute them.

* * *

Multiple scoring options are always a bonus, and I realised the top-up work I had done had made me much more confident about a duel with Mitchell Johnson. For this match in particular, I was conscious of sending out the right message: if you are looking to go short at me, expect to be hit. There are certain situations that develop in the game where you feel you cannot do this – for example, when opponents have got two men posted back on the boundary and another catching around the corner, it would be foolhardy – but on other occasions, if you trust the bounce of the wicket and feel that the field is set so that you can take it on, then why not? It was about taking one of his strengths, his most productive ball, and transforming it into one of my most productive shots.

In contrast, one of my previous strengths was becoming a bit of a concern. It was like Groundhog Day: same bowler, same delivery, same dismissal. Although there were other dismissals in between, it was not the first time I had departed edging a drive at Mitchell Starc, and there had been that Brad Haddin miss at Cardiff too, of course. I've never considered myself to have a technical issue against left-armers, so after some reflection I accepted I was becoming a victim of my own positivity. Being marginally out with the judgement of length came with a heavy price. Getting the balance right is the challenge. Ideally, you don't want to get out to that stroke at all. But if you are able to score a lot of runs from it, you have to weigh up whether the risk is worth the reward. It was a length ball that I had gone after as if it was a fuller delivery. I had not been as precise as I would want to be and had gifted Adam Voges a conventional slip catch.

Not for the first time, Moeen Ali and Stuart Broad then complemented each other perfectly as a batting partnership at a vital stage of a contest. They are both left-handers, of course, but they clearly capitalise on bowlers struggling to alter length because of their differences in height. Here, they restored English momentum with their 87-run partnership inside 20 overs, and having a lead as big as 145 runs even after losing a clutch of wickets ensured we remained well on top heading into that second innings.

The two of them were so important to us getting bigger scores and big leads in the matches that we won in the summer. When a tail wags effectively it gives you such belief heading into the next innings and none of us could give them enough credit for the way they played. In the twelve months since Stuart had been hit in the face by a bouncer against India, there had been a lot of debate about whether he had lost all confidence as a batsman. He had not managed many significant scores in the interim and if there was an attack to exploit any fears about short-pitched stuff, then this Australian one was it. But what we do know for certain about Stuart Broad is that he responds to the grandest occasions. So to those of us who share a dressing room with him it was no surprise that he kept coming out and playing the way he did. The fight he displayed summed up his character. The bigger the stage, the better he performs.

To do what Stuart did took a tremendous amount of bottle. When you play international cricket, being brave is a necessity because facing bouncers goes with the territory. As a batsman, you accept that you are going to have to face plenty and that you will get hit a few times. But for those that bat down the bottom, being hit can seriously erode confidence. Considering his horrific experience, it was only to be expected that he would be tentative.

There was a time not so many years ago when people considered him to be a bowling all-rounder, but England's period of success between 2009 and 2013 meant that he spent a large period of time with reduced onus on his batting. By the time that started to change, he was perhaps not used to walking to the crease in the same pressure situations. Netting is one thing, you can do it as much as you want, but if you are not a genuine batter and do not spend time out in the middle, it is very hard to keep your game in order. But we know just how much work he did in practice so that he could contribute again, and for him to look so much more accomplished against the short stuff was a credit to his commitment.

In his pomp, Broad is a very difficult cricketer to stop and he provided a great start to Australia's second innings by immediately switching to round the wicket to Chris Rogers and producing a repeat dismissal of first innings. But the irresistible force of our attack at the most pivotal stage of the series proved to be Steven Finn – whose triumphs on that second evening must have made the breakdown of his bowling action in Australia in 2013–14, which led the then England one-day coach Ashley Giles to dub him 'unselectable', seem an age ago. Finn is not the kind of man to hold a grudge and there was no malice in the comment. He had simply lost the skills that made him so selectable in the first place.

The reprise of those skills resulted in an unbelievable spell, arguably the best of his career, to decimate Australia's batting. It was a mixture of high pace and great control, making it very hard for any new batsman who came in to settle. Throughout his career, his danger ball has generally been the one that nips back in, and the Australians will no doubt have been ready for that, having played against him before. He gets the ball to climb big on batsmen and it can tend to follow their hands, which is deadly when the ball is delivered at high pace. But he showed the skill he has developed as a fast bowler by swinging the ball consistently too.

As a cordon, during that second innings we were very comfortable that the ball was going to carry if he got an edge, and it always felt like the next ball had your name on it. Thankfully, we were able to take some really good catches, and it must have been an amazing experience for him. There must have been times in the previous eighteen months when he wondered whether he would get the opportunity again, having slipped down the pecking order and seen various others come in ahead of him. I don't think he could have wished for a better return to the team.

Propelled along by David Warner, who appeared to be playing a different game to the rest of his team, Australia were 62–1 when Finn dug one in to Steve Smith to force an error. A spiralling top edge provided a second success before tea and Edgbaston was rocking during a magical over shortly after the interval, when Michael Clarke was turned around and Adam Voges felt for one outside off-stump to provide catches to the slips and leave Finn on a hat-trick. Although Steve could not complete the fairy tale, Mitchell Marsh was uncomfortable against him too, surviving a challenge to a not-out lbw on umpire's call after the ball was shown to be clipping the bails before allowing another delivery to go straight through him. Finn, such a likeable man who refuses to take himself too seriously, had done some serious damage. People like him showed that this England team and English cricket in general has a bit more depth than some would have given us credit for before the series.

Finn had broken the back of Australia's batting, and a two-day finish seemed a real possibility when Jimmy Anderson, whose first-innings figures of six for 47 were his fourth-best figures in Test cricket, was reintroduced and quickly ended Warner's typically pugnacious innings of 77 – a leading edge from an attempted turn to the leg-side looping to cover. Australia at 111–6 were still 34 runs in arrears.

The one dampener on all this was Jimmy suffering inter-costal discomfort soon afterwards. He tried to continue but realised midway through his run-up that doing so would only make the problem worse. After he left the field, I was asked to complete the final three balls of the over, and instinctively we all knew that we would not see him bowl another ball in the contest, and perhaps the series for that matter. When a fast bowler feels his side like that, more often than not it's game over for quite a while. Side strains do not heal easily. Some will say that it was better to lose him then, with a 2–1 lead in the series in sight. But no matter the state of play, losing someone of his calibre was a massive body blow to us as a team. As leader of the attack, he sets the tone and a pitch like that was made for him.

Australia were only eight runs ahead when Mitchell Johnson spooned Finn's first ball back to backward point. But you expect a team of such quality to fight back, and Peter Nevill and Mitchell Starc were able to withstand our push that evening. Conversely, there was enough wiggle room for us not to panic.

For a lower-order player, Starc has a really good eye and he was successful in pursuit of his favourite stroke, driving through the off-side whenever the ball was full. In contrast, Nevill was very patient, looking for us to go to him rather than chasing any width. He tucked well off his legs and did not look to do much else, which was a mature way of playing for someone in only his second Test match. He effectively eliminated the risk of being dismissed caught behind in conventional manner, which meant our best way of getting him out appeared to be via a leg-side tickle.

First of all, late that evening, on 35, with the Australians on 160–7, he offered a tough chance off Stuart Broad that Jos Buttler could not cling on to. Then, when Jos did take a spectacular catch next morning, shortly after Nevill reached his half-century, umpire Chris Gaffaney turned down our appeal. The fact we had used up our two reviews on leg-before appeals the previous evening was frustrating, especially as replays showed we had been correct in our assumption that the ball had brushed the batsman's glove on its way through.

That let-off on 196–7 was followed by another Nevill strangle 21 runs later and, thankfully for us, it was third time lucky. Jos covered the ground to take the ball high to his left, following a deflection off Steven Finn, and the raising of Aleem Dar's finger came as something of a relief. Hot Spot confirmed Nevill's fate, after a challenge, and a mode of dismissal that always looked likely despite not being one you plan for had been rubber-stamped. It became obvious that it could be a way to get him out because of how he had adjusted to playing. It was obvious that he was being more deliberate in getting further across his stumps to cover the off-stump, after being bowled by Jimmy Anderson leaving one alone in the first innings. This time, he was much more precise in his estimation of where his off-stump was and he played and left the ball really well.

* * *

After the departure of Australia's last recognised batsman, it was a question of how quickly we could wrap up the tail. They rode their luck for a while during that morning session, and although he may have been feeling as agitated as some of the others amongst us, Alastair Cook pulled his usual trick of appearing calm and reassuring everyone else that all was OK. When you have been on top for so long, it is easy to start panicking if the opposition have a sustained spell of resistance or counter-attack, but the senior players recognised that there was no need to panic.

In fact, after play on the second evening, Ian Bell had urged us to be patient, when he said, 'Let's not think we have to bowl them out for next to nothing from here. We don't have to win the game by ten wickets or by an innings. Let's just keep plugging away and if they get a 150-run lead, accept it. We'll knock it off. That's fine.'

When you are involved in a hectic, wicket-heavy session like that one on the second evening, it can scramble your thoughts. The game had taken place at such high tempo that we needed to be ready for it to slow down or be stretched in length, if Australia were good enough to make that happen. Naturally, when you get into that kind of dominant position, you want to get it finished as quickly as possible. But the key is to retain your composure.

I was pleased to do this, from a personal point of view, when Josh Hazlewood slashed at a Ben Stokes delivery – the ball flew to third slip and hit me rather than me grab-bing it, to be honest, but I held on to my right. It made me think of all the work we had done in Spain and to reproduce it out in the middle when it mattered most was a real thrill. It took us one full hour to claim those final two wickets, as Starc tried to hit them to a total that provided them with a sniff of bowling us out. He was last out, for 58, going for another aggressive shot off Moeen Ali in the final over before the second new ball was available.

A chase of 124 – the figure we required to retake the lead, can be tricky, and there has been plenty of evidence of this in Ashes cricket over the years. Recall the 1981 series, when Australia were bowled out for 121 chasing 151 on the same ground, and 111 in pursuit of 130 in Botham's match at Leeds, or even the 2005 series when England got to their 129-run target with seven wickets down.

On this occasion, he went out so positively that within forty minutes the requirement had been reduced to 80, with Ian Bell, in early once more, charging us through the new-ball spell. Getting out of the blocks as quickly as that can deflate the opposition. It also eradicated any lingering nerves amongst those of us watching on from the sidelines.

He had got to 20 by hitting five of his first nine deliveries to the boundary when he was given a reprieve by Michael Clarke at second slip off Mitchell Starc. Strangely, he almost played it off the face of the bat, and I greeted this with a yelp of 'What's he done?' from the dressing-room balcony. Thankfully, Clarke put it down, following a well-developed tendency in cricket: when you are not scoring runs consistently and you have a lot on your plate, as Clarke did, such as questions about your captaincy, negativity seems to follow you. Here was a reliable slip catcher unable to hold on to what looked like a regulation chance. You would expect him to catch that chance nine times out of ten.

It was just the stroke of luck we required. While that first-innings knock was an important one for Bell himself, this one was important for the team. In that situation Starc is as dangerous as anyone on the world scene because he swings the new ball and is a genuine wicket-taker. He did not have many runs to play with but is capable of doing sensational things, and had already accounted for Alastair Cook with a beauty. If Clarke had held on to that catch and they had got another wicket straight away, it could have been a totally different story.

As it was, I arrived at the crease at 51–2 in the 12th over. It was a great passage of play to be a part of: the expectation of the crowd, the Australians throwing everything at us, Bell keeping the scoreboard moving to alleviate the pressure. When we got it down to 40 required with eight wickets standing I knew we were virtually home. It was at that point that Bell deftly ran a ball from Starc down to third man for his second fifty of the match.

It was a carnival atmosphere, although not for Mitchell Johnson. The crowd remained all over him from start to finish, not even relenting late into that second innings. It can't have been nice to be subjected to such verbal hostility, and as an opposition player you cannot help but smile when their most dangerous bowler is being taunted, even if he does say publicly that he's enjoying the banter.

To be honest, he was doing some strange stuff in response to their goading. Bowling round the wicket, he pulled up in delivery stride to me one ball and then bowled from about 23 yards with his next. In that kind of situation you have to really concentrate. It half felt like he was playing up to the crowd and half felt like he was trying to throw me off as well. Even though it appeared to be driven by a bit of fun, I couldn't really tell whether that was truly because the Test had gone or he'd done it after coming to the end of his tether.

Towards the end, with Australia forced into placing men around the bat – at slip, short leg and leg-slip – I had licence to attack Nathan Lyon. It was good to connect well with a couple of sweeps to the boundary, one so perfectly that it travelled into the stands at midwicket. And to hit the winning runs off Mitchell Marsh was a special moment too, although from a batting perspective, Ian Bell had to take the plaudits. No one, however, would have denied that Steven Finn was the right choice as Man of the Match.

One of the questions asked in the aftermath of the match was why this England team was so inconsistent. Our sequence of win, loss, win, loss, win, loss, win had not been produced in more than 140 years of Test cricket. Analysing the make-up of our team probably helps to explain why we were the trailblazers in the up-and-down stakes. Normally, in a Test series you discover that one team grabs the initiative and runs with it. But although we are capable of getting into good positions because we are a very talented side, we are also an inexperienced one, and with inexperience come mistakes. Several of our players were featuring in their first full Test series at home.

One of our areas of weakness had been an inability to maintain consistency across the full five days. Simply, we had to eradicate allowing bad half-hours to ruin the game. There were times in our hot-and-cold run when that contributed massively to the end result – most obviously in Barbados but also against the New Zealanders at Leeds, when we could not withstand a good spell in helpful bowling conditions and relinquished an unbelievable position of strength. Without doubt, the test of this team will be how we respond to these situations in the longer term. When opponents have got on top of us, we have found it very difficult to pull the situation back. Equally, sides have struggled to do that to us.

Not that Australia were better for their greater experience. Amidst criticism from ex-players for overlooking wicket-keeper Brad Haddin, their chairman of selectors, Rod Marsh, had said 'there was no option' but to select Peter Nevill. Their captain, Michael Clarke, then revealed his own frustration at not being able to influence the series as he would have liked, when he said, 'I think it's always going to be hard to beat any opposition when they've got eleven and we've only ten. At the moment that's how it feels. With my performances so far, I certainly haven't led from the front.'

If we were the ones under pressure just a few days earlier, the situation had flipped. We were now the ones in control of the destiny of the urn. And it led to a straight-talking match debrief from our coach Trevor Bayliss.

'Lads, this is one night of your lives I am asking you not to go mental. Sure, have a drink or two to celebrate. Just don't make it a 2 or 3 a.m.-er. We can be a part of something extremely special next week if we are absolutely right physically, so don't overdo it with the booze. Let's make sure our bodies are in good condition for back-to-back Tests,' he said.

These words might have been viewed as something of a downer in the immediate aftermath of a Test match win. Test wins, and especially Ashes ones, are to be celebrated. But the bigger picture, as Trevor made clear, was that there was a series to win, and it could be won with one match to spare. Until that point, I can honestly say the thought had not crossed my mind.

The caveat from Trevor, if we sacrificed a few hours of fun, was 'If you win at Trent Bridge, you can go as mental as you want.'

England v Australia
(3rd Test)

Played at Edgbaston, Birmingham, on 29–31 July 2015

Umpires:	Aleem Dar & CB Gaffaney (TV: M Erasmus)
Referee:	RS Madugalle
Toss:	Australia

AUSTRALIA

Batsman	Dismissal	Runs	Dismissal (2nd)	Runs (2nd)
CJL Rogers	lbw b Broad	52	lbw b Broad	6
DA Warner	lbw b Anderson	2	c Lyth b Anderson	77
SPD Smith	c Cook b Finn	7	c Buttler b Finn	8
MJ Clarke*	b Finn	10	c Lyth b Finn	3
AC Voges	c Buttler b Anderson	16	c Bell b Finn	0
MR Marsh	c Buttler b Anderson	0	b Finn	6
PM Nevill†	b Anderson	2	c Buttler b Finn	59
MG Johnson	c Stokes b Anderson	3	c Stokes b Finn	14
MA Starc	c Buttler b Broad	11	c sub (JE Poysden) b Ali	58
JR Hazlewood	not out	14	c Root b Stokes	11
NM Lyon	b Anderson	11	not out	12
Extras	(lb 7, nb 1)	8	(b 2, lb 9)	11
Total	(36.4 overs)	**136**	(79.1 overs)	**265**

ENGLAND

Batsman	Dismissal	Runs	Dismissal (2nd)	Runs (2nd)
A Lyth	c Voges b Hazlewood	10	lbw b Hazlewood	12
AN Cook*	c Voges b Lyon	34	b Starc	7
IR Bell	c Warner b Lyon	53	not out	65
JE Root	c Voges b Starc	63	not out	38
JM Bairstow	c Nevill b Johnson	5		
BA Stokes	c Nevill b Johnson	0		
JC Buttler†	lbw b Lyon	9		
MM Ali	c Warner b Hazlewood	59		
SCJ Broad	c Marsh b Hazlewood	31		
ST Finn	not out	0		
JM Anderson	c Nevill b Starc	3		
Extras	(b 6, lb 4, w 4)	14	(w 2)	2
Total	(67.1 overs)	**281**	(for 2 wkts) (32.1 overs)	**124**

ENGLAND	O	M	R	W		O	M	R	W
Anderson	14.4	2	47	6		8.3	5	15	1
Broad	12	4	44	2		20	4	61	1
Finn	10	1	38	2		21	3	79	6
Ali						16.1	3	64	1
Stokes						11	3	28	1
Root						2.3	0	7	0

AUSTRALIA	O	M	R	W		O	M	R	W
Starc	16.1	1	71	2		6	1	33	1
Hazlewood	15	0	74	3		7	0	21	1
Johnson	16	2	66	2	(4)	7	3	10	0
Marsh	7	2	24	0	(5)	1.1	0	8	0
Lyon	13	2	36	3	(3)	11	1	52	0

Fall of wickets:

	Aus	Eng	Aus	Eng
1st	7	19	17	11
2nd	18	76	62	51
3rd	34	132	76	–
4th	77	142	76	–
5th	82	142	92	–
6th	86	182	111	–
7th	94	190	153	–
8th	110	277	217	–
9th	119	278	245	–
10th	136	281	265	–

Close of play:	Day 1: Eng (1) 133–3 (Root 30*, Bairstow 1*, 29 overs)
	Day 2: Aus (2) 168–7 (Nevill 37*, Starc 7*, 55 overs)

Man of the Match:	ST Finn
Result:	**England won by 8 wickets**

10 MISSION ACCOMPLISHED

JIMMY Anderson's Test record at Trent Bridge is officially ridiculous. Conditions in Nottingham are usually perfect for his brand of swing bowling, and if he could roll up the pitch and bottle the microclimate and carry them round with him in a suitcase, I am sure he would. The question was how was this England team going to cope in the absence of an injury victim who had claimed 53 wickets in eight appearances here at a smidgeon over 19 runs apiece? We need not have worried. A feature of our team throughout the Ashes was that whenever we truly needed someone to step up, they did. In this case it was hometown hero Stuart Broad.

Everyone knows how successful Jimmy has been, and during the previous Ashes match there, my first in 2013, he took ten wickets, including keeping his cool to take the crucial final one to seal victory with Australia needing only 15 runs to force a result of their own. So not only did he have good history on the ground, but good history on it against Australia. He even got his highest Test score there in the match against India in 2014. You would have got a good price on someone putting his exemplary numbers in the shade, but Broad used his own knowledge of Nottingham to deliver his best-ever spell in an England shirt.

Despite being unavailable due to his side strain, it was decided by Alastair Cook and Trevor Bayliss that keeping Jimmy with the squad would be beneficial. With his family away on holiday, he had been Broad's house guest between Tests. When you are not playing, it can be very hard to stick around a team environment, both before and during a match, and you end up feeling like a bit of a spare part. The fact he did so showed how committed he was to contributing to our success in any capacity possible. He was desperate to win. Desperate to help us achieve our goal even though he couldn't contribute physically. From the management perspective, it was a shrewd move because even though he wasn't going on the field, it still felt as if you had that experienced member of the attack in the side. He just never left the dressing room.

The fast-bowling group worked really well together throughout the series, chatting through their plans for different pitches and atmospheres, and that continued even though Jimmy was unavailable. He was there offering advice on practice days, providing a slightly alternative viewpoint to what the coaches might say. By that stage, he had already completed his intense early-morning fitness sessions in his bid to get back for the final Test at The Oval. He had also taken to wearing an oxygen mask daily to quicken the healing process. To see a senior player like that, someone who has played for so long, doing shuttle runs on the outfield when we arrived highlighted to everyone else how special it is to be able to represent England. Jimmy had more than 100 caps to his name and had nothing to prove, but he hated missing just one match. Doing all that extra work demonstrated exactly what a good role model he is – it showed the guys on the fringe of selection the commitment required for their practice. He wanted to give himself every possible chance of being fit when Cook flipped the coin for the fifth and final time on 20 August.

In fact, as a team we put extra emphasis on being ready for ball one of the Trent Bridge Test. Less than twenty-four hours after completing victory at Edgbaston, and having been asked to go easy on the knees-up, it was decided that we would factor an extra practice day into our preparations. It was not overly taxing – the most strenuous activity for the bowlers was our football kickabout, before a rub, swim and general relax – with the emphasis for everyone on their batting. Anyone who wanted extra throw-downs was accommodated. Getting there ahead of schedule felt extremely beneficial. It provided extra time to talk things through and assess the wicket.

The previous year the pitch against India had been the flattest imaginable. To put it into context, Jimmy Anderson scored 81 on it. The International Cricket Council officially marked it poor. Groundsman Steve Birks took the unusual step of issuing a public apology for it after the opening day's play. This time, however, he produced one which was not dissimilar to the one we'd played on at Edgbaston. The one against India was arguably rolled to death, but this one was a lot fresher, and that made it a very important toss to win.

Once we had won it, we had to make the most of the favourable conditions and, thanks to Stuart Broad, we did. By the end of one of the craziest first overs in history Australia were 10–2. Even when you are feeling positive about taking early wickets, you daren't dream of things going that well. The target is to get a couple of early wickets to put yourselves in a good position, but they came so much faster than we could ever have anticipated, and to get Chris Rogers for a duck – incredibly, his first in Test cricket, a remarkable stat for an opening batsman – was sensational. Rogers had been in rich form throughout the summer, scoring fifties in every Test leading up to this point, so we could not have begun any better.

Although Broad did not get his line right immediately, going for four leg-byes to get Australia's scoreboard moving, he did not take long to locate his line and length and Rogers provided Alastair Cook with a straightforward slip catch. Then, three balls later, after being shovelled into the leg-side for a couple and driven square for a boundary, he nicked Steve Smith off to me at third slip. It was a very conscious effort by Stuart to get the ball full, and undeterred by being punished a couple of times, he got the greatest reward. The key was to get the batsman to keep coming at him. He did, and pandemonium ensued as a packed house recognised that the ball had nestled in my hands.

Half an hour earlier our chat had focused on luring the Australian batsmen into strokes slightly away from the body. This suggested it had been a perfect estimation of how to make the most of the conditions. But knowing exactly what you have to do is one thing; having the skill and control to deliver it is another.

The roar of the crowd that morning was amazing, and it was exactly the kind of atmosphere you would want a fresh opposition player to be subjected to. It brought to the crease Shaun Marsh, who had yet to play in the series and had been drafted in to allow Michael Clarke to drop down to number five.

Within two deliveries from Mark Wood, who had won the selection vote for the vacated bowling place ahead of Liam Plunkett and Mark Footitt, the change in the order had become irrelevant as the pair were brought together when David Warner got an inside edge on a brute of a delivery – short of a length, it nipped back to provide Jos Buttler with a straightforward catch. Emulating Broad, it was mightily impressive of Wood to stand up to the extra responsibility in the absence of Jimmy. In this instance, taking the new ball.

Whilst Stuart was an experienced cricketer, taking the first over of a Test match was not something he had done before. He had always had Jimmy in front of him in the pecking order and before that he'd played in a team along-side Steve Harmison and Andrew Flintoff. Here, he took on the mantle and shone. This epitomised his character.

When you take three wickets in the first eight balls – not that it was a situation many of us had experienced before – it is important to stick to the plan you had when you entered the field and not go chasing further inroads. With such an unbelievable start, you have to expect a partnership to develop at some point.

It didn't. They just kept nicking the ball and we kept catching it. It was an astonishing spell of cricket to be involved in. And it wasn't just Broad's once-in-a-lifetime session. That morning we held on to some blinders. At the top level, you always talk about getting into strong positions by claiming all the half-chances on offer. At Lord's we had not taken any of them, but here everything that went to hand was claimed – partly because the ball was so hard that they all flew quickly, and sometimes that helps. At top speed they can just stick.

There was no better example of this than when Adam Voges edged thick and low, and Ben Stokes contorted his body to cling on, one-handed, just above the turf, even though the ball had technically gone past him. As soon as it was struck, I thought it was four and so, from my position two men away, when I saw Ben fling himself down and hold on I just went mental. To see it was to believe it, and even then some struggled. None more so than Broad, whose reaction proved to be one of the images of the 2015 Ashes. As Ben rose from the turf, Stuart placed his hands over his mouth in disbelief, a pose that was copied by club cricketers celebrating wickets all around the country that weekend, I am sure.

I have come to expect that kind of freakish intervention in match situations from Ben, who nevertheless kept taking the mickey out of himself, saying that the only reason he managed to hold on was the clawed nature of his right hand. Four years ago in a County Championship match between Durham and Lancashire at Chester-le-Street, he had to have his right index finger pinned after dropping a fierce chance offered by Paul Horton caused a dislocation. The lasting damage of that injury is that the tip of that finger now points at 45 degrees. He was joking that the 'claw' was what helped him hang on. It cost Australia a wicket but it almost cost us a man too: in his excitement, Ben went to hug Jonny Bairstow and effectively rugby-tackled him to the ground. This moment summed up what you get with Ben. His intensity in the field, and the standards he sets, are of the highest quality. That means that he is one of those players who, even when having a bad day with bat or ball, can give something back to the side. Players like him can get you a wicket from nowhere.

If there were any lingering doubts about bowling first, they had long been quelled by this point, with Australia 21–5. Having performed well as a unit bowling first in the previous match, it would have made it an easier decision. Ironically, typical of a fast bowler wanting to put his feet up, Broad had insisted that we needed to bat first. But we all knew what was coming because Cook had informed us of his intention in the team huddle that morning.

When you feel as if the ball is coming to you every single time it's released by the bowler, it's a really strange place to be in. It is not something you experience very often as a slip fielder, but it was a credit to the menace and control that Stuart in particular bowled with that this was the way I felt at third slip. I took three catches that innings, the two left-handers Mitchell Starc and Mitchell Johnson in the same over, and it was bizarre how often the ball was flying off the edge.

My brother Bill was one of England's three twelfth men that morning and because it was quite chilly he was on coffee duty for the three of them. He went upstairs in the Trent Bridge pavilion to get a round in just after the 11.05 a.m. start but ended up having to go up and down the stairs three or four times before completing it. Every time he got up there, another wicket fell and he would have to run out to the middle to bring our team drinks on. Three-quarters of an hour had passed by the time he got that cuppa.

Test match cricket's pace has definitely quickened since I began playing it just three years ago but the speed of this one was amazing. It was like a Test match in fast forward. Like a highlights package played on double speed. By the drinks break, the Australians were seven wickets down.

Given that we were attacking and leaving vacant areas for the batsmen to exploit, the control of Broad in particular, backed up by Wood and Steven Finn, was mightily impressive. The batsmen simply couldn't take advantage of them because we just kept taking wickets.

At the start of the innings, Broad needed one wicket to make it to 300 victims in Test cricket, but by the end of it, quite ridiculously, he had pulled level alongside Fred Trueman on 307. It's obviously been a good couple of years for him, because I remember his 200th. Or should I say his wait for his 200th. In the Lord's Ashes Test of 2013, Peter Siddle edged one and the ball went straight into my hands at third slip – and straight out again.

Stuart had got really arsey with me during the barren spell of 50 overs that followed, subjecting me to lots of chuntering along the lines of: 'Why couldn't you catch it? All I needed was one catch.' Of course, you expect that kind of thing from disappointed bowlers and I felt bad denying him his moment, as I undoubtedly should have caught it. Now, I look at it another way. If I had, he wouldn't have had the chance to take his 300th on his home ground of Trent Bridge. To see him walk off with the match ball in his hand, figures of 8–15 representing the best figures in Ashes cricket by anyone other than Jim Laker, was surreal.

Australia. 60. All out. Stop and pause for a moment. Look again. I am not sure it gets any better than that. It was as if we'd played a trump card at just the right time in the series, and if we needed any more evidence that things were going our way, it was provided when, having bowled at Australia under quite heavy cloud cover, the sun came out to coincide with our response. It was as if Trevor Bayliss was in the dressing room operating a weather dial. Suddenly, the sun was beating down on the pitch, and Alastair Cook and Adam Lyth came through three overs before lunch unscathed.

With the advantage ludicrously weighted in our favour, we almost had to approach the innings as though we were batting first. The onus on us was to build a platform and so, despite the loss of Lyth and Ian Bell in quick succession, we did just that. Of course, we expected Australia to bowl well and they did so initially, but with such a minuscule score on the board, it didn't take a lot to deflate them.

There had already been a few edges when one flew from Cook's bat off Mitchell Starc and Michael Clarke and Steve Smith appeared to be at odds as to whose catch it was. Smith reacted late and could not pouch it, providing us with a stroke of luck. We were only five runs ahead at that stage and, glancing around the field, you could see the disappointment etched on Australian faces. When you are at the non-striker's end you cannot wish to see anything better than that. Whenever you get an indication that you are on top it makes your life so much easier as a batsman. If anything, I had not been ruthless enough in this kind of situation in the past and here was a chance to capitalise on a position of strength.

From the moment we went past them into the lead, everything seemed to go in our favour. They started to chase wickets, providing more balls to score off, and that eased any pressure. Whenever the scoreboard is ticking, life feels so much easier, and just as we had at Edgbaston, we got it ticking. Even though Cook went on the eve of tea, we were moving away from our opponents.

With regards to my own batting, my movements were as good as they had been at any stage in the series. One shot in particular told me exactly the kind of touch I was in: when, on 12, Mitchell Johnson bounced me and I pulled him, with two men back, straight into the gap for four. The ball had come right out of the middle. Johnson's most destructive ball, which I had struggled with previously and even had some minor concerns about this very series, had been crunched. In that moment I felt in complete control. In my head I'd removed his most effective ball from his armoury. I am not sure if that was what was going through his head, but the message that I was there to take him on could not have been any clearer.

At the point Jonny joined me, at 96–3, he had faced only a dozen balls in the series. He rode a couple of ferocious deliveries off Johnson that got him jumping around early on, but as we started accumulating runs he played more and more freely. Jonny is the kind of player who is very hard to stop when he gets into his stride. It's not unusual for him to score a couple of boundaries an over when he's in this kind of form and he did so on a trio of occasions.

It's an ability that means you never feel stuck when opponents have an economical twenty-minute period.

In all, we put on 173 in 34 overs. It's not like one-day cricket, when you have to score at a certain rate, but restricting the maidens of a bowler like Nathan Lyon, their go-to guy for maintaining control, made the captaincy job that much more difficult for Michael Clarke. Because Australia possess a couple of strike bowlers, it is down to others to keep the scoring rate to a minimum while they are resting out in the deep.

The only major disruption to our stand was caused not by the opposition but by an external factor. Although I couldn't have been in a better place mentally, physically things were different immediately after tea. Having sat down for twenty minutes during the interval, my lower back completely seized up. I know that given that I was in form, and into the 30s by this stage, it must have caused a few moments of anxiety for those watching on television at home, but despite my grimacing I knew it wasn't going to prevent me carrying on.

I'd experienced exactly the same problem in the West Indies, so I knew what was happening. When that situation occurs, my back just needs warming up a bit. My body had been warm throughout the morning but the period of inactivity had cooled it down. It is something I have had to contend with for quite some time now and thankfully it hasn't restricted me from playing to this point.

There is no doubt that it looks worse than it is and it only actually requires some attention from the physio, as I received from Craig de Weymarn on the Trent Bridge pitch, to get going again. Yes, it is slightly uncomfortable at times, but it is manageable – it is not as though I am in absolute agony and can't play on. How it would affect my ability to bat was naturally my primary concern when it first happened in December 2014, on the one-day tour of Sri Lanka. I was worried it might stop me being able to get my weight forward and back, but it has not at all.

Since then Craig, in conjunction with the England strength-and-conditioning coach Phil Scott, has put together a programme to strengthen that area. It has meant adding extra warm-up and stretching exercises to my daily routines – predominantly around match days – to ensure I am loose when we head out onto the field. As with many back niggles, it has required stretching the hamstrings out fully first thing in the morning. To be right on top of it is really important. I am determined it is not going to stop me playing at any point.

Another unexpected challenge was thrown down to me not long after I moved into the 90s with two powerful cuts for four off Mitchell Johnson. It wasn't only a part-time bowler that Michael Clarke brought on to test me; it was the one opponent with whom I have a bit of history. He had also turned to David Warner's medium pace in the same circumstances at Cardiff. I was desperate not to get out to him, of course, and so while there was a part of me content in the knowledge there would be more opportunities to score and I would be able to rotate the strike comfortably enough, at the same time I was wary of relaxing too much and giving it away. A back-foot punch to the point boundary in Warner's second over eradicated any such worries. Another punch, into the Nottingham air, acknowledged my third Ashes hundred. Hundreds do not come any more special. The innings had presented a chance to push England towards a series victory and I had taken it.

The sound of R-O-O-O-O-O-T reverberating around the stands, as it did then, is one I will never tire of. Most of the time you are trying to shut out external distraction while batting, but when things are going really well for you it's nice to let the crowd noise in. To see the emotions of people around the ground gives me a real buzz. It's almost like being fed energy when they chant like that in unison. It is very distinctive and the first time I heard it, it did make me think, 'Why are they booing me?' In fact, it became a running joke inside our dressing room that whenever a new player came into the team, established lads would talk about the crowd jeering me, and how unjust it was, amongst themselves. Apparently, they've reeled in plenty of fish with that wind-up. As a kid you dream of a crowd singing your name, and when it echoed around Headingley when I celebrated my maiden Test hundred off the New Zealand attack in 2013, it sent shivers down my spine.

That first evening and the following morning – after we closed on 274–4, Jonny Bairstow unfortunately flicking straight to square leg with a hundred in his sights – represented one of the only times I felt Australia went away from their normal game plan to me. Generally, they bowled two lengths at me – very short or very full. But in this game, with my movements spot on, my leaving of the ball decisive and my stumps covered with precision, I felt I had the upper hand on the best balls each of the Australian attack could deliver. As a batsman you are always striving to be in control in any duel with a bowler. And Australia are not normally a team to give an opponent an easy ride. But I felt they were a little guilty of this whenever we lost a wicket at the other end. They always seemed keen to be bowling at the new batsman, allowing me to take singles in a bid to expose them early. Tactically astute, some might say. But un-Australian, nevertheless. This was certainly the case when nightwatchman Mark Wood came in. They tried to bowl as much as they could at him in a quest for another wicket to strengthen their position overnight and then again when we resumed.

On that first evening, Wood came out with a real determination to get through to the close. In my mind, I considered that if he could hang around next morning, I could get going at the other end. As it was, the opposite happened.

On three occasions, he hit Mitchell Johnson deliveries through or over the off-side field, and watching him dismantle the attack for that short period was reminiscent of a destructive top-order player. He has potential to become a genuine all-rounder at number eight in the long run, in my opinion. He was playing these audacious strokes against the world's most hostile fast bowler. Two more fours off Johnson followed soon after I departed.

Mitchell Starc's ability to swing the older ball both ways made it tricky first thing. With the newer ball, at times it is a lot easier to see which side of the ball is shiny and which is not, but as it gets older he is very good at covering this up and making it hard to pick out of the hand which way it is going to swing. In this instance, with it also being soft, it was difficult to force him away for runs, and trying to do so cost me.

Of course, this was a recurring theme for me as I followed one outside off-stump, but once again it was a gamble I was willing to take. Perhaps I should have taken a little bit more time to get set that morning, but he went across me at high pace and I fell into his trap and was out for 130.

Starc bagged further rewards soon afterwards, but a stand of 58 inside eight overs from Moeen Ali and Stuart Broad – 31 of them coming from the first thirteen deliveries with the second new ball – swelled the advantage further. With their latest alliance in its infancy, Trevor Bayliss had instigated a conversation with Alastair Cook about the possibility of declaring. 'Why not?' he asked. We were obviously in a strong position, with a good score on the board, and although the wicket was still pretty good, we were so far ahead of the game that if we could sneak a wicket before the lunch break it would further undermine the Australians.

Cook considered it for a few overs and realised it was the thing to do, soon after the ninth-wicket pair were separated. It was a really positive move. In terms of the match situation there was absolutely no need to force anything since we held all the cards, but not only had their entire side been dismissed cheaply in the first innings, both their opening batsmen were on a pair. Pulling out twenty minutes before lunch would test their mettle. No one wants to face three overs in a mini-session like that. There is no more uncomfortable time to bat.

Armed with a 331-run advantage, we didn't achieve the early breakthrough Cook targeted and for the first hour after lunch we were quite sloppy, in fact, chasing things a little rather than sticking to what had made us successful on the opening morning. So in our discussion at the drinks break, which Australia took on 77–0, Cook demanded the bowlers focus on being really consistent in the areas they were going to bowl. It would have been easy for the team to start flapping after that disappointing start to the second innings, and Cook was looking to reassert our control.

Australia, scoring freely, would not have required too much longer to begin entertaining thoughts of getting back into the game despite their huge deficit. But Cook's back-to-basics policy was to reap spectacular rewards. He set more defensive fields for a short period, waiting to attack again once we had separated their prolific opening pair.

By this point we had already floored two slip chances and, to add to our frustration, when we got a nick that I caught, diving to my left at third slip, Mark Wood, bowling at the pavilion end, overstepped. Initially our negative feelings were against Aleem Dar, the umpire, for not telling Wood he was close to the line. But our frustration transferred onto Woody when we discovered he had been told. You don't want to have to bowl fifteen wicket-taking balls in an innings. Attention to detail on things like that will only make this England side sharper. Wood was doing himself a disservice by challenging the line so much.

Thankfully, however, his Durham team-mate Ben Stokes marked an excellent first few overs from the Radcliffe Road End by locating the edge of Chris Rogers's bat for the second time in nine deliveries, and a carbon-copy catch from me at third slip stood on this occasion.

From that point onwards it was like a mini-replica of the first innings up until tea, as Australia slumped from 113 without loss to 136–4. Stokes bagged the first three and then played his part in a brilliant execution of a team plan. Our smart cricket got its rewards. During the series, our team talks regularly featured discussions about David Warner's tendency to hit the ball in the air just in front of square, off both front and back foot, and how if you were the man fielding at point, this should be taken into consideration. As we stood in the slips that afternoon, Cook and I discussed how Smith could be quite similar to Warner early in his innings. He is a batsman who likes to throw his hands at the ball and while he hits boundaries as a result, he doesn't always keep the ball down.

Our plan to put a fielder there was actually to make him think twice about playing square and look to play straighter down the ground. In turn, that might encourage a more regulation edge. So, in implementing it, Cook subtly told Stokes to plug the gap square where he anticipated the ball was most likely to go. Instead of making a big deal, positioning him with precision in the exact spot he wanted and drawing attention to it, he trusted Stokes to read the game. He couldn't have placed himself any better. When the big drive came out and Ben pulled off the low catch it felt like a real success for attention to detail.

I was pleased with my catching in this match and the series in general. Over the years I have not been the best fielder but working on consistency and relationships with the other slip fielders in Spain definitely helped. Intensive practice to both left- and right-hand batsmen – because the angles at which the ball comes and the way you have to dive obviously differ with each – proved crucial. So extensive was the work that I even got used to catching the ball fingers up and fingers down depending on the height. It sounds simple but it takes some getting used to.

My second legitimate one off Stokes's bowling, accounting

for Shaun Marsh, was much more conventional. Ben was a threat with the ball throughout that second innings, but never more so than in his evening spell just after the floodlights had been switched on. He might not have been everyone's favourite to push us towards victory with a bucketload of wickets – but when he got the opportunity he took it.

Ben had experienced a quiet couple of Test matches and when that happens you know he is never far away from doing something out of the ordinary. He was unplayable at times, and the left-handers in particular struggled against him. It wasn't just a replication of Jimmy Anderson, it was a replication of Jimmy Anderson at his best, and after the game, sharing a beer, Jimmy was in awe of how Ben had bowled. To have England's leading wicket-taker, one of the best swing bowlers to have played the game, reacting like that is the compliment of all compliments.

But for that astonishing first-innings effort from Stuart Broad, Ben's display would have been good enough for Man of the Match. The skill and control he displayed for sustained periods might not necessarily have been associated with his bowling previously, yet those at Durham will tell you he gets it to go through the air further than anyone at the club. During that early-evening passage of play, he set up Peter Nevill an absolute treat, shaping a couple of deliveries away before angling one back in to claim an lbw with no shot offered. There was one very full delivery to

Mitchell Johnson that swung so late it made the batsman look silly – his feet were nowhere near it.

Since his recall in the spring of 2015, Ben has made some fantastic contributions to the England team and the beauty of his bowling is that, while it is obviously second to his batting, he has the ability to play so many different roles. The aggressor, who bowls short, banging the ball into the wicket, with a full follow-up delivery; the defensive holding role, bowling one side of the wicket and drying up the runs; or the attacking swing bowler. To be able to play three different roles, not always to perfection admittedly, makes him such an attractive proposition. The challenge now is for him to get better at each facet. To have that kind of player up your sleeve is a massive asset for a captain.

Because of his action – quite front-on, with a tendency to get his hand the left side of the ball in delivery – he naturally swings it across the left-handers. But what he likes to do most is to get the ball to go the other way, and that makes him very awkward to face – because he does it with little noticeable change.

One of the features of this stunning display was that the ball would hoop one way and then almost swing the other at the last moment. I'm not sure that Ben could even tell you how he does that. It must be a combination of his action and getting the seam in exactly the right position. But to witness it from the slips is truly amazing.

When he lured Johnson into a false drive at 6.21 p.m.,

holding the match ball aloft to the crowd, there was that element of excitement knowing that we were so close. Around the field you could sense that everyone had the same thoughts: 'Let's do this tonight.' Unfortunately, bad light prevented any suggestion of taking the extra half-hour to finish the job. Typically, Cook maintained his calm exterior and kept us in check as we got back into the dressing room. I am sure he wanted his hands on the urn that night as well, but this was a time for composure.

On the third morning, Ben was on the money straight away, and backing up that spell with another one of high class justified Cook's decision to continue with him at the other end to Mark Wood, who had four balls of an over to complete from the Pavilion End. Wood is a nightmare for the lower order to face because of his skiddy action and ability to swing the ball at a pace close to 90 mph. That must be really hard for guys when they are not proficient batsmen and are new to the crease. From experience in the nets, I can say that the biggest problem when facing him is that he is on to you before you know it.

Our Durham pair could not have bowled better that morning, providing a mixture of high-class yorkers, such as the one that spectacularly did for Hazlewood, and swinging deliveries flirting with the outside edge, like the one that flew from Mitchell Starc's bat to Ian Bell at second slip from a Stokes delivery.

A wicket apiece left us on the verge, and with Australia nine down I had all sorts of thoughts about fancy knee-slides, fist-pumps and piggybacks when the time for celebration arrived. Of course, that was all forgotten when, from the sixty-second delivery of the day, the moment arrived. Instinctively, we all did the same thing. It is one of the great photographs from the series: all of us with arms aloft to signify that Nathan Lyon had just crashed the ball into his stumps via an inside edge off Wood.

You spend so much time working together, towards one goal, that when the moment finally comes, it's the one thing you've not planned for. I know personally, as we jumped up and down in a group hug on the edge of the pitch, that there was a healthy amount of pride at the achievement mingled with a touch of relief that we had managed to get across the line. Around me were ten mirror images. Elation reflected in each and every face. There were guys in that group who had enjoyed really strong series and been dominant throughout and others who had struggled. But if you had been in the middle of the throng it would not have mattered who you looked at. You would not have been able to tell which guys were which. And that was the most incredible thing about this incredible team.

It was about a group of players who had been able to accomplish a collective goal. There is no better feeling when you are looking back through a series of this magnitude than to consider there was always someone, if you

England v Australia
(4th Test)

Played at Trent Bridge, Nottingham, on 6–8 August 2015

Umpires: Aleem Dar & S Ravi (TV: M Erasmus)
Referee: RS Madugalle
Toss: England

AUSTRALIA

CJL Rogers	c Cook b Broad	0	c Root b Stokes		52
DA Warner	c Buttler b Wood	0	c Broad b Stokes		64
SPD Smith	c Root b Broad	6	c Stokes b Broad		5
SE Marsh	c Bell b Broad	0	c Root b Stokes		2
MJ Clarke*	c Cook b Broad	10	c Bell b Wood		13
AC Voges	c Stokes b Broad	1	not out		51
PM Nevill†	b Finn	2	lbw b Stokes		17
MG Johnson	c Root b Broad	13	c Cook b Stokes		5
MA Starc	c Root b Broad	1	c Bell b Stokes		0
JR Hazlewood	not out	4	b Wood		0
NM Lyon	c Stokes b Broad	9	b Wood		4
Extras	(lb 11, nb 3)	14	(b 20, lb 16, w 1, nb 3)		40
Total	(18.3 overs)	**60**	(72.4 overs)		**253**

ENGLAND

A Lyth	c Nevill b Starc	14
AN Cook*	lbw b Starc	43
IR Bell	lbw b Starc	1
JE Root	c Nevill b Starc	130
JM Bairstow	c Rogers b Hazlewood	74
MA Wood	b Starc	28
BA Stokes	c Nevill b Hazlewood	5
JC Buttler†	b Starc	12
MM Ali	c Smith b Johnson	38
SCJ Broad	not out	24
ST Finn	not out	0
Extras	(b 14, lb 2, w 2, nb 4)	22
Total	(for 9 wkts dec) (85.2 overs)	**391**

ENGLAND	O	M	R	W	O	M	R	W
Broad	9.3	5	15	8	16	5	36	1
Wood	3	0	13	1	17.4	3	69	3
Finn	6	0	21	1	12	4	42	0
Stokes	21	8	36					6
Ali	6	0	34					0

AUSTRALIA	O	M	R	W
Starc	27	2	111	6
Hazlewood	24	4	97	2
Johnson	21.2	2	102	1
Lyon	10	1	47	0
Warner	3	0	18	0

Fall of wickets:			
	Aus	Eng	Aus
1st	4	32	113
2nd	10	34	130
3rd	10	96	136
4th	15	269	136
5th	21	297	174
6th	29	306	224
7th	33	320	236
8th	46	332	242
9th	47	390	243
10th	60	–	253

Close of play: Day 1: Eng (1) 274-4 (Root 124*, Wood 2*, 65 overs)
                      Day 2: Aus (2) 241-7 (Voges 48*, Starc 0*, 62.2 overs)

Man of the Match: SCJ Broad
Result: **England won by an innings and 78 runs**

were not able to perform, who had got your back. Full credit to the coaching staff for creating the environment where that mentality thrived, but also to the unit itself, because ultimately we came through it together. Obviously there were minor disagreements on things out on the field, but no one holds grudges and that's the template you want of a team moving forward. When your backs are against the wall, you want to know you are all in it together.

A good proportion of us had come to learn how brutal Ashes cricket can be, having won comfortably in 2013 and then suffered the ignominy of a 5–0 whitewash in the return series later that year. In an England v Australia conflict you win or you lose; there is no middle ground. And while we had ended 599 days of waiting to answer that 2013–14 humiliation, the inevitability was that Australia's team would be dismantled.

First evidence of this to us in the opposing team came at the post-match presentation when Michael Clarke, speaking to Mike Atherton, confirmed, despite a pre-match denial that he was considering quitting, that the Oval Test match would be his last before retirement. Later, it emerged that he had been emotional at the team hotel on the Friday night and had told a few people of his intentions, but we didn't find out until after the ceremony. When he said that he needed his number four batsman to come off the plane following defeat at Edgbaston, we knew he was struggling and it is always a boost when you have the opposition captain under the pump.

Not that we could claim his derailing as a concentrated tactical ploy. As with any great player, you try to target them during periods of struggle and the more balls you can bowl in a challenging area at the top of off-stump the better. With a player like Clarke, you want to get him before his feet really get going. That's when you've got your best chance of dismissing him, and even when he fought through fifty minutes at Trent Bridge, we kept plugging away and Wood was rewarded with a nick to Ian Bell at second slip. Obviously, he felt under enough pressure to move himself down a spot in the order and to sacrifice Mitchell Marsh, his all-rounder, in the process, but the change did not help.

'You never want to walk away from the game but I think my performances in this series and the last twelve months have not been acceptable to me. I pride myself on leading from the front, so that's been disappointing. You build yourself up for the big tournaments, the big series. One-day cricket is about the World Cup and Test cricket is about the Ashes,' Clarke said. 'I certainly tried my best, the boys tried their best and we got outplayed. We got beaten. Now it's time for the next generation of players, the next captain to have his opportunity to try and build the team and get them ready for the next Ashes series.'

Clarke was a brilliant servant to Australian cricket and you could feel the respect for him on our balcony as we joined in to applaud his career with the other 17,000 people at Trent Bridge. Credit to him as a player for that. You don't have to like opponents, and I know he was not Mr

Popular with everyone, including some of the guys huddled around me, but when it came to ability and performance, there was 100 per cent respect.

As a team, we were aware he was taking a bit of a battering from the press back in Australia. But even then I cannot imagine retiring from international cricket was an easy decision to make. After all, he still possessed an outstanding career CV. Even though he was defeated twice in series over here, his record as captain of Australia was exceptional, winning twenty-four of his forty-seven matches, and elevating his batting average to 51.92 from a career return of just under 50 in the process. Half his twenty-eight hundreds came during this time.

As a kid I admired the way he looked to take the attack to the opposition. He played spin really well and on the rare occasions I bowled to him, I always felt that he was in control of the situation, not me, even if the ball was spinning. It shouldn't have done.

Following Clarke's emotional address, there were tears on our side of the divide too. Yes, Alastair Cook cried. You don't even have to know him personally to realise that was most unlike him. He's normally a very calm, down-to-earth, matter-of-fact, emotions-intact sort of guy, especially in press conferences. But the culmination of what he had been through since the start of his previous Ashes series as captain – be it his personal struggles in form, or questions over his leadership – and what we had achieved against expectation here all seemed to come bubbling to the surface.

To come through the other side and build a new team clearly made him extremely proud. Few had given us a chance, but we had played like a band of eleven brothers and clicked at the right times. 'We've done something I didn't think was quite possible at the beginning of the summer,' he told those who remained to join the celebrations – and I don't think a single person left.

From the group's perspective we are extremely proud of what Cook achieved this year. He made a significant change of style in his captaincy, allowing himself to open up and not be afraid to speak to previous captains, take advice off people he might not necessarily have before, and turn to aggression as a default position. He drove that style of play from within our dressing room. Allowing himself to change gained our utmost respect. The team he took over had a lot of established players in it and he had to adapt to having fewer dead-cert performers in his team. Credit to the ECB for sticking with him as captain, because we reaped the rewards and I believe we will continue to do so.

The feeling of ecstasy did not leave me for the rest of the day, through forty-five minutes of post-match speeches, multiple laps of honour and a couple of hours signing autographs around a ground still bursting at the seams with people. Our relationship with the crowds is important to this England team – we take our responsibilities seriously but place an emphasis on having fun and this revealed itself in our interactions that afternoon. Never more so than when we forced Mark Wood to get his imaginary horse out to play. It's genius, and seeing him larking around like that in match situations when things aren't going your way, or a session's dragging, gives you a bit of a lift. The novelty for him – since doing it for the first time in an England shirt after taking his first Test catch at Lord's – may have worn off. But it hasn't for the public, judging by the crowd reaction to his gallop on the boundary edge.

My own off-field performance got decent reviews too. Veuve Clicquot had kindly donated a few bottles of champagne for our consumption in the dressing room but obviously, boys being boys, we sprayed it instead of drinking it. My grandpa Don always tells me that instead of popping them to spray, I should be slipping one or two into my bag to bring home for him. But when you are as giddy as we were, you will seize on any opportunity to soak other folk. Particularly a Sky Sports commentator, as Jimmy Anderson proved when he completely drenched Ian Ward – to the point that Wardy reckoned he was getting feedback from his earpiece.

It had been during the interview between the pair directly before this incident that I had seen our Albert Einstein team mask lying on the table and taken the opportunity to get into camera shot wearing it. When they went back to the studio, Wardy then challenged me to do an interview with it on for a bit of fun.

When he started the interview by saying, 'Hi, I've got Bob Willis here with me,' I'd been dropped in at the deep end. Initially, I'd just planned to talk like an old man that had sneaked into the dressing room but he had thrown down the gauntlet and so I got into Bob mode. I have always tried my hand at impressions because I like a bit of a giggle – we all have a go at taking off the commentators, past players and each other in the dressing room – but I wouldn't say I was particularly good at any of them. But I'd heard Bumble do his Bob a few times on commentary and with a couple of ales already inside me I just went for it. 'Send him down!'

Right: One of the challenges for me heading into the series in South Africa was facing Dale Steyn, someone I had never come up against before.

Below: It was an emotional moment when Jonny Bairstow scored his hundred in Cape Town. You could see how much it meant to him.

Left: This was one of my best hundreds for England as the surface in Johannesburg was difficult and it was a crucial Test match.

Below: AB de Villiers (centre) is one of the players I admire for his ability to transfer his skills across all formats. It was credit to our attack that they muzzled him during the series.

I am extremely proud to have played alongside James Taylor. An extraordinary player, a model professional, a great team man and an even better bloke.

Winning in South Africa is right up there amongst my most enjoyable Test moments.

The Gayle Force blew us away in our opening game of the World Twenty20.

Up against it, needing a win to stay in the competition, we performed exceptionally under pressure against the South Africans.

I thought this was a good idea at the time – but looking back hitting that full toss from Kagiso Rabada into the deep was borderline stupid.

Captain Morgan: we took our lead from Eoin during the World T20, practising what he preached.

'Yes, no, maybe, cheers Stokesy.' A calamitous run-out cost me my wicket against Afghanistan.

The semi-final against New Zealand was as good as we played all tournament – bring on the World Cup final.

It was a brave decision to bowl me for the second over but the plan to get Chris Gayle out went even better than expected.

No words can help in this situation. Ben Stokes was devastated but good teams share the burden of disappointment.

Everything started to sink in during the post-match presentation. We were absolutely gutted to have fallen just short after a phenomenal effort throughout the tournament.

Carlos Brathwaite is a big man, and he came down on us like a ton of bricks in that final over. His ball striking was phenomenal under pressure.

Brathwaite puts us on the verge of defeat with a dream-shattering strike.

All credit to West Indies for out-performing us when it mattered.

11 A PLACE IN HISTORY

SATURDAY, 8 August: Ashes winner and world number one Test batsman. Sunday, 9 August: Yorkshire League drinks carrier.

They say a lot can change in twenty-four hours, but this deterioration in status was quite drastic. Not that I minded. As you can probably imagine, I was in a world of pain the day after the night before and sitting around was only going to make it feel worse, so when I got home that lunchtime I popped along to Abbeydale Park to get some fresh air to clear my head and watch Bill and the rest of the Sheffield Collegiate first XI take on Harrogate.

The previous evening I had necked a few drinks in the Trent Bridge dressing room as my England team-mates toasted my reaching of the summit in the Test batting rankings, amongst other things. Until it was mentioned in the aftermath of our victory – by an innings and 78 runs – I had no idea I had nipped in ahead of Steve Smith at the top, but to do so was something I was extremely proud of, naturally.

In Nottingham, the people we chatted to in our revelry

were full of hearty congratulations. Typically, the lads at Collegiate were less complimentary. You can always rely on your mates to keep you grounded. Forty-eight hours earlier Bill had been running drinks for us at Trent Bridge, and here I saw a chance to reciprocate after a little egging-on from some of the club members watching. So I toddled off to the bar to make up the squash and then had to jog on into a huddle of lads I'd known for years. I was like a lamb to the slaughter.

They were all taking the mick out of me, complaining that I might be the world's best batsman, but I was also the world's worst maker of orange cordial. 'It's a bit weak, this,' they complained. 'Shouldn't you be off scoring a double hundred somewhere?' Being there for that five minutes was really nice for me. I always like going to watch the lads I grew up with playing their club cricket and to see them enjoying it as much as I used to, and as much as I enjoy playing international cricket now.

In the immediate aftermath, it was also nice to share a momentous series victory like that with friends and family. On that surreal Saturday afternoon, Mum and my grandpa Don had been amongst those celebrating in the dressing room with the other families. Dad was miffed because he couldn't make it, having committed to playing in a golf competition earlier that week. He was present for the first two days and had intended to come back on the Saturday afternoon, but that plan was deemed redundant when we rushed through the Australian batting on the Friday evening. He was desperate for us to produce something even more spectacular so that he could have stayed and soaked it in. Bill was absent too, because of back-to-back Yorkshire League games that weekend.

Having Grandpa there was really special, though, because from being a little whippersnapper up to my teenage years he ferried me absolutely everywhere to play cricket. To be able to share a moment like that with him filled me with pride. He's a classical Yorkshireman and on his 80th birthday a couple of weeks later he told me how proud his father would have been to know that his great-grandson played for Yorkshire, let alone England. If he'd known I would go on to wear the white rose, he would have fallen off his chair, because he lived for and loved the game.

With something tangible to drink to, we all gave it a pretty good go that evening and we remained in the dressing room until nearly ten o'clock. Our parents, partners and in some cases children had all been present at some point during the celebrations but after the champagne and snacks in the afternoon, the girls left us to make a proper night of it. Carrie, I am pleased to report, got right into the spirit of things and had to be tucked up in bed before we headed into Nottingham city centre – at roughly the same time as Alastair Cook's two-year-old daughter, something I have not let her forget since.

In all seriousness, that long-haul day of celebration with our loved ones around was something that will stick with me for ever, no matter what I go on to achieve in my career.

It also featured the first singing of a brand-new England team song, the product of the creative talents of Jimmy Anderson and Mark Wood. It is not for public consumption – some privileges need to be contained within the four walls of the dressing room. All I can say is that after all the emotions, the highs and lows you go through on the field, standing there being able to sing it with the ink barely dry and the Ashes in the bag was so enjoyable. We'd all been given a hymn sheet and half an hour to learn the words. Such fun times.

Most of the people we partied alongside until the early hours were in high spirits too, coming up to us expressing how they'd enjoyed watching us and what we'd done for the country. When you hear stuff like that, it fulfils what we pledge to deliver as the national team. We want our followers not only to be interested in the score but to be there with us as part of what we are trying to achieve.

The week-long gap between the fourth and fifth Tests allowed us some down time to take stock of our achievements. I'd never been one to study the international rankings and although it was a nice fleeting accolade – when Michael Vaughan congratulated me he said, 'Hope you last a little longer than the three weeks I did!' – that kind of thing has no real relevance to my career ambitions. What I really want to do is help England win Test matches. That's how you get your most enjoyment as a player. I would much rather be drinking cold beers with the other lads at the end of the game than have my individual efforts lauded by strangers. Sure, to be number one, with the likes of Steve Smith, Hashim Amla and A.B. de Villiers beneath me, was a pleasing sign of how far I'd come in three years as an international cricketer.

But there was a sense of unfinished business from a team perspective. One further chance for victory remained before the closure of the Test match summer and it would leave a longer-lasting impression if achieved. No England side had won 4–1 against Australia at home before and here was our chance to make history. Keen to avoid his players falling into the trap of treating the fifth and final match as a dead rubber, Alastair Cook took the time to ring each and every member of the squad individually during the break to remind us how special it would be to become that team. He asked us to concentrate on how good it would sound to say we had beaten the Australians 4–1.

Naturally, part of you just wants it all to be over so that you can get your hands on the urn, but the desire to win truly outweighed any sense of complacency that week. To beat a team that began as pre-series favourites in such comprehensive fashion would have been a great reward for our endeavours. Any England team that managed that would be remembered alongside other great teams of the past, and to be honest, we needed something like that to catalyse our efforts. It was decided that, with the series result decided, worsening Jimmy Anderson's healing side by recalling him was not a risk worth taking but, for the record, anyone thinking that our standards slipped that week would be wrong. Our intensity in net sessions and in fielding practice was as high as it had been throughout the seven weeks. We approached it in exactly the same way as the previous four matches and were shaping up really nicely. We just wanted to crack on with finishing the job. Winning matches does that to you, and one of the things we spoke about in the build-up to this match was that one more victory would also put us second in the Test standings behind South Africa.

We were pleased to welcome a guest of honour for our first practice session at the Kia Oval on the afternoon of Tuesday, 18 August, as Roy Hodgson, the England football manager, came to watch. Earlier that day he'd met up with Peter Brukner, Australia's team doctor, who had worked under him at Liverpool. As he likes cricket, he hung around to see us train after lunch and this gave us a real thrill. As you have probably realised by now, the highlight of our training sessions is our football warm-up, and naturally enough we were all keen to impress.

For a bit of fun, Roy called us into a huddle before we started and told us how much he'd enjoyed watching us play throughout the summer, how much he'd admired our achievements and, for humour value, added, 'Look, lads, there's a Euro 2016 qualifier around the corner and as far as I'm concerned everyone is up for selection against San Marino. Make sure you put in a strong performance.' Of course, this drew a few laughs, but not as many as moments later when, from the back of the group, a voice chimed, 'Cheers, gaffer.' It was a perfect piece of comic timing. It was typical Moeen Ali. You might not get this from his quiet on-field persona, but Moeen is quite outgoing and very funny. You can always find him in the middle of what's going on in our dressing room.

The mood remained light in the build-up thanks to the Cricket United fundraiser that asked current and past Ashes players to sketch team-mates for charity. Obviously we didn't spend huge amounts of time drawing them, but to have a laugh and caricature your mates was good fun, and I have to admit that Freddie Flintoff's one of me was outstanding, the cheeky sod. Of course, I've always had a reputation for looking young for my age and others will tell you that he summed me up perfectly by putting me in an ECB nappy. I got my own back with a take on his physical state at the time of the visit to Downing Street and the ride on the open-top bus back in 2005, as well as doing one of that memorable winning team. I've always been a pretty handy sketcher and art was my best subject at school after PE. To be involved in any way in the raising of around £20,000 for three charities was extremely satisfying.

There was also some pranking that Tuesday night ahead of a Yorkshire Cricket Club dinner at Lord's. The five of us from the club in the final Test squad were asked to go along with our former second XI coach, Paul Farbrace, who stitched Adil Rashid up a treat that night. It was a black tie do but as we were on Test duty, we were told to go in our England suits. When Rash asked whether he needed a tie, Farby playfully told him no, which naturally caused a right commotion when we got there to find everyone was dressed to the nines. It meant a dash to the Lord's reception to enquire whether they had any lost property. Beggars can't be choosers in that situation and he ended up walking back into the Long Room bar with an egg-and-bacon number covered in stains.

There was an awkward moment for me too when we walked into the Long Room and saw the seating plan. As he is a former Yorkshire player, and a highly popular one at that, I was aware that Darren Lehmann would be in attendance. But as he is also Australia's coach I didn't fancy sitting next to him on the top table. He proved excellent company, however, and I made a conscious effort to talk to him about anything other than the Ashes. We were there to celebrate Yorkshire's history, not the history of the Ashes, and more specifically the first County Championship title since Lehmann was a player in 2001. When the conversation inevitably did turn to the A-word, he was very complimentary about the way that England played.

He was a good sport when it came to his part in the Q&A too. In fact, he had the floor in stitches when he spoke about the Trent Bridge Test, and how he'd felt like an RAF pilot in the parachute regiment. He said he seemed to be waving batsmen out of the door as quickly as the parachutists – telling each one in turn 'go, go, go' every time the green light came on. That bit was fine. The difficulty was when I was on the end of the questions and was expected to answer, with Lehmann next to me and Andrew Strauss and Colin Graves, two of my bosses at the ECB, on the other side of the table. But I negotiated my way through it all without incident – I think.

As it happens, I remain indebted to the man sitting alongside me that evening. I'd had some dealings with Darren way before he became Australia coach. First of all in 2006, when Yorkshire Under-15s had a game against Lancashire Under-15s at Old Trafford as the warm-up to an Andrew Flintoff benefit match. People were pouring in to watch this match and for us it was a real thrill to play in front of such a big crowd. Because Lehmann and Anthony McGrath were playing in the game, they popped over to coach us. I opened the batting and, playing to type, couldn't hit the ball off the square. I only faced perhaps twenty balls in the ten overs I was in and had a dozen to my name, but one of the two coaches was not happy. I could see Darren on the sidelines, waving his hands at me and mouthing, 'Play some shots!' His brutal assessment, after I was dismissed, was that if I wanted to play for the full Yorkshire team, I'd have to score quicker than that.

Four years later, at the start of the 2010–11 winter, I was dispatched to Adelaide for five months to play for grade club Prospect at the weekends and attended the Darren

Lehmann Academy in the week. The man himself became Queensland coach that Australian season, so we didn't see a lot of him, but the sessions we did do helped progress me as a player.

As a 19-year-old, spending an extended period of time away from home, playing in different conditions and having to do things for myself helped no end in terms of personal development. There wasn't just cricket to take care of. I also had to organise myself off the field, much as a student does when they head off to university, I imagine. It was a little bit of a student lifestyle at times too, especially when it came to socialising. My local pub, The Windmill, was a regular haunt. Then, on Thursdays, it would be a trip to the General Havelock for a late one. But there was a responsibility when it came to the weekend – as the club's overseas player, I was expected to perform and that meant scoring runs every Saturday. This period was good for me and I returned home feeling a more rounded person and feeling good about my game.

As much as anything he said about playing the game, it was the Lehmann batting drills that stuck in my mind. One was to crank the bowling machine up to a speed somewhere between 80 and 85 mph and take a position half a dozen yards out of the crease to face it. In effect, you were facing a pace bowler 16 yards away rather than 22. You would do so for a few deliveries, then edge a little bit closer. The same process was repeated until you no longer felt able to hit the ball properly. Then it was time to go back to where you started. Despite no changes being made to the speed setting, the effect was that the bowling now felt really slow. Of course, it's an illusion created by sharpening your reaction time – an excellent technical preparation for facing fast bowlers. Once you've combated 85, you might raise it a notch or two, all the way up to 90.

Another one he taught us involved putting a whiteboard down on the playing surface and loading the bowling machine with tennis balls. He would turn the machine up to maximum speed and when these balls hit the whiteboard, instead of being absorbed temporarily in the surface as they would on AstroTurf, they would skid off at high pace. Using tennis balls in this way was very good for practising against short-of-a-length stuff and genuine bouncers as they would sting the ribs rather than crack them if you got in a tangle. That was the first time I did that kind of stuff, although some of the lads I play with now do similar things with a whiteboard and those spongy chew balls you throw to dogs.

His approach to spin was an eye-opener. He was absolutely adamant that spinners should not be allowed to bowl at you, simply existing to be treated with complete disdain. He used to tell us what a joke it was that he had taken so many wickets in first-class cricket with his slow left-armers. In his eyes, he saw facing spinners as an opportunity to get from 10 to 50 as quickly as possible. That was a mentality I'd certainly never considered before. So I came back from Australia thinking that I had to find ways of dominating spin. I might not be as dominant or aggressive as he was, but I've always tried to make sure I'm in control against it.

In the final Test at The Oval it was swing and seam, not spin, that were expected to be the predominant factors and the decent amount of cloud cover in the vicinity provided good reason for Alastair Cook to ask Australia to bat first after winning the toss on 20 August. But, although we bowled well at the start, we didn't get the rewards we deserved. We absolutely dominated, to the extent that Australia had managed only 19–0 after fourteen overs when drinks were taken.

In assessing the first hour you would have concluded that we were in control and the pressure was on our opponents. But the balance of power flipped immediately. The very next over felt like a turning point: David Warner counter-attacked and Chris Rogers doubled the score he managed in his first forty-two deliveries by hitting his forty-third to the boundary. Sometimes a natural break in the game can disrupt one side and allow the other to gain momentum. By the end of the session, Australia were scoring at three runs an over.

It was as if Australia had learned their lessons from their first hour at Trent Bridge – and that is exactly the kind of reaction you expect from a quality side. Their innings featured big opening stands more often than not, but in retaliation throughout the five matches our strength more often than not was to follow breaking it up by taking a cluster of wickets. This time we couldn't do that, despite the fact that, bar the second hour of that first morning, we bowled well all day. Yet we only had three wickets to show for it.

Our chances of fighting back diminished on the second morning when, immediately after Ben Stokes dismissed Adam Voges, Finn took a wicket with another no-ball. As a result, we were denied two in two deliveries and two new batsmen at the crease with the score on 332–5. Instead, Steve Smith, no doubt nervous nearing his hundred, was reprieved. Just as had been the case at Trent Bridge, we were having to create more chances than necessary. Steve remained on 99 wickets – perhaps it was his desperation to get to 100 that made him overstride.

Having done it twice, it must have felt like it wasn't going to happen. In Nottingham, it was Peter Nevill who prospered and here Smith went on to transform the 92 he had when Jos Buttler claimed the catch behind the wicket into 143. Finn finally got his man – and had reached three figures in between with the removal of the recalled Mitchell Marsh – but we have high standards and he will have been livid with himself. It contributed to Australia posting 481 when it might have been 100 fewer.

During my Long Room Q&A with Yorkshire supporters three days earlier, I had been quizzed about facing high pace and I answered that I didn't think any batsman in the world particularly enjoyed facing it. I told everyone in the room that it was quite intimidating to have someone like Mitchell Johnson stood at the end of his mark preparing to run in and bowl bouncers at you. Even though at times you might feel comfortable against it, it would be wrong to say it was an enjoyable experience. Rightly or wrongly we were told that Jacques Kallis, one of the great players of fast bowling in the modern era, said that he only started to play it better once he accepted that it was intimidating and quite uncomfortable. He wouldn't be the only one.

No wonder then, with Lehmann listening intently, that when I went out to bat at The Oval I got a peppering. Although I hit my first ball for four over point off Peter Siddle – a last-minute selection ahead of Pat Cummins – the transformation from Trent Bridge, where I felt really fluent in my movements, was incredible. At the start of any innings I like to get bat on ball and be dominant. Even if I don't feel 100 per cent in control from ball one, I always like to give that impression. So that even if I am leaving the ball, I am doing it in a very assured way. But from that boundary ball onwards they denied me the chance.

Michael Clarke, in the final Test of his career, proved very astute at this point, putting Johnson on, placing two men back and therefore making it hard to take him on. I certainly couldn't do so in the game situation – two wickets down early, requiring 282 to avoid the follow-on. Being unable to be aggressive contributed to my lack of fluency, I am sure. Sometimes you go out to bat and things just click. On other occasions they don't. I wasn't timing the ball, my feet were not going as well as they had previously and I just felt as though I was fighting myself for form.

Although I had opted to battle through it, eventually I got a good ball off Mitchell Marsh. I don't think I nicked it, but there was a big noise and they referred it. It was very similar to Ben Stokes's dismissal of Michael Clarke in the first innings. He referred it after being given out by the on-field umpire but lost his challenge. Here, Australia were trying to overturn another on-field call and although there was no Hot Spot mark on the TV replays, there was a spike on Snicko.

From 60–2 we were blown away. My dismissal followed swiftly on the heels of that of Ian Bell. By the close of play we were eight down for 107 and our dreams of a 4–1 win were long gone. Peter Siddle deserved a lot of credit for this turnaround for the Australians. Having not played at all throughout the series, he came in and performed really well, bowling consistent areas to build pressure at both ends.

He may not have got an abundance of wickets as a reward, but he definitely made it easier for the guys he was bowling in tandem with. He was brought in to provide control, something the Australians expected but did not necessarily get from Josh Hazlewood; he had not played a great deal of Test cricket leading up to the series and comparisons to Glenn McGrath were not helpful. That's a big name to have to live up to, and while Hazlewood is undoubtedly a quality bowler – someone destined to be on the international scene for a long time – being expected to replicate the game plan of one of the greatest fast bowlers of all time in your first Ashes series would be hard for anyone.

It was evident that Michael Clarke – to whom we had provided a guard of honour when he came out to bat in the first innings to show our respect – was determined to say goodbye to his career on a high. If someone serves their country for that long and returns such good numbers, it merits recognition. There was to be no sentiment from us once he was at the crease, of course, and I'm sure he wouldn't have expected it to be any other way. He was equally ruthless in pursuit of victory, even changing tactics to do so.

Typically, Australia like to bat again and we weren't sure if they would enforce the follow-on after they wrapped up our innings for 149 on the third morning. Their preference is to hammer away at you, demoralising you in the field by swelling their 200-plus lead quickly and getting out of range. It is a policy that serves a double purpose: it provides their bowlers with some respite and makes sure they don't have to bat last on a deteriorating wicket. On this occasion, with the forecast for poor weather later in the match in mind, Clarke chose, in his last match as captain, to enforce the follow-on for the first time.

For our part, we realised that if we could get off to a

good start, it could have an effect on their bowlers' legs towards the end of that third day. Unfortunately, we didn't.

Uncomfortable with my ducking-and-diving policy against Johnson in the first innings, I reflected that my success against him had been a product of taking him on. So I vowed that if he gave me any opportunities to score this time I would take them. That meant if he went short, I would go hard at the ball. Of course, when you are following on, it looks terrible when it doesn't come off and you are caught at fine leg, as I was after a dozen overs at the crease.

But there had been occasions earlier in the series, and indeed against New Zealand earlier in the summer, when I did take it on early and no one said anything critical. They don't tend to when you hit the ball for four or get off strike. Yet, if you get caught on the hook, it's seen as inexcusable and foolish. It's one of cricket's curiosities to me. No one says anything if you get out trying to block. I am of the belief that if the shot is a strength of a batsman, then you should go for it.

Look at someone like Glenn Maxwell in one-day cricket: he plays the reverse sweep as much as, if not more than, the cover drive. When he gets out reverse sweeping, no one grumbles, because it's a shot we know he plays regularly and successfully. Of course I am going to get out hooking if I play it a lot, but I believe I am going to get plenty of runs doing so too. The decision I made in this particular game didn't work out, unfortunately. If I had played the same stroke off a bowler operating from the Vauxhall End, the ball would have ended up ten rows back and the reaction to hitting a six would have been that I was being positive, looking to take the game to Australia. To my mind, that's the same shot and should not be considered differently.

When you are out in the middle you have a split second to make a decision. Maybe I could have lined him up a bit longer and got out of the way of a few more, but I decided I was ready and perished, the ball steepling straight to Mitchell Starc on the rope at fine leg.

Alastair Cook's decision to revise his game paid greater dividends. In the first innings he got what had appeared to be an unplayable delivery off Nathan Lyon that gripped on the pitch. The turn directed it past his outside edge into the top of off-stump. It would have been very easy for him to dismiss that delivery as a jaffa, as I did, but he came off, looked at it and came to the conclusion that his downfall had been caused by getting stuck on the crease. He said he had been done for length and needed to get out to the ball a bit more. Which is exactly what he did in the second innings, in almost exaggerated manner. He'd worked hard at doing exactly that during the morning practice and it shows how good a player he is that he was able to make such a big adjustment in such a short space of time.

His five-and-a-half-hour innings on that third day really was a valiant effort. He played out of his skin to make batting look a lot easier than it was. When wickets are going down at the other end, it's never easy to retain the strength of character and discipline in your own game. He did that extremely well and got deep into the final half-hour of the day. It was just three overs from the close, in fact, when Clarke's punt on Steve Smith's leg-spin was to have a devastating impact. A few pies were followed by an absolute belter that spun and took a little feather of an edge on its way to short leg.

It was a real shame Alastair fell 15 runs shy of that elusive hundred against Australia, because although he provided some valuable contributions across the five matches, all top-order batsmen crave that big score. But Australia are always dangerous with the new ball and so Cook's performances in the series were vital. Even 30s and 40s – allowing guys like myself and Ian Bell to come in and benefit during easier periods – can prove crucial to the team's health. Openers pride themselves on setting up games, so that the bowlers have the opportunity to take twenty wickets. He'd managed that without the moment of personal glory.

Both times in London, the Australian bowlers appeared to be more at home than us. In those conditions, when there was nothing on offer sideways and little in the way of pace or bounce, they seemed to know what lengths to bowl. Both the Lord's and Oval pitches were not very responsive and they were better at getting something out of them. Mitchell Marsh was a good example of this, as was Peter

Siddle: bowlers who look to bowl wicket to wicket, hit the pitch hard and give the batsmen nothing. That is exactly what you have to do as a seam bowler operating in Australia. The Dukes ball alters the dynamic somewhat, as it does tend to swing around a bit more. That makes it harder to control, and when it is seaming around, you generally need to bowl that little bit fuller. Australians are not necessary as accustomed to this as their English counterparts and so our attack was more threatening when conditions were most English. The series was not won by the amount of runs we scored but by taking twenty wickets in three out of five games.

At The Oval, with a race against the rain that was expected to arrive on Sunday afternoon and not cease until the fifth evening, the Australians kept finding ways to take wickets. And on one occasion – in the ninth over after tea – they did so despite contravening the laws of the game. When Jonny Bairstow jabbed a delivery to short-leg off Nathan Lyon, he turned, tucked his bat under his arm and walked off, I could not believe it. Straight away I realised he should not have been out because, during the completion of an extremely smart catch, the ball clearly struck the helmet worn by the fielder, Adam Voges. Jumping to my feet, I made my way to the front of the dressing-room balcony and tried to get Jonny to stop short of leaving the field, without making too much of a scene.

Once you cross that boundary line it's game over as far as your innings is concerned and as Jonny had fallen foul of this before, I couldn't believe what I was seeing. Back on the 2012–13 tour of India, he was called into the England team as a replacement for Ian Bell, who had returned home for the birth of his first child. In the first innings of that second Test, just before lunch, facing the slow left-armer Pragyan Ojha, Jonny popped the ball to silly point, and as Gautam Gambhir grasped for it, it brushed the grille of his helmet. I had never experienced that kind of situation before – but although taken unawares I became involved in what happened next.

A couple of minutes later, Andy Flower, then England coach, saw the replay on the TV in the dressing room and said, 'That shouldn't be out.' With the dismissal occurring on the eve of the interval, all the players had left the field together and Jonny had come back in, taken all his kit off and gone round to the gym to release some anger by throwing some weights around. As twelfth man, I was used as the messenger, to fetch him back. Meanwhile, Flower went to the umpires to see whether the dismissal was going to stand, as it should not within the laws of the game.

Of course, Jonny got really excited when I ran over and told him he might still be batting and that he needed to come and put his pads back on. However, not long after we had returned to the dressing room, Flower came back with the bad news – because he had walked off the field he had effectively given himself out. Jonny's face dropped and he went back to hammer that gym.

Surely, I thought, having had that experience at the

Wankhede Stadium, it would stick in his mind? I couldn't believe he didn't stay the other side of the boundary line.

After he came to sit down in the viewing area, I decided to give him five minutes to calm down, before asking, 'You know that hit his helmet, don't you?'

'What?'

We had a discussion about the incident and he got angry again. The only positive from it all is that the next time it happens he will think twice about walking off. On this occasion, he might have preferred not knowing. His departure coupled with that of Ben Stokes in the same Nathan Lyon over decreased our chances of staving off defeat, although while Cook remained there was always hope.

Overnight we were 203–6 and now that we couldn't beat them 4–1, we wanted to at least hang on for a wet-weather draw if possible. By the time that lunchtime rain arrived, however, we had lost two further wickets and the three-hour interlude simply delayed the inevitable. Australia were deserving of their innings victory, but losing the match after so desperately wanting to finish on the right note meant emotions were hard to handle.

After the initial disappointment, Cook told us, 'Lads, let's discuss this at another time. Tonight is about celebrating what has been a great series for us.'

Trevor Bayliss's follow-up was something like 'Let's get pissed.'

England v Australia
(5th Test)

Played at The Oval, London, on 20–23 August 2015

Umpires: Aleem Dar & HDPK Dharmasena (TV: S Ravi)
Referee: JJ Crowe
Toss: England

AUSTRALIA

CJL Rogers	c Cook b Wood	43	
DA Warner	c Lyth b Ali	85	
SPD Smith	b Finn	143	
MJ Clarke*	c Buttler b Stokes	15	
AC Voges	lbw b Stokes	76	
MR Marsh	c Bell b Finn	3	
PM Nevill†	c Buttler b Ali	18	
MG Johnson	b Ali	0	
MA Starc	lbw b Stokes	58	
PM Siddle	c Lyth b Finn	1	
NM Lyon	not out	5	
Extras	(b 1, lb 24, w 6, nb 3)	34	
Total	(125.1 overs)	**481**	

ENGLAND

A Lyth	c Starc b Siddle	19		c Clarke b Siddle	10
AN Cook*	b Lyon	22		c Voges b Smith	85
IR Bell	b Siddle	10		c Clarke b Marsh	13
JE Root	c Nevill b Marsh	6		c Starc b Johnson	11
JM Bairstow	c Lyon b Johnson	13		c Voges b Lyon	26
BA Stokes	c Nevill b Marsh	15		c Clarke b Lyon	0
JC Buttler†	b Lyon	1		c Starc b Marsh	42
MM Ali	c Nevill b Johnson	30	(9)	c Nevill b Siddle	35
SCJ Broad	c Voges b Marsh	0	(10)	b Siddle	11
MA Wood	c Starc b Johnson	24	(8)	lbw b Siddle	6
ST Finn	not out	0		not out	9
Extras	(b 1, lb 7, nb 1)	9		(b 12, lb 18, w 7, nb 1)	38
Total	(48.4 overs)	**149**		(101.4 overs)	**286**

ENGLAND	O	M	R	W		O	M	R	W
Broad	20	4	59	0					
Wood	26	9	59	1					
Stokes	29	6	133	3					
Finn	29.1	7	90	3					
Ali	18	1	102	3					
Root	3	0	13	0					

AUSTRALIA	O	M	R	W		O	M	R	W
Starc	8	3	18	0	(2)	16	4	40	0
Johnson	8.4	4	21	3	(1)	16	2	65	1
Lyon	10	2	40	2		28	7	53	2
Siddle	13	5	32	2		24.4	12	35	4
Marsh	9	2	30	3		16	4	56	2
Smith	1	0	7	1					

Fall of wickets

	Aus	Eng	Eng
1st	110	30	19
2nd	161	46	62
3rd	186	60	99
4th	332	64	140
5th	343	83	140
6th	376	84	199
7th	376	92	221
8th	467	92	223
9th	475	149	263
10th	481	149	286

Close of play:
Day 1: Aus (1) 287–3 (Smith 78*, Voges 47*, 79.4 overs)
Day 2: Eng (1) 107–8 (Ali 8*, Wood 8*, 40 overs)
Day 3: Eng (2) 203–6 (Buttler 33*, Wood 0*, 79 overs)

Man of the Match: SPD Smith
Result: **Australia won by an innings and 46 runs**

He might be Australian, but it was pretty evident how much he'd enjoyed being part of a success like this, both from a personal and team perspective. There was nothing false about his excitement. It was completely natural. Both he and Paul Farbrace remained reluctant to be part of any public celebrations, preferring to shove us into the limelight, but we weren't having a bit of that and wanted to get them involved as much as possible. After all, they were integral to what we had achieved.

It was nice to share a few dressing-room beers with some other Australians too. Alastair Cook invited Michael Clarke's team over, just as he had done at Cardiff after the first Test, and it was lovely to spend a couple of hours chewing the fat. Our invitation to them at the start of the series had been viewed with scepticism in some quarters, but it was a genuine one, not made solely because we had won that first Test.

The subject of inviting the opposition in for post-match drinks every match, win, lose or draw, had been discussed during our four-day camp in Spain. With regard to that initial invitation at the SWALEC Stadium, Clarke said he would have a little think about it and let us know. But when Cook and I were on the way to the press conference, we bumped into Darren Lehmann. 'Thanks very much for the offer, but we'll do it at the end of the series, not now,' he said.

That was fair enough. It's been the done thing for some time on the international circuit. But had Australia been hosts and the offer been the other way round, we would have gone. One of the things Cook has been strong on developing is a team culture, and that means that although we want to play good, aggressive, hard cricket on the field, we want to be well-meaning and good-spirited off it. The two-Test series against New Zealand was a perfect example. They came in both times.

We want to show as a team that after several days of hard contest the result doesn't matter – that we are the sort of side that respects our opposition regardless of it, and will happily socialise and chat about the game, life in general or whatever else comes up in conversation once everyone has left the field for the final time. Once it's over, it's over. Disagreements can be left on the field. There's no need to carry bad blood over the boundary with you.

So that evening, as soon as my old mate Davey Warner came in, I made a point of going up to him immediately.

'Come on, mate, let's have a beer,' I said.

'I'm all right, mate, I'm not drinking tonight.'

'Why not?' I asked. 'Are you scared of getting drunk and punching someone, or something?'

It was quite a safe thing to say in that environment, and drew a few laughs from players on both sides of the equation; the fact his colleagues found it quite amusing helped break the ice.

There was no real civility between the pair of us through the series. In fact, we didn't really speak at all, and I was quite surprised how much he left me alone, given our history. Certainly in the past, he had a reputation for being a lot louder. More like he had been when Ben Stokes walked out to bat in that second innings at The Oval.

'There's not a cat in hell's chance you will bat out for a draw here, Ben,' Warner told him.

'No. I've got about as much chance as you have of winning the Ashes this year, mate,' was Ben's perfect retort. Unfortunately, having shut Warner up, he was out in the same Nathan Lyon over as Jonny Bairstow.

It was nice that Warner and I ended up having a conversation. I am sure there will be other things that arise in the future – you almost want a bit of spiciness in Ashes cricket, a villain on the opposition – but this put that particular incident to bed for me.

It was also good to have proper chats with Mitchell Starc and Nathan Lyon, former team-mates I have known for a long time. I had a bit of a go at them for ignoring me all series, ribbing them that it was because they were too big for their boots these days. We reminisced about times gone by playing for Yorkshire, where Mitchell was our overseas player in 2012, and Prospect, the Adelaide grade club where I played with Nath.

Mitchell had been very quiet towards me throughout the five matches, whereas Nath tended to speak about me rather than directly to me on the field, trying to take the mickey out of me whenever he could. During the first Test match, for example, he was standing over the stump microphone saying, 'Mate, can you put some deodorant on, you stink!'

He was saying it out loud to get in my head, to affect my concentration. I didn't stink, honestly. But his pseudo-nastiness didn't wash with me. He's one of the least malicious guys you could wish to meet. It just made me chuckle. And to have friendly banter in a high-intensity environment can relax you.

It was certainly quite a different backdrop to that at Prospect, the club where we played alongside each other for five months in 2010–11. When I arrived for that stretch in October, he was working on the ground staff at the Adelaide Oval and was yet to play any first-class cricket. Things changed in January 2011 when he was selected for South Australia in the pre-franchise Big Bash League, and his journey from groundsman to international cricketer in the space of twelve months was under way. It all happened so quickly, and I remember when he came back from being picked in the Big Bash, I walked over for a conversation with him and he brushed me off. I gave him a bit of stick, tongue in cheek, for being a bit too 'big time'. He was mortified that anyone would think that of him, and that tells you what a good bloke he is.

My change in status had not been quite as rapid, but to sit reminiscing with him as winner of the Compton-Miller Medal, awarded for being Man of the Series in the 2015 Ashes, was a sign of how far I had come. In nominating me, Australia's coach Darren Lehmann cited 'outstanding knocks in bowler-friendly conditions at key moments'. To be frank, as a batsman, that's exactly what you want to be remembered for – because it means you have contributed to victories. Looking back at the series, there weren't huge amounts of runs scored, partly because of the wickets and partly because on more than one occasion one side batted only once in a match. Conditions were conducive to swing bowling and so contributions of 30 to 40 here and there were a lot more valuable than they might have been in past Ashes. Hundreds were even more precious.

That award was a nice surprise. To be fair, Stuart Broad was deserving of something too, having finished up as the leading wicket-taker, with twenty-one. He was to get an altogether different surprise, however, as the dressing-room snipper made a final incision for the summer.

Throughout the series, Broad had made it clear to everyone not to go near his lucky pair of green socks. They were to be tampered with on pain of death. Therefore there had been a good amount of restraint shown towards him for the previous six weeks. At that point of the evening, our celebrations were winding down and there were only a few lads left waiting for their cabs back to the team hotel and he was one of that dwindling number. With the socks out of bounds, the opportunity had been taken to take the scissors to another item amongst his belongings – unbe-known to him, a huge hole had been cut out of the bottom of his holdall. As it had been standing upright in the hours after the game, he was none the wiser. Only when he came to pick it up, throwing both straps over his shoulders, did his parting gift become clear. Picking all his kit up off the floor was the last thing he would have wanted to do after a skinful.

As we left the ground that night in pitch black, we got our own personal souvenir photos, the pick of which had to be Alastair Cook, signing off for the summer with a Ben Stokes salute on horseback. Or, more accurately, zebra-back, having mounted the model Investec one at the front gates.

Cook was to play again in the County Championship for Essex, but as far as I was concerned, that was it for 2015. During that final Test match Trevor Bayliss told me he thought the time was right for me to have a bit of a break. While I was desperate to play in the one-day series against the Australians, I accepted that I had played a lot of cricket over the previous eighteen months. The selectors foresaw that a combination of a heavy winter schedule and the fact that I was a member of Test, one-day and Twenty20 teams meant there would be few other opportunities to give me meaningful time away from cricket. As I am keen to continue playing all three formats, it made sense. It's important to stay fresh and keep feeling you can give absolutely everything each time you play rather than allow yourself to become lethargic.

Part of top-level cricket is getting used to losing your

place due to selection issues. Although I always hate giving up my spot, this time it was done with a view to making sure I was at my best when I did return. I have always believed if you are a good enough player, then you fight your way back through performances, even if someone has done well enough to merit retention in your absence. If I had played in the series and got three or four low scores, I wouldn't have expected to be selected at the start of the winter just because I had performed well previously. I am a massive England fan and I want us to win every time the side plays. Of course I want to be a part of it, the one out there doing the damage, but the bigger picture is that we have World Cups coming up in the future and we have to develop quality and depth for that.

As for the summer I was leaving behind, I would be lying to suggest I hadn't been hungry for more runs. It would have been nice to have made some valuable contributions in that last Test match, for example. But to have taken 460 runs off that Australian attack and done some real damage to their hopes of being successful meant I had achieved everything I had set out to. On reflection, I felt a sense of pride and accomplishment by the end of the series. Being able to sit back and consider not only what we had achieved as a team but also the personal performances I had produced was really pleasing.

Taking that final wicket at Trent Bridge, and then standing on the stage with all the lads at The Oval, bubbling up the champagne ready for a spray, were the two really special moments for me.

Everyone focuses on the replica urn when it comes to Ashes cricket, but there is also the Waterford Crystal Trophy that goes with it. After the presentations, I took care of it, making sure it got back into the dressing room safely. It was soon full of beer and my dad and I were taking the obligatory selfie with it when Jimmy Anderson pranked us.

We play this stupid drinking game after a match with rules similar to that of cricket. You have to protect the bottom of your cup like you would your stumps. Quite simply, a part of your body must be covering the bottom or it is vulnerable. If you don't cover it with a finger or thumb and someone touches it and appeals you are 'out' – and that means emptying whatever is in the glass. So when Jimmy sneaked up behind us, tapped the bottom of the trophy and shouted, 'Howzat?', we had to finish several pints between us.

Having Dad there alongside me toasting the occasion, drinking from the glass urn, was special. After all, it was he who started me off on this journey back in Sheffield twenty or so years ago, when the real thing was in Australian hands. Our parents all played their part in helping us fulfil our dreams of returning it once more and that early evening provided a throwback to my Saturday afternoons as a boy when mum would take Bill and I down to watch dad play. Only it wasn't the Collegiate first XI bowling to us on the outfield at Abbeydale. Instead, it was Stuart Broad bowling to our fielding coach Chris Taylor's little lad Jonty; it was Joseph Bell, son of Ian, and Ben Stokes' boy Layton running around kicking a football. And this wasn't the toasting of a Yorkshire League victory. Stood chatting on the outfield with mum and dad, and Carrie, I surveyed one big happy family, and reflected that our job for the summer was complete. We had brought home the Ashes.

12 SO NEAR AND YET SO FAR

THIS was not a moment I had prepared for. As a boy, dreams are of the glorious moments: the hitting of the winning runs, being mobbed by your team-mates after taking the decisive catch, lifting a trophy. Yet, four mighty swings of Carlos Brathwaite's bat had just succeeded in shattering our World Twenty20 Cup hopes.

As Ben Stokes, the bowler on the end of the blows, sat on his haunches, head bowed, on the side of the Eden Gardens pitch, it was hard to know what to do. Ben is not only a team-mate, he's a good friend. We have played a hell of a lot of cricket together over the years and enjoyed lots of success. But how should I react in this situation? Should I go and give him a hug? Or allow him to have his own space? As I say, it's not something that you practise for.

Not knowing what else to do, I chose to put my arms around him as he remained motionless in the same position. 'Great effort, mate. Keep your head up,' I told him.

To be honest, it was hard to find any appropriate words in the circumstances. In that situation, more than the words themselves, I reckon you've got to let the person know that you're with them.

As an individual, naturally it is devastating to be on the verge of victory and then abruptly plunged into despair; looking around the faces of the whole England team I could see the story of our collective disappointment. We had worked so hard throughout the World Twenty20 and we had come so far as a side, even over the space of one tournament, that losing the final to West Indies in such a manner hit everybody hard. Ben was naturally gutted, as you would expect of a bowler failing to defend 19 runs off the final over, but in that situation you share the pain. It is not for Ben to bear. In good teams the burden of disappointment falls on everyone, and you could see from the reactions that the main concern was to make sure he was all right.

Moods are infectious. One smile can trigger another. Gloom spreads across faces in the same way. The images of us, as West Indies celebrated their astonishing last-gasp triumph, showed that we had given everything. In that snapshot of time we were hollow, and to see as fiery a character as Ben in such a dejected state pulled on the heartstrings.

As a mate, I knew he had given absolutely everything he had, and as a cricketer I knew he had not missed his mark by much in attempting to get his yorkers in – in Twenty20 cricket the margins between success and failure with every delivery are so small. Ultimately, he missed, and fell foul of some of the cleanest ball-striking imaginable in the most high-pressure situation Carlos Brathwaite will ever find himself. Fair play to him, because a couple of those sixes were absolute monsters.

One thing we know is that Ben will be putting his hand up to bowl again if, as is the aim, we get into similar big-match scenarios in future. He is one of those blokes who wants to be asked to perform when everything is on the line. Equally, as an England cricketer, when you look round the field and ask yourself who you would want to bowl, it would be him, because you know how good he is, how skilful he can be and the character he shows nine times out of ten in that kind of situation. His death bowling in the previous two matches against Sri Lanka and New Zealand had been one of the major reasons we got to the final in the first place. A couple of dot balls would have killed off West Indies' chances.

It had been an absorbing match and a fitting final, I believe, for a thrilling tournament. Indian fans love Twenty20 cricket and the atmosphere when India play in any limited-overs cricket is absolutely electric. Eden Gardens is a stadium notorious for its extremely loud crowds and for players not being able to hear themselves think as a result but, to be honest, for whatever reason it did not reach the volume I was expecting. Supporters were still out in force, wanting to watch some great cricket, but

I couldn't help feel that it would have been very different if we had been playing India in a one-day international on that Sunday, April 3.

So the game might have felt more tense for those watching than us out on the field. Throughout it felt as though we were in relative control, despite losing a couple of early wickets and scoring 20–30 runs fewer than we would have liked, and you could see things unfolding for us in a calm manner. In contrast, that last over of mayhem went in a flash. Credit to West Indies, though, because that is how they'd played their cricket throughout the whole tournament. They backed themselves at the back end to clear the ropes. In that respect they were deserved champions, because they planned what they wanted to do and carried out those plans in all the games that mattered.

Similarly, our own performances during those three weeks in India reflected the spirit we had developed as a Twenty20 team. Whenever we needed to scrap and fight during contests we did so, and it didn't take mid-match conversations between us England players during the final itself to confirm we would need to do so again, having not managed a big enough total on a very good Kolkata surface. Knowing we had only a 156-run target to work with, our defence of such a total had to be spot on.

After being asked to bat, we were also in a spot of trouble after losing a couple of wickets inside the first two overs. In that situation, I have learned not to panic.

If anything, being 8–2 made me consider how long a

batting line-up we had. Equally, I knew how West Indies would continue to be aggressive in search of more wickets, so there would be scoring opportunities. With my own game now feeling transferable across all three of cricket's formats, I had confidence that batting normally and playing good cricket shots would bring rewards. Even when Eoin Morgan was dismissed soon afterwards, I knew it would only take one partnership of substance to bring the game back into the balance, and that if that was alongside Jos Buttler, we would potentially be in a really good place. If Jos stays at the crease for 30 balls, the run rate tends to climb dramatically with minimal fuss, and sure enough, when we were in tandem, it looked as if we were on for a big score.

If I'm being brutally honest, I got carried away with the size of total we needed, and after Jos got out as one of three quick wickets, I chose the wrong option. In that situation, I was the set batsman, I had just reached 50, and although I was not necessarily worried about running out of partners, I was intent on facing as many balls as possible. For one, it's always harder for new batsmen coming in than it is for those who have been in the middle for a while. Naturally, when you feel good at the crease, you want to take the strike as much as you can. But in managing the situation I got a little bit too clever. My intention was to get a boundary early in the over and then look to rotate the strike with my new partner, Chris Jordan. Getting an early four takes the pressure off the other guy.

In hindsight, maybe I overthought all this a bit. I am not sure the option to paddle Brathwaite to the boundary was necessary at that point. Sitting back in the dressing room, I glanced up at the scoreboard. When it hit home there were still six overs left I was furious with myself. On the other hand, it was in keeping with the attitude that had served this England side so well – whenever there was a positive option, we took it. I had to stand by my decision.

The fact that we have an extremely long batting order helped ensure we posted a score that was enough to be a winning one – given the pressure players tend to feel chasing in a final – if we managed to get early wickets. And those plans for early wickets involved yours truly. Leading up to the game, as soon as we knew West Indies were our opponents, talk turned to how we would get rid of Chris Gayle, the man whose blitz had derailed us in our opening match of the tournament in Mumbai. His hundred that night was an awesome display of Twenty20 innings management and clinical striking, and it was clear that we might have to rethink our strategy to him.

It was Ottis Gibson, our bowling coach, who had suggested that I should bowl in the powerplay, particularly if Gayle was on strike. Ottis and I been watching the golf on television at the team hotel one evening, and chatting about this and that. As a former coach of West Indies, he had seen Gayle flummoxed by occasional off-spinners before, and so the next day, after Gibbo had floated the idea to Eoin Morgan, I bowled at practice. Although we had stuck to a plan throughout the group stage, this was a final, and to win might involve taking a risk. Not for the first time our positivity was rewarded.

Although Gayle was at the non-striker's end for the second over of West Indies' chase, Morgs summoned me to bowl. The intention for my first ball was actually to get Johnson Charles off strike by cramping him for room and forcing him to take a single off his hip. Having watched footage of Gayle batting against spin early in an innings, it was noticeable that he likes to take a few balls to get in if he has time on his side, as he did in this instance. From our perspective, we thought it would be a good thing to get some dots on him early. But our outlook was altered when, instead of working one, Charles whacked my first delivery straight up in the air, high enough to ensure the batsmen crossed before Ben Stokes took the catch.

Here was my chance to bowl at Gayle. Unfortunately, my first delivery was a bit wide – ideally I wanted to attack the stumps to keep in as many forms as dismissal as possible. Even then, it seemed as if he had fluffed his shot straight to point. But a measure of the man's strength is that – despite it being a mishit – the ball still sailed five foot over the fielder's head for four. The second, in my attempts to bowl straighter, turned into a bit of a slot ball. As soon as it left my hand I anticipated it going out of the park. But, somehow, Gayle had totally mistimed his stroke again. Yanking my neck backwards, once again I saw Stokesy was getting under it. With hands like his, there is no one you would rather have in that position.

What an amazing start. David Willey's first over had gone for just one, so immediately West Indies had been under pressure to attack me. Partnerships you develop with the ball can be as vital as a batting partnership at the start of an innings, and we began it with great momentum. At that stage there was a real buzz about us, one that got louder when Willey trapped Lendl Simmons in the next over.

Undoubtedly, the biggest moment of the match came immediately after the powerplay concluded, when Liam Plunkett forced Marlon Samuels into an edge behind. Even when Jos Buttler's scooped catch was referred, we were still excited about it, and in the heat of the moment could not understand how the third umpire had managed to overturn the decision. Only later, when we came off the field and looked at it on a normal television, did it seem quite clear that it had scraped the grass. It was frustrating that it was then Samuels who went on to win the game for West Indies, but the very fact that he did showed the margins involved at Twenty20 level.

There was a lot made afterwards of how excessively Samuels and the rest of West Indies team celebrated. They had obviously experienced a lot of issues with their own cricket board in the build-up to the tournament and there-fore winning meant a huge deal to them. You could see that with their emotional response to Brathwaite's stunning finale. I tried not to look at them too much while we were still on the pitch, and I didn't think too badly of them, because I know when you are in a winning scenario like that it is very difficult to control that sense of euphoria. Some suggested it did not look good, that it was excessive and that they came across badly, but they had just won a World Cup and that meant we needed to cut them some slack. From a personal point of view I believe you conduct yourself in the same way regardless. For me that means you are gracious in defeat, congratulating your opponents on their success, and applaud them receiving their medals at the presentation.

That presentation drew the line under things a little bit for us all. Things had been rather muted until that point but, back in the dressing room, conversations broke out and we reflected on some of the special moments of the tournament.

Some of the things we had achieved as a group were downright ridiculous. Guys were shouting across the room at each other, recalling wickets, catches and shots, and it was a very different atmosphere to when we had sat in the same seats an hour earlier in the immediacy of defeat. You can't dwell too long on events once they've happened, and the sombre mood was transformed when we turned our phones on to read messages from friends and family. People we held in high regard were telling us how proud they were of us, and so although disappointment lingered deep down, placing our achievements into context helped return smiles to our faces.

In effect, getting into that position in the first place had required us to win the equivalent of five finals. Having lost our first game to West Indies, every match we played from then on carried the threat of us being eliminated from the competition if we lost. To perform as we did with that being the equation was an incredible effort, and in every single game we found ourselves in some sort of sticky situation.

Halfway through our second Group 1 match, we were asked to chase a World T20 record of 230 to defeat South Africa, a team that had just defeated us 2–0 in a bilateral series. Less than a quarter of the way into our third match, against Afghanistan, at 57–6, we were looking down the barrel again, so it wasn't as if the failure of one department was letting us down. Against Sri Lanka, in what was effectively a quarter-final, it took the end-of-innings expertise of Stokes and Chris Jordan to halt Angelo Mathews' charge. While a similarly strong finish with the ball in the semi-final restricted New Zealand to 153–8 when it had looked at one stage as if they would be posting somewhere in the region of 190. Whenever we were in trouble, someone dragged situations back our way, and although certain players enjoyed very strong tournaments, if you looked at our entire squad everybody contributed, and Eoin Morgan was flawless as captain in pressure situations.

Rather than this being the end, afterwards we reflected on this tournament being the start of something really special for this England team, and this group of players.

We want to play exciting cricket and make people want to watch us. And I want to be at the heart of that. There is so much in the bank to fall back on now as a group, to learn as we strive for improvement, and there is a general desire to work harder from all involved. It never feels like we are standing still. We are always striving for improvement.

To be frank, I headed into the tournament asking questions about my own game. I did not possess a huge amount of Twenty20 experience, so I was still trying to find a way of being successful when we arrived. Neither in South Africa a month earlier, nor in the warm-up games once we'd arrived in India, did I feel I had played the spinners that well. Twice I lofted to deep extra cover off spinners in practice matches, and yet that is not a shot I generally play. My thinking had become scrambled. Thankfully, Mahela Jayawardene, our batting coach for the event, offered advice to make things clearer. My boundary options lay elsewhere – strong on the slog sweep, I also pull and cut well when bowlers drop short. Yet, for some reason, I had abandoned these for riskier aerial strokes. Working with Mahela was good for me: recognising my ability to flick and ramp the seamers, he told me to paddle the spinners as well, encouraging me to try to get the ball over the wicketkeeper's right shoulder. Doing that successfully delivers four runs every time, and it was something I enjoyed incorporating into my game.

To finish as second leading run scorer behind Virat Kohli

was pleasing, chiefly because it meant my contributions were counting towards results. Never more so than when I hit a 44-ball 83 against the South Africans at the Wankhede Stadium. It was an innings spawned from anger.

As we left the field after conceding 229 runs in a whirl-wind 90 minutes Eoin Morgan had run over to tell me I would be dropping down the order so that our bigger hitters could try to get us ahead of the required rate. Ben Stokes would be going in at number three. Tactically, although I knew it was the right thing to do if we were to have any chance of hauling that target down, as a batter who prides himself on scoring runs, it naturally hacked me off. Thinking that I might be an afterthought in this thrilling pursuit got me into a really good place mentally. The one caveat, Morgs told me, was that I would go in at number four if we lost two wickets inside the opening six overs.

There was a lot of ego involved, I guess, but I could not have felt more ready to prove that I was a player who could adapt to scoring at this kind of rate. When you are employed to score top-order runs, you expect to go in at the start, and self-belief is essential if you want to be successful. The fact I was angry certainly helped with the aggression required.

The situation I walked into was one I relished, and had undoubtedly been improved from an England perspective by the extraordinary start provided by Jason Roy and Alex Hales. To take 48 runs off the opening 13 deliveries of an innings is freakish, but in the circumstances we needed freakish. It bought us valuable time. Another added helping hand was provided by South Africa's bowlers getting the ball to reverse swing: with the bounce of the wicket so true, the fact they had seen it reverse meant they concentrated on bowling yorkers – effectively what they would revert to at the death – very early on. This simply played into our hands.

A matter of a few weeks earlier, the South Africans had enjoyed success against us because of their ability to vary the pace in mid-innings. Yet I can remember facing just two slower balls. It made their pace bowlers very predictable to hit. When the ball reverses it can be harder to control, and bowlers can find it challenging to get both their length and their line spot on when aiming for the block-hole. It requires them to aim outside the line of where they want the ball to go, and, with batsmen moving around the crease, the skill becomes even harder to deliver.

I used this to my advantage in executing a shot that drew some attention – the one that from my 29th ball that brought up my half-century - a reverse ramp for six off Chris Morris. When Faf du Plessis brought third man up at the start of that over, it signalled that Morris would be bowling nice and full; weighing things, up the stroke was a really strong choice amongst my options. As I surveyed the field, I realised the only way I could get out playing it was if I didn't commit to it fully. I certainly knew the consequences of this from practice the previous day, when Trevor Bayliss had whanged one down at me with his dog sling and I pulled out right at the last second, top-edging it straight into my bicep. The bruise was a warning not to be a wuss. It is a high-risk stroke from a safety point of view but, once you go down to play it, there's not really much else you can do, and if you connect the result is high reward. With the asking rate at 10 runs an over at that stage, I decided, as Morris was halfway towards me for that third ball of the 15th over, that I would use his speed to generate the pace off the bat. I wanted him to bowl at the stumps – if it's wider it's hard to get your hands at the ball and you need to create an angle to deflect it precisely. In that regard, it couldn't have been better directed, and the great thing about connecting with it as I did was that I didn't need to do it again. The fielder stayed back at third man from then on, forcing midwicket to be brought up instead and allowing us to hit with the swing over his head.

Being involved in a chase like that is exhilarating, and Jos Buttler is a master of these kinds of situations. So his words when we were pitched together in the middle settled me down completely. 'Look around the field, see their faces, and remember how we felt when we were fielding. They're under a lot more pressure than we are right now. They were expected to win this game at halfway, and it looks like they have thrown it away with the start we have got,' he said.

His assessment freed me up completely. When you consider the scenario, with the board confirming we needed 119 from 62 balls, that sounds a bizarre statement. In the same over, from JP Duminy, I rocked back and hit a six, and felt a release as I did so. I knew we would win the game. Soon, South Africa started bringing guys back into the attack earlier than they wanted to. Kagiso Rabada came back on, Dale Steyn was asked to bowl in the middle overs, and when the opposition go away from what they planned to do, it only serves to increase your confidence. For our part, we were able to follow through with our plan to be conservative against the leg-spinner Imran Tahir, restricting his impact as a wicket-taker at a cost of allowing him to send down his four overs for just 28, as we knew how difficult he would make life for new batsmen to the crease.

When next we came together in the semi-final against New Zealand, I did all the talking. Jason Roy had given us such a fantastic start once again that it was about completing the job without taking undue risks. Although Jos arrived at the crease on a hat-trick, we only required 44 runs for victory from the thick end of eight overs. With no pressure on to score quickly, I told him to concentrate on knocking off five runs at a time initially. He knocked a few around and so did I until, with the equation at a run a ball from the final four overs, I dinked a reverse sweep off the leg-spinner Ish Sodhi that went for four.

'Right, five more runs, Jos,' I said.

'Don't worry about that. Let me do the counting from now on,' he replied.

I managed a single from the second ball of the over. The next three balls went 4, 6, 6, and with two to win we sneaked an over-throw. Jos was clearly in the mood and smoked the first ball of the next over into the stands too. I ran down to him and he just stood with his arms aloft chanting: 'We're going to Calcutta!' Looking back at the bench, everyone was going mad; in cricket there is no better feeling than being in at the end when you win the game. Contrast that to the emotions we were to feel post-match at Eden Gardens.

The World Twenty20 was the last of three challenges for us over the winter, and one which incorporated some amazing individual performances and some heroic efforts. If we were to build on our Ashes success from the previous summer, we had to prove we could be competitive away from home in challenging conditions.

As it turned out, the three-match series against Pakistan proved to be a little bit of a missed opportunity for us. Cricket in the United Arab Emirates throws up lots of challenges. Firstly, it is ridiculously hot. 'It's bloody obvious that it's not comfortable but these are the conditions we have to contend with, so let's not moan about it,' Alastair Cook told us after our second training session. In typical fashion, he then made light of fielding for the best part of two days after losing the toss in the first Test in Abu Dhabi to hit a career-best 263. He played an unbelievable hand. It was a lesson to the rest of us in discipline in uncomfortable conditions.

It also taught us the importance of staying in the game.

To get a first-innings lead after conceding in excess of 500 at the Sheikh Zayed Stadium was an outstanding effort, and when we went out to bowl for a second time we were simply brilliant. Our seamers James Anderson and Stuart Broad showed their experience by bowling cutters and waiting for Pakistan's batsmen to make mistakes, and Adil Rashid showed the character I have come to appreciate as a team-mate at Yorkshire to bounce back from a first-innings struggle to claim a five-wicket haul on debut. From the moment we reduced them to four wickets down, I knew we would bowl them out, and a match that had appeared dead would return to life.

In the end only the light scuppered us, and Pakistan were very smart in defending the 99-run target, bowling as few overs as possible without it being unfair to hold us at bay. Not to get over the line was a bit deflating, but it nevertheless showed the surprises Test cricket can throw up. For four days people had commented on how rubbish the pitch was and how it was the dullest imaginable. Yet we got to the last two hours and it was some of the most exciting Test cricket I have ever played in. We nearly did it when, after the first innings scores, we had no right to do so.

In Dubai, a Wahab Riaz-inspired collapse cost us the match. We could simply find no answer to his reverse swing, and I was one of those who fell into the trap of playing the ball away from my body. It was a mode of dismissal that was to plague me and prevent me making the three-figure contribution I craved. Just as in the summer, I was getting past 50 and then getting out, and my inability to convert starts was really beginning to frustrate me. It made me consider what was behind it. Was it fitness? Was it concentration? Was I simply overthinking things? Was it simply coincidence that I was making batsman errors at the same point in my innings so frequently? It was hard to put my finger on a reason and I decided to just trust my game. It was probably important not to think about it too much. Although batsman error is not something to be ignored, if I had hit the balls that were getting me out for four, as I had been doing previously, there would be no problem at all. Let's face it, you don't play shots to get out, you play shots to score runs. Maybe I was simply picking the wrong balls. I am not a massive believer in form. To me if you are a good player you will always be a good player. Yes, there will be times when your footwork is not quite as good as you would like, or your head is getting the wrong side of the ball, but the bottom line is you're still a good player. Things can sometimes just click back into place for you. Thankfully, from a Test cricket point of view, they did so – after Adil Rashid narrowly failed to avert a 2–0 scoreline with his fronting of a fifth-day rearguard at Sharjah – on the tour of South Africa.

We had unearthed a method that worked against Australia, and South Africa are a similar team. One that is aggressive, looks to take wickets with the ball and generally attack you whenever possible. So the challenge for us was finding a way of replicating what we had done in the Ashes against the team that was rated number one in the world. To score a hundred in a warm-up encounter filled me with confidence, and I know that Ben Stokes felt the same after coming back from a shoulder injury incurred against Pakistan to make a hundred of his own.

Our new-look batting line-up – including Alex Hales, Nick Compton and James Taylor – stood up manfully to South Africa's pace attack throughout the four-match campaign and, having overcome a team including the returning Dale Steyn to go 1–0 up in Durban, Stokes struck a psychological blow I believe was integral to our series victory.

We might not have won the second Test in Cape Town. Indeed, in a bizarre twist we might have lost it, which was mental considering that we posted 629. But Ben's innings – the fastest 250 in Test history – asserted an authority over our opponents that would influence what would happen later in Johannesburg.

He had looked in fine touch both during our partnership on the first day at Newlands, and alongside Jonny Bairstow during the evening session, following my dismissal. Unfortunately, however, so clean was his hitting on the second morning that I actually missed part of the 'I was there' day.

Because I was already out, I thought I would alter my usual routine, wait to do my usual pre-play throw-downs until we had done all the team stuff, then head over to the nets half an hour before the start, anticipating that I would only miss the first 10–15 minutes of play. That way I could still have a long practice without getting in the way of guys still to bat who wanted to have a meaningful hit of their own.

Out the back at Newlands, there are no replay screens; all you can hear is the crowd. Ben was on 74 overnight, and although I was back round within quarter of an hour, I missed his special moment. Hearing the commotion, Mark Ramprakash, our batting coach, and I ran through to see 100 by his name, having surged there inside four overs. But, in truth, he was only just beginning. He struck the ball so purely all morning, and afternoon, and just kept going. I couldn't get my head around it. At the other end, Jonny Bairstow dovetailed his innings really smartly, showing a lot of maturity about his game to reach a maiden hundred. It would have been very easy to get drawn into a bit of a hitting contest and throw his wicket away.

What Ben was doing was extraordinary – hitting Morne Morkel over long-on for six, hitting Dane Piedt's off-spin into Claremont and various other Cape Town suburbs and clearing the boundary by several metres with those crunching pulls every time Kagiso Rabada bounced him. It was such special batting that the South Africans had no idea what to do. Who would? Eleven sixes in an innings of just 198 deliveries. You don't see that kind of thing in any cricket, and witnessing it is something that will stand out throughout my whole career. It was also the contribution in that series that emphasised to us that South Africa – albeit missing their attack spearhead Steyn – were not impregnable. We saw we could dismantle them if we applied ourselves.

In playing my part in doing just that in Johannesburg, I also got that monkey off my back. Not since the Ashes had I got a Test match hundred, and in the context of the match we needed it. On the first morning at the Wanderers, Stuart Broad had been really ill, to the extent that he did well to get through the day, so dismissing them for 313 was a reasonable effort.

Yet South Africa would have considered themselves to be on top when Ben joined me in the middle on the second afternoon. His very presence at the crease seemed to spook them, and it soon became pretty evident that they had no idea where to bowl at him. It was a wicket that was quite spicy and therefore the key was to make people play on the front foot, yet they went short at him early, whicg simply encouraged him to carry on where he left off in Cape Town by playing his shots.

For a period of just over an hour either side of tea we really took the game to them and out of their control. Ben's aggressive stroke-play helped this but, from a personal perspective, it was also a pleasing period as there had been a bit of chat about how this pitch would sort me out. During the second innings in Cape Town, I had spliced one off Kagiso Rabada that just dropped short of the wicketkeeper, which caused AB de Villiers to warn me: 'You may have got a few runs here, but let's see how you are in Jo'burg where there is pace and carry.'

His words stuck in my mind, and I did quite a lot of work in practice leading up to the match with the intention of meeting fire with fire. On a wicket like that there is always a ball with your name on it, so you have to think about attacking first and foremost, the variety of batting that proved to be so successful in the Ashes summer.

As soon as Ben arrived they went from bowling consistently at the top of off-stump to various other methods, and it meant I got looser stuff to hit too. To make the most of it was satisfying, because of the number of times I had got beyond 50 and not converted. On more than one occasion I had told myself: 'You're an idiot, you're throwing away hundreds here.'

When I nicked off early on the third morning, I could not have envisaged that there would not be a fourth day's play. With a lead of just ten runs it effectively became a one-innings game. Enter Broad.

Despite having a go at South Africa's openers pre-lunch, some poor deliveries allowed them to go in unscathed having wiped out the deficit. In contrast, when we came back out for the afternoon session, our attack showed how disciplined it can be if the pitch is aiding us. It was barely believable how similar this passage of play was to the one that had taken place in Nottingham five months earlier.

Seeing Broad at the back of his mark, from my vantage point in the slips, it felt as though there could be a wicket every ball. Spells like this have become his forte, and our close catchers felt the ball was destined for their hands. It did not end up in mine but, after an extremely disappointing fielding performance in Cape Town, it was a pleasing response. We simply caught everything, including two catches at short leg by James Taylor that were the equal of any ever taken in that position. Broad's masterclass of 6–16 meant I had the honour of clipping the winning single later that evening – one that concluded with us toasting another series victory. There are no moments I cherish more.

ACKNOWLEDGEMENTS

THIS book recounting the incredible events of the 2015 Investec Ashes series, and indeed the tumultuous period that led up to it, came to fruition not solely because of my own efforts but the endeavors of players I am proud to call England team-mates.

Being an international cricketer is about more than just what happens on the field. The hard times we endure make the successes all the sweeter, and I hope there are many more to be shared in the future. To all those who have been part of my journey as an England player so far – thank you.

I am grateful to Hodder & Stoughton for allowing me to tell my tale of this great summer. Roddy Bloomfield and his team of Fiona Rose and Tim Waller were always patient and understanding despite deadlines looming as menacingly as the second new ball.

I would like to thank Richard Gibson for capturing my thoughts and presenting them in these pages. He was less demanding of my time than he was of my tea and biscuits. It was fun.

To those who have supported me: the many coaches from schoolboy level upwards who have contributed so heavily in my development, and to all at ISM who work so hard on my behalf, in particular Neil Fairbrother; who has become not only a great adviser but a great friend, thank you.

Finally, none of this would have been possible to achieve without the love and support of those closest to me. To be successful you need a strong support network and that starts with your partner. It takes a special person to put up and fit in with the life of an England cricketer, and that sums up my girlfriend Carrie. Always there to listen; she's my best friend.

Like all the best stories, mine had a good beginning too, and for their roles in it I am indebted to Mum, Dad and my brother Bill. I owe each of you, as well as the rest of our wonderful family, for all the adventures we have made, and the highs and lows we have shared over the years. I could not have done any of it without you.

PHOTO ACKNOWLEDGEMENTS

WENN Ltd / Alamy Stock Photo, Anthony Devlin / PA Archive/PA Images, Bob Thomas/Getty Images, Gareth Copley/Getty Images, David Munden/Popperfoto/Getty Images, Phil Walter/Getty Images, Jan Kruger/Getty Images, Phil Noble / PA Wire/Press Association Images, NOAH SEELAM/AFP/GettyImages, Morne de Klerk/Getty Images, INDRANIL MUKHERJEE/AFP/Getty Images, Akila Chinthaka/REX Shutterstock, Shaun Botterill/Getty Images, SAEED KHAN/AFP/Getty Images, Hagen Hopkins-IDI/ IDI via Getty Images, Michael Steele/Getty Images, Ricardo Mazalan / AP/Press Association Images, Sky Sports, Mitchell Gunn/Getty Images, Kieran Galvin/REX Shutterstock, Sarah Ansell/REX Shutterstock, Jan Kruger/ Getty Images, Stu Forster/Getty Images, Rui Vieira / AP/ Press Association Images, Nigel French / PA Wire/Press Association Images, Sport Arabia Worldwide Ltd and Desert Springs Resort, Kirsty Wigglesworth / AP/Press Association Images, Philip Brown, PAUL ELLIS/AFP/Getty Images, Ryan Pierse/Getty Images, Jon Super / AP/Press Association Images, Andy Hooper / Associated Newspapers/REX

CAREER STATISTICS

Compiled by Benedict Bermange

TEST CAREER

CAREER

	M	Inns	NO	Runs	HS	Avge	SR	100	50	Ct	Balls	Wkts	Avge	RPO	BB
Test Matches	39	72	10	3406	200*	54.93	53.52	9	19	41	1239	12	51.08	2.96	2-9

AGAINST

	M	Inns	NO	Runs	HS	Avge	SR	100	50	Ct	Balls	Wkts	Avge	RPO	BB
Australia	14	27	3	991	180	41.29	47.28	3	4	12	459	7	38.14	3.49	2-9
India	6	9	3	611	154*	101.83	52.31	2	4	6	96	1	38.00	2.37	1-5
New Zealand	7	13	0	514	104	39.53	50.49	1	3	10	150	1	68.00	2.72	1-7
Pakistan	3	6	1	287	88	57.40	54.45	0	3	4	48	0		4.87	-
South Africa	4	8	1	386	110	55.14	63.38	1	3	4	162	0		2.85	-
Sri Lanka	2	4	1	259	200*	86.33	56.79	1	0	1	48	0		2.87	-
West Indies	3	5	1	358	182*	89.50	73.21	1	2	4	276	3	33.66	2.19	2-22

COUNTRY

	M	Inns	NO	Runs	HS	Avge	SR	100	50	Ct	Balls	Wkts	Avge	RPO	BB
Australia	4	8	1	192	87	27.42	33.27	0	1	2	192	0		3.06	-
England	21	38	5	2002	200*	60.66	55.79	7	9	26	495	9	29.11	3.17	2-9
India	1	2	0	93	73	93.00	32.63	0	1	0	6	0		5.00	-
New Zealand	3	5	1	88	45	17.60	30.55	0	0	1	60	0		3.10	-
South Africa	4	8	1	386	110	55.14	63.38	1	3	4	162	0		2.85	-
UAE	3	6	1	287	88	57.40	54.45	0	3	4	48	0		4.87	-
West Indies	3	5	1	358	182*	89.50	73.21	1	2	4	276	3	33.66	2.19	2-22

CONTINENT

	M	Inns	NO	Runs	HS	Avge	SR	100	50	Ct	Balls	Wkts	Avge	RPO	BB
Africa	4	8	1	386	110	55.14	63.38	1	3	4	162	0		2.85	-
Americas	3	5	1	358	182*	89.50	73.21	1	2	4	276	3	33.66	2.19	2-22
Asia	4	8	2	380	88	63.33	46.79	0	4	4	54	0		4.88	-
Australasia	7	13	1	280	87	23.33	32.36	0	1	3	252	0		3.07	-
Europe	21	38	5	2002	200*	60.66	55.79	7	9	26	495	9	29.11	3.17	2-9

WHERE

	M	Inns	NO	Runs	HS	Avge	SR	100	50	Ct	Balls	Wkts	Avge	RPO	BB
Neutral	3	6	1	287	88	57.40	54.45	0	3	4	48	0	-	4.87	-
Home	21	38	5	2002	200*	60.66	55.79	7	9	26	495	9	29.11	3.17	2-9
Away	15	28	4	1117	182*	46.54	49.68	2	7	11	696	3	104.00	2.68	2-22

YEAR

	M	Inns	NO	Runs	HS	Avge	SR	100	50	Ct	Balls	Wkts	Avge	RPO	BB
2012	1	2	1	93	73	93.00	32.63	0	1	0	6	0	-	5.00	-
2013	14	27	2	862	180	34.48	40.64	2	3	8	366	3	54.66	2.68	2-9
2014	7	11	3	777	200*	97.12	58.02	3	3	7	138	1	56.00	2.43	1-5
2015	14	26	3	1385	182*	60.21	63.70	3	10	24	585	8	40.25	3.30	2-22
2016	3	6	1	289	110	57.80	65.09	1	2	2	144	0	-	2.75	-

RESULT

	M	Inns	NO	Runs	HS	Avge	SR	100	50	Ct	Balls	Wkts	Avge	RPO	BB
Won	15	26	4	1767	182*	80.31	64.30	7	8	22	309	7	15.71	2.13	2-9
Lost	13	26	1	650	88	26.00	40.02	0	5	12	492	3	106.00	3.87	2-55
Drawn	11	20	5	989	200*	65.93	49.67	2	6	7	438	2	92.50	2.53	2-22

INNINGS

	Inns	NO	Runs	HS	Avge	SR	100	50
1	39	4	2226	200*	63.60	55.60	8	10
2	33	6	1180	180	43.70	50.00	1	9

MATCH INNINGS

	Inns	NO	Runs	HS	Avge	SR	100	50
1	17	1	932	200*	58.25	55.24	3	4
2	22	3	1294	182*	68.10	55.87	5	6
3	17	1	709	180	44.31	60.18	1	6
4	16	5	471	87	42.81	39.84	0	3

JOE ROOT

POSITION

	Inns	NO	Runs	HS	Avge	SR	100	50
2	10	1	339	180	37.66	40.69	1	1
3	7	1	197	87	32.83	38.40	0	1
4	18	2	874	130	54.62	59.57	2	7
5	28	4	1755	200*	73.12	60.53	6	8
6	8	2	241	77	40.16	37.13	0	2
7	1	0	0	0	0.00	0.00	0	0

SERIES

	Venue	Season	M	Inns	NO	Runs	HS	Avge	SR	100	50	Ct	Balls	Wkts	Avge	RPO	BB
v Ind	Ind	2012/13	1	2	1	93	73	93.00	32.63	0	1	0	6	0	5.00	-	-
v NZ	NZ	2012/13	3	5	0	88	45	17.60	30.55	0	0	1	60	0	3.10	-	-
v NZ	Eng	2013	2	4	1	243	104	60.75	57.44	1	1	3	18	0	0.33	-	-
v Aus	Eng	2013	5	10	1	339	180	37.66	40.69	1	1	2	96	3	11.33	2.12	2-9
v Aus	Aus	2013/14	4	8	1	192	87	27.42	33.27	0	1	2	192	0	3.06	-	-
v SL	Eng	2014	2	4	1	259	200*	86.33	56.79	1	0	1	48	0	2.87	-	-
v Ind	Eng	2014	5	7	2	518	154*	103.60	58.66	2	3	6	90	1	33.00	2.20	1-5
v WI	WI	2014/15	3	5	1	358	182*	89.50	73.21	1	3	4	276	3	33.66	2.19	2-22
v NZ	Eng	2015	2	4	0	183	98	45.75	59.60	0	2	6	72	1	36.00	3.00	1-7
v Aus	Eng	2015	5	9	1	460	134	57.50	67.05	2	2	8	171	4	33.75	4.73	2-28
v Pak	UAE	2015/16	3	6	1	287	88	57.40	54.45	0	3	4	48	0	4.87	-	-
v SA	SA	2015/16	4	8	1	386	110	55.14	63.38	1	3	4	162	0	2.85	-	-

CAREER STATISTICS

HOW HE HAS BEEN DISMISSED

	Times	Total	%
Bowled	10	62	16.12
Caught fielder	18	62	29.03
Caught keeper	26	62	41.93
Lbw	6	62	9.67
Other	0	62	0.00
Run out	2	62	3.22
Stumped	0	62	0.00

HOW HE HAS TAKEN HIS WICKETS

	Times	Total	%
Caught fielder	9	12	75.00
Lbw	3	12	25.00

HIS TEST CENTURIES

Score	Team	Against	Venue	Season
200*	England	Sri Lanka	Lord's	2014
182*	England	West Indies	St George's	2014/15
180	England	Australia	Lord's	2013
154*	England	India	Nottingham	2014
149*	England	India	The Oval	2014
134	England	Australia	Cardiff	2015
130	England	Australia	Nottingham	2015
110	England	South Africa	Johannesburg	2015/16
104	England	New Zealand	Leeds	2013

BEST BOWLING FIGURES

Bowling	Team	Against	Venue	Season
2-9	England	Australia	Lord's	2013
2-22	England	West Indies	North Sound	2014/15
2-28	England	Australia	Cardiff	2015
2-55	England	Australia	Lord's	2015
1-5	England	India	Southampton	2014
1-6	England	Australia	Nottingham	2013
1-7	England	New Zealand	Lord's	2015
1-34	England	West Indies	Bridgetown	2014/15

BOWLERS DISMISSING HIM

Bowler	Times	M
RJ Harris	5	8
TG Southee	4	7
MA Starc	4	8
MG Johnson	4	9
TA Boult	3	7
NM Lyon	3	12
CH Morris	2	2
MJ Henry	2	2
Rahat Ali	2	2
DL-R Piedt	2	3
JO Holder	2	3
K Rabada	2	3
JR Hazlewood	2	4
RA Jadeja	2	5
PM Siddle	2	10
SR Watson	2	10
PP Chawla	1	1
V Permaul	1	1
AD Mathews	1	2
ANPR Fernando	1	2
HMRKB Herath	1	2
JE Taylor	1	2
KJ Abbott	1	2
MD Craig	1	2
Pankaj Singh	1	2
Yasir Shah	1	2
MR Marsh	1	3
Wahab Riaz	1	3
Zulfiqar Babar	1	3
BP Martin	1	4
I Sharma	1	4
Bhuvneshwar Kumar	1	5
N Wagner	1	5

CAREER STATISTICS

BATSMEN HE HAS DISMISSED

Batsman	Times	M
S Chanderpaul	2	3
CJ Anderson	1	1
EJM Cowan	1	1
DM Bravo	1	3
S Dhawan	1	3
Usman Khawaja	1	3
PM Nevill	1	4
MA Starc	1	8
MG Johnson	1	9
MJ Clarke	1	14
SPD Smith	1	14

HIS TEST MATCHES

StartDate	Against	Venue	Batting	Bowling	Fielding
13/12/2012	India	Nagpur-J	73 & 20*	0-5	
06/03/2013	New Zealand	Dunedin-UO	4 & 0	0-8	
14/03/2013	New Zealand	Wellington	10	0-6 & 0-12	
22/03/2013	New Zealand	Auckland	45 & 29	0-5	1 ct
16/05/2013	New Zealand	Lord's	40 & 71		2 cts
24/05/2013	New Zealand	Leeds	104 & 28	dnb & 0-1	1 ct
10/07/2013	Australia	Nottingham	30 & 5	dnb & 1-6	1 ct
18/07/2013	Australia	Lord's	6 & 180	dnb & 2-9	
01/08/2013	Australia	Manchester	8 & 13*	0-18	1 ct
09/08/2013	Australia	Chester-le-Street	16 & 2	dnb & 0-1	
21/08/2013	Australia	The Oval	68 & 11		
21/11/2013	Australia	Brisbane	2 & 26*	0-5 & 0-57	
05/12/2013	Australia	Adelaide	15 & 87		
13/12/2013	Australia	Perth	4 & 19	0-4 & 0-24	1 ct
26/12/2013	Australia	Melbourne	24 & 15	dnb & 0-8	1 ct
12/06/2014	Sri Lanka	Lord's	200* & 15	0-7 & 0-7	
20/06/2014	Sri Lanka	Leeds	13 & 31	0-9	1 ct
09/07/2014	India	Nottingham	154*	0-6 & 0-22	2 cts
17/07/2014	India	Lord's	13 & 66		1 ct
27/07/2014	India	Southampton	3 & 56	dnb & 1-5	
07/08/2014	India	Manchester	77		1 ct
15/08/2014	India	The Oval	149*		2 cts
13/04/2015	West Indies	North Sound	83 & 59	dnb & 2-22	2 cts
21/04/2015	West Indies	St George's	182*	dnb & 0-29	2 cts
01/05/2015	West Indies	Bridgetown	33 & 1	1-34 & 0-16	
21/05/2015	New Zealand	Lord's	98 & 84	0-6 & 1-7	3 cts
29/05/2015	New Zealand	Leeds	1 & 0	dnb & 0-23	3 cts
08/07/2015	Australia	Cardiff	134 & 60	dnb & 2-28	2 cts
16/07/2015	Australia	Lord's	1 & 17	2-55 & 0-32	
29/07/2015	Australia	Birmingham	63 & 38*	dnb & 0-7	1 ct
06/08/2015	Australia	Nottingham	130		5 cts
20/08/2015	Australia	The Oval	6 & 11	0-13	
13/10/2015	Pakistan	Abu Dhabi	85 & 33*	0-13	
22/10/2015	Pakistan	Dubai	88 & 71	dnb & 0-26	2 cts
01/11/2015	Pakistan	Sharjah	4 & 6		2 cts
26/12/2015	South Africa	Durban	24 & 73	0-11	2 cts
02/01/2016	South Africa	Cape Town	50 & 29	0-54	1 ct
14/01/2016	South Africa	Johannesburg	110 & 4*		
22/01/2016	South Africa	Centurion	76 & 20	dnb & 0-12	1 ct

CAREER STATISTICS

HIS BATTING PARTNERS

Partner	Inns	Unb	Runs	Best	Avg	100	50
IR Bell	28	4	1092	177	45.50	3	6
AN Cook	25	0	1064	158	42.56	3	5
JM Bairstow	12	0	620	173	51.66	2	2
BA Stokes	13	0	519	161	39.92	2	2
GS Ballance	6	0	514	165	85.66	3	0
MJ Prior	8	0	414	171	51.75	3	0
MM Ali	10	0	359	101	35.90	1	2
JC Buttler	6	0	349	134	58.16	1	2
JM Anderson	6	1	293	198	58.60	1	0
IJL Trott	8	0	289	123	36.12	1	2
SCJ Broad	9	0	281	78	31.22	0	3
NRD Compton	6	0	244	71	40.66	0	2
MA Carberry	5	0	198	62	39.60	0	1
KP Pietersen	8	0	198	111	24.75	1	0
JWA Taylor	6	1	164	73	32.80	0	1
CJ Jordan	3	0	143	82	47.66	0	1
LE Plunkett	3	0	104	81	34.66	0	1
TT Bresnan	2	0	99	99	49.50	0	1
GP Swann	2	0	60	60	30.00	0	1
MA Wood	2	0	28	28	14.00	0	0
CT Tremlett	1	0	21	21	21.00	0	0
CR Woakes	1	0	9	9	9.00	0	0
ST Finn	1	0	0	0	0.00	0	0
MS Panesar	1	0	0	0	0.00	0	0

HE HAS SCORED 3406 TEST RUNS OFF 6363 BALLS, CONSISTING OF:

940	Singles
286	Twos
91	Threes
383	Fours (of which five were all-run)
1	Five
14	Sixes

JOE ROOT

HIGHEST SCORES

Score	Against	Venue	Season
125	South Africa	Centurion	2015/16
121	Sri Lanka	Wellington-W	2015
113	India	Leeds	2014
109	South Africa	Johannesburg	2015/16
107	West Indies	North Sound	2013/14
106*	New Zealand	Nottingham	2015
104*	Sri Lanka	Pallekele	2014/15
104	New Zealand	Birmingham	2015

BEST BOWLING

Bowling	Against	Venue	Season
2-15	West Indies	North Sound	2013/14
2-46	Australia	Brisbane	2013/14
1-11	Australia	Melbourne	2013/14
1-20	Australia	Birmingham	2013
1-21	Sri Lanka	Hambantota	2014/15
1-24	West Indies	North Sound	2013/14
1-27	Scotland	Christchurch-HO	2015
1-34	New Zealand	Nottingham	2013
1-47	West Indies	North Sound	2013/14
1-58	Australia	Southampton	2013

CAREER STATISTICS

HIS ODI CAREER

StartDate	Against	Venue	Batting	Bowling	Fielding
11/01/2013	India	Rajkot-K	0-51 (9)	1 ct	
15/01/2013	India	Kochi	36 (50)	0-5 (2)	1 ct
19/01/2013	India	Ranchi-H	39 (57)	1 ct	
23/01/2013	India	Mohali	57* (45)	0-24 (5)	
27/01/2013	India	Dharamsala-H	31 (49)	0-34 (5)	
17/02/2013	New Zealand	Hamilton	56 (64)		
20/02/2013	New Zealand	Napier	79* (56)	1 ct	
23/02/2013	New Zealand	Auckland	28* (56)		
31/05/2013	New Zealand	Lord's	30 (40)	0-15 (2)	
02/06/2013	New Zealand	Southampton	28 (27)	0-16 (3)	
05/06/2013	New Zealand	Nottingham	33 (50)	1-34 (5)	1 ct
08/06/2013	Australia	Birmingham	12 (17)	1-20 (5)	1 ct
13/06/2013	Sri Lanka	The Oval	68 (55)	0-27 (3)	1 ct
16/06/2013	New Zealand	Cardiff	38 (40)	1 ct	
19/06/2013	South Africa	The Oval	48 (71)	0-22 (3)	
23/06/2013	India	Birmingham	7 (9)		
08/09/2013	Australia	Manchester	3 (15)	0-13 (2)	1 ct
11/09/2013	Australia	Birmingham	12 (24)		
14/09/2013	Australia	Cardiff	0 (1)	0-9 (1)	
16/09/2013	Australia	Southampton	21 (36)	1-58 (6)	1 ct
12/01/2014	Australia	Melbourne	3 (23)	1-11 (2)	
17/01/2014	Australia	Brisbane	2 (8)	2-46 (9)	
26/01/2014	Australia	Adelaide	55 (86)		
28/02/2014	West Indies	North Sound	37 (48)	1-47 (9)	
02/03/2014	West Indies	North Sound	23 (43)	2-15 (5)	
05/03/2014	West Indies	North Sound	107 (122)	1-24 (3)	
09/05/2014	Scotland	Aberdeen	17 (6)		
22/05/2014	Sri Lanka	The Oval	45 (41)	0-7 (1)	1 ct
25/05/2014	Sri Lanka	Chester-le-Street	0 (3)	0-1 (1)	1 ct
28/05/2014	Sri Lanka	Manchester			
31/05/2014	Sri Lanka	Lord's	43 (68)	0-40 (6)	
03/06/2014	Sri Lanka	Birmingham	10 (11)	0-25 (6)	1 ct
27/08/2014	India	Cardiff	4 (4)	0-14 (3)	
30/08/2014	India	Nottingham	2 (7)	0-27 (4)	
02/09/2014	India	Birmingham	44 (81)		
05/09/2014	India	Leeds	113 (108)		
26/11/2014	Sri Lanka	Colombo-RPS	2 (8)	0-12 (2)	
29/11/2014	Sri Lanka	Colombo-RPS	42 (57)		
03/12/2014	Sri Lanka	Hambantota	48* (48)	1-21 (2)	
07/12/2014	Sri Lanka	Colombo-RPS	36 (49)	0-29 (6)	

10/12/2014	Sri Lanka	Pallekele	104* (117)	0-21 (5)	2 cts
13/12/2014	Sri Lanka	Pallekele	55 (76)	0-4 (1)	
16/12/2014	Sri Lanka	Colombo-RPS	80 (99)	0-22 (5)	
16/01/2015	Australia	Sydney	5 (15)		
20/01/2015	India	Brisbane			
23/01/2015	Australia	Hobart	69 (70)	1 ct	
30/01/2015	India	Perth	3 (2)	1 ct	
01/02/2015	Australia	Perth	25 (37)	1 ct	
14/02/2015	Australia	Melbourne	5 (12)	0-11 (1)	2 cts
20/02/2015	New Zealand	Wellington-W	46 (70)		
23/02/2015	Scotland	Christchurch-HO	1 (3)	1-27 (5)	1 ct
01/03/2015	Sri Lanka	Wellington-W	121 (108)	0-12 (2)	
09/03/2015	Bangladesh	Adelaide	29 (47)	0-6 (1)	2 cts
13/03/2015	Afghanistan	Sydney	2 cts		
09/06/2015	New Zealand	Birmingham	104 (78)	1 ct	
12/06/2015	New Zealand	The Oval	6 (10)	0-20 (3)	
14/06/2015	New Zealand	Southampton	54 (63)	0-21 (3)	2 cts
17/06/2015	New Zealand	Nottingham	106* (97)	0-10 (2)	
20/06/2015	New Zealand	Chester-le-Street	4 (5)		
11/11/2015	Pakistan	Abu Dhabi	0 (7)	0-12 (3)	
13/11/2015	Pakistan	Abu Dhabi	63 (77)		
17/11/2015	Pakistan	Sharjah	11 (14)	2 cts	
20/11/2015	Pakistan	Dubai	71 (71)		
03/02/2016	South Africa	Bloemfontein	52 (58)		
06/02/2016	South Africa	Port Elizabeth	38 (64)		
09/02/2016	South Africa	Centurion	125 (113)	1 ct	
12/02/2016	South Africa	Johannesburg	109 (124)	1 ct	
14/02/2016	South Africa	Cape Town	27 (25)		

HIS TWENTY20 INTERNATIONAL CAREER

Start Date	Against	Venue	Batting	Bowling	Fielding
22/12/2012	India	Mumbai	2 cts		
15/02/2013	New Zealand	Wellington-W	1-15 (2)	1 ct	
29/08/2013	Australia	Southampton	90* (49)	0-27 (1)	
31/08/2013	Australia	Chester-le-Street	1* (1)	1-25 (3)	
29/01/2014	Australia	Hobart	32 (24)		
31/01/2014	Australia	Melbourne	18 (14)		
02/02/2014	Australia	Sydney-O	11 (21)	1-13 (1)	1 ct
20/05/2014	Sri Lanka	The Oval	5 (7)	1-16 (2)	1 ct
07/09/2014	India	Birmingham	26 (29)		
23/06/2015	New Zealand	Manchester	68 (46)		
27/11/2015	Pakistan	Dubai	20 (16)		

CAREER STATISTICS

30/11/2015	Pakistan	Sharjah	32 (22)		
19/02/2016	South Africa	Cape Town	8 (12)		2 cts
21/02/2016	South Africa	Johannesburg	34 (17)		1 ct
16/03/2016	West Indies	Mumbai	48 (36)		
18/03/2016	South Africa	Mumbai	83 (44)	0-13 (1)	
23/03/2016	Afghanistan	Delhi	12 (8)		2 cts
25/03/2016	Sri Lanka	Delhi	25 (24)		1 ct
30/03/2016	New Zealand	Delhi	27* (22)		
03/04/2016	West Indies	Kolkata	54 (36)	2-9 (1)	1 ct

INDEX

INDEX